Understanding Your Child
from Birth to Sixteen

David Elkind, Ph.D.

Professor of Child Study
Tufts University

Understanding Your Child from Birth to Sixteen

Allyn and Bacon

Boston London Toronto Sydney Tokyo Singapore

Copyright © 1994 by Allyn and Bacon
A division of Paramount Publishing
160 Gould Street
Needham Heights, Massachusetts 02194

Library of Congress Cataloging-in-Publication Data
Elkind, David, 1931–
    Understanding your child from birth to sixteen/David Elkind.
      p. cm.
    Includes bibliographical references and index.
    ISBN 0-205-15971-0
    1. Child Psychology.   2. Adolescent psychology3. Child rearing.
    4. Parenting.   I. Title.
BF721.E368   1993
93-39529   155.4—dc20
                                                                         CIP

Photo credits:
Elizabeth Crews: Chapters 1, 2; Robert Harbison: Chapter 5; Stephen Marks:
Chapters 7, 9, 10; Jim Pickerell: Chapters 3, 4, 6, 8; Brian Smith: Chapter 11.

Printed in the United States of America
10 9 8 7 6 5 4 3 2   99 98 97 96 95 94

Contents

Preface

This is a difficult time to be rearing children. Certainly one could have said the same for parents rearing children during the Depression or for mothers rearing children alone while their husbands fought in World War II. There is an important difference, however. During those earlier periods in our history there was a lot of social support for healthy child rearing. Schools were child-, rather than curriculum-, centered and did not treat education as if it were a race. The media saw fit to protect children, and banned the use of foul language, nudity, and explicit sexual language and behavior. Although there was violence, it was rarely as graphic as the violence presented to young people today. Moreover, children were not seen as little salespeople who could cajole their parents into buying products advertised on television.

The lack of contemporary social support for healthy child rearing is shown in other ways as well, most deplorably in the nationwide lack of affordable, accessible, quality child care for all parents who need it. The need for child care grows, in part at least, out of the changed economics of our society. At mid-century, even a blue-collar worker could earn enough to support the family if his wife chose to stay home when the children were young. That is no longer the case. Today, the majority of white-color, as well as blue-collar, families require two incomes just to maintain the standard of living one working parent provided in an earlier era. Many single parents work two jobs to try and keep up with the bills. The lack of quality child care is the most widespread and serious problem for contemporary parents.

Still, the family survives, and the majority of children grows up to be responsible, decent folk. The reason is that despite the contemporary lack of social support for healthy child rearing, parents find ways and means to do a good job; it is just a much more stressful and more tiring, if no less pleasurable and rewarding, undertaking than it was in the past. Given these circumstances, parents need all the help they can get. In this book I make an effort to provide several kinds of help. First of all, I provide a few strategies for countering society's lack of social support for healthy parenting. Second, I provide information about the normative stages of development, about how children think and act at successive age levels. Finally, I occasionally suggest some techniques for dealing with perennial child-rearing issues.

In addition, however, I would like to suggest several general principles of child rearing that I believe every father and mother should have in their parenting tool box. These general principles derive from our vast accumulation of research and clinical experience with children and families over the past century.

The first principle is that it is always better to "start tough" and ease up as children mature than to start "easy" and get tougher as children get older. For example, consider parents who are firm with their infants and who continue to set clear and consistent limits with care and love as their children grow older. When these children reach adolescence, their parents can allow them considerable freedom. By this age, the teenagers have internalized (built into their own personalities) the limits and social responsibility they learned when young. In contrast, parents who fail to set limits, or instill manners, when children are small have a hard time asserting discipline when their children are grown into teenagers.

A second principle is to deal with issues when they are hot and not when they are cold. If a child engages in an action that needs to be addressed, it should be done at the time it occurs and not put off until later. For example, if a child says something rude or disrespectful, it should be dealt with then and there. While the incident is fresh, a parent's emotions are genuine and easy to see. If you tell the child how much what he or she has said has hurt you or made you unhappy, that feeling is tied directly to the child's remark. Should you wait until later in the day, your anger will have abated and the child probably will have forgotten the incident and likely deny it if you bring it up. Nor should this immediacy be relegated only to negative events; immediately expressing joy at a child's success is also much more effective than delaying that reaction until later.

A final principle is simply to share yourself with your child whenever possible. In this day and age when parents are working so hard just to maintain a reasonable standard of living, they often feel guilty about not spending enough time with their children. When they do have time to spend, they often feel that they should do something special and "fun." This may mean going for outings or to lessons or to sports activities. While these activities are fun, they waste the precious little time parents do have for their children.

With a time famine, such as the current one we are experiencing, it is essential that parents use the available time for sharing themselves with their children. By this I mean that we involve our children in the activities that need to be done or that we enjoy doing. If we have children only for the weekend, then we need to do the things we ordinarily would do: go shopping, do the laundry, mow the lawn. If we have the time and love to fish, we should take our children fishing. If you love to read, take your children to the library or an interesting book store. If you love sports, take the child to a ball game. What is essential is that we involve children in our real lives, not in some fantasy world that separates us, rather than brings us together, as family.

There are no easy answers, no simple paths to successful child rearing. We have already covered the many features of contemporary life that make child rearing more difficult than it was in the past. Nonetheless, rearing children continues to be one of the most, if not *the* most, rewarding and gratifying activities of our lives. You don't have to be a special kind of person to be an effective parent. Individuals with quite different personality and child-rearing styles do an excellent job of child rearing and take great satisfaction from so doing. I hope that this book, in some small way, contributes to your comfortableness with, as well as your enjoyment of, parenting.

*Understanding Your Child
from Birth to Sixteen*

1

The Infant
and the Young Child

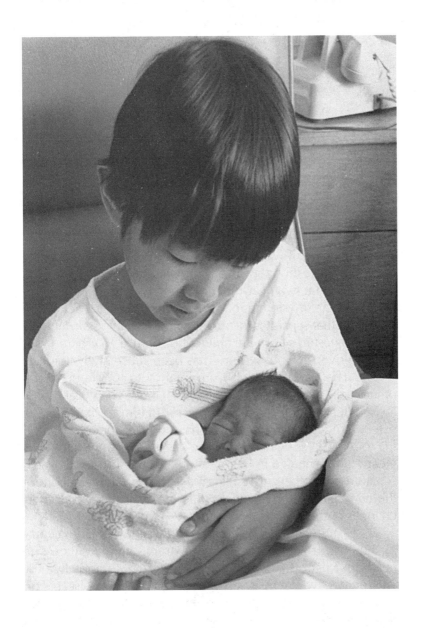

1

Personal and
Social Development
in the Infant

The infancy period, roughly the first two years of life, is certainly one of the most important and remarkable eras in the entire life cycle. Within two short years, a squalling, uncoordinated bundle of wants is transformed into a walking, talking individual with strong social attachments and a will of his own. To be sure, the two-year-old has a long way to go before maturity, but the transformation—the enormous "leap" across the boundary that separates the infant who can only use instinctive cries and gestures from the child who can use an arbitrary, socially derived symbol system—has been successfully made.

The transformation from infancy to toddlerhood has other facets as well. Toward the end of the second year of life, the toddler shows that he has a concept of himself that, to some extent, guides and directs his behavior. In his prideful "no's," the toddler gives evidence that he has a concept of self that is clearly differentiated from that of others. It is this sense of self, separate from others, that helps make the social interactions of the two-year-old qualitatively different from the social interchanges of the infant.

If human infancy is a period of extraordinary accomplishments, it is also a period of extreme vulnerability. The newborn infant is exposed, for the first time, to a totally new environment where he is susceptible to a variety of diseases for which he has, after a period of immunity, to build up fresh defenses. The infant is vulnerable, too, because he is dependent upon others to meet his most elementary needs. Even more important, the infant is socially vulnerable; without the necessary minimum of love and physical parenting, the delicate, budding sense of self-worth and trust in others can be badly damaged. The price of the remarkable transformation that occurs in infancy is thus the extreme vulnerability of the baby to the vagaries of the biological, physical, and social worlds.

"You forget how small they are" is a comment the parents of young infants hear again and again from parents whose offspring are full grown, or at least half grown. Infants are indeed small, at least from the adult perspective. The average infant at birth has a head-to-feet length of about 20 inches and weighs about 7.5 pounds. The body proportions of an infant are far different than they will be later, and the length of his head is about a fourth the length of his body. His head, moreover, has about the same circumference as his chest, and his arms and legs are quite short. To get some idea of the problems these proportions impose on a young infant, we have only to imagine our problems if our head were the size of a large beach ball while the rest of us remained the same size.

Although the infant makes tremendous progress during the first two years of life, he does not start from a zero baseline. At birth the infant has a number of adaptive reflexes, such as the *startle pattern*, which can be elicited by sudden sharp sounds, and the *sucking reflex*, which can be induced by stroking the infant's lips. Newborn infants also exhibit a powerful *grasp reflex*. This reflex is so strong that if the infant grabs a finger on each of your hands, you can easily lift him into the air.

In addition to reflexes, the young infant also has some sensory abilities at his disposal soon after birth. He can discriminate among loud, sudden, and other sounds, and he can also distinguish between sweet and bitter water solutions. Visually, even the young infant shows a preference for more complex patterns, such as newsprint, over less interesting patterns, such as lines. Infants can also distinguish between a picture of a normal human face and one that has the facial features all jumbled up.

Although the baby's ability to make sounds is relatively undeveloped, he can nonetheless convey his emotional states through cooing and crying. The ability to distinguish different sounds appears quite early; indeed, there is some evidence that it can occur while the infant is still in the womb. Some investigators have demonstrated that a fetus can recognize the mother's voice and responds differently to it than to other voices. Unfortunately, some workers in the field have exaggerated the significance of this finding. They argue that one can educate the child while it is still in the fetal stage by talking to it, reading to it, playing music to it, and so on. Although these practices would seem to do no harm, it is also unlikely that they accomplish much of what is promised or intended.

As the infant develops over the next few years, maturation follows several typical patterns. Generally, growth is from the "head" to the "tail," and the infant can control his head movements before he gains control over the movement of his legs. Growth also progresses from the center of the body toward the outside or periphery. A child can flail his arms before he can oppose his thumb and his forefinger. In the same way, the older infant will learn to walk long before he learns to curl his toes.

Sociocultural Change

Child-rearing practices are very much affected by the sociocultural climate in which the child is reared. Less than a century ago, parents were urged to toilet train a child early, by the age of three or four months, if the child was not to be spoiled. Parents were also urged to sew up the sleeves of the infant's bedclothes so that he could not touch his genitals or suck his thumb. Breast-feeding has at various times been strongly advocated or dismissed as an unnecessary burden upon the mother. Fashions in child rearing are more widespread and more changeable for the infancy period than they are for any other stage of childhood.

Fortunately, not all infant child-rearing practices are subject to fashion, and some have shown a definite direction in keeping with our growing knowledge about child development. Since the last decades of the nineteenth century, for example, there has been a trend away from a moralistic approach to infant behavior. Young children are no longer regarded as imbued with original sin, shown in such behavior as willfulness or masturbation. Thanks to the work of Austrian neurologist and founder of psychoanalysis Sigmund Freud and American psychologist and pediatrician Arnold Gesell, we now recognize that many infant behaviors, such as interest in the genitals, is common to all children and is a natural phase of child growth. We also accept the fact that children can be, and often are, mischievous without being evil or bad.

Another progressive change in our understanding of infant child-rearing practices has occurred in the domain of breast-feeding. Breast-feeding was once seen to be healthy for all children, but we now know that this is not always the case. Some infants may be allergic to breast milk, and some mother's milk may be harmful. An extreme case is that of HIV-positive mothers who breast-feed. Their infants are more likely to evidence the HIV virus than similarly affected mothers who do not breast-feed. The virus is not transmitted through the milk, but rather from the blood that may come, say, from a scratched nipple. There are no absolutes when it comes to breast-feeding.

In addition to the health considerations, psychological factors also have to be taken into account. For example, if a mother wants to breast-feed her infant, this will generally have beneficial effects. Such a mother will use the feeding period to fondle, caress, and engage in one-way conversation with her baby. On the other hand, if a mother, for whatever reason, does not want to breast-feed her infant, she probably should not do so. If she does breast-feed feed her infant out of a sense of obligation or guilt, she will communicate her mixed feelings to her infant. Her breast-feeding itself will convey love, caring, and tenderness, but her physical stiffness and dislike of the activity will convey dislike and rejection. Infants are very good at reading affective messages. When these messages are conflicting, this may weaken the child's sense of trust and security. Accordingly, whether or not a mother breast-feeds her infant is much less important than her consistent attitude of loving and caring.

One of the most significant changes in our conception of child rearing over the last fifty years has been in our perception of the parenting role. Up until mid-century, women were regarded as imbued with "maternal love," an instinctual need and desire not only to care for her infant but to subordinate all of her own personal talents and ambitions for the sake of her offspring. We recognize today that although the birth of a child is a major event in a woman's life, it is not the beginning and end of her life. Women can and do pursue careers at the same time that they are caring, competent, and effective mothers.

Today, the concept of maternal love has been replaced by the concept of shared parenting. According to this idea, mothers are no longer the only ones capable of giving their children the love and care they need in the early years. Increasingly, fathers are playing a larger role in child rearing. The concept of shared parenting, however, encompasses relatives such as grandparents and also nonfamilial caregivers. Mothers who are free to realize their own talents and abilities are often better mothers than women who may have stayed home out of a sense of obligation or duty.

There is a growing consensus among professionals today that even infants can be reared by nonfamilial caregivers without any negative effects. What is most important is not who gives the care but rather the quality of the care itself. For example, infants in a quality child-care arrangement with one adult for every three infants that is housed in a safe, clean, warm, and protected place will generally do very well. Infants in such situations may get as much attention or more than they would in a home where the mother was caring for several children and trying to run a household at the same time.

What this new perception of parenting provides are new options for parents. When the concept of maternal love held sway, women did not have the option of pursuing a career and of realizing their abilities and talents. Today, thankfully, they have that option, and more than 50 percent of mothers with children under the age of six exercise it. Some women may, however, not choose to pursue a career and may opt instead to stay home and do the bulk of the child rearing. That is another option, and it is as demanding and as fulfilling a choice as that of pursuing a career. Some fathers, too, may opt to stay home with their children as "househusbands" while their wives work. The point is that these are choices that are not good or bad, but simply different and equally rewarding life paths.

What we see today, then, is an important distinction between the infant's need for parenting, which is well established, and the mythology about who must do the parenting. Mothers who have little inclination to be with their young children full time now can accept the fact that this is not a reflection on their feminity. Nor will it have untoward effects upon the infant. As long as the infant is adequately and consistently cared for by a qualified child-care provider and as long as the mother spends some time with her infant each day, he will do fine. A mother who comes home tired but energized by a challenging job will relish the few hours she has with her child. In contrast, a frustrated, unhappy, stay-at-home mother may resent the many hours she has to be with her offspring.

Sociocultural change is affecting the role of the father as well as that of the mother. Child-care activities, such as feeding or changing the baby, are no longer regarded as unmanly. Many fathers today also want to be present at the birth of their child. Some may even request parental leave so that they can be with their child full time during the early months of life. Such fathers take a greater share of responsibility for feeding, changing, and bathing the baby than was probably true for their own fathers. Although contemporary mothers continue to do the bulk of the child rearing and housekeeping, fathers participate more and more comfortablely in child care than was true even a quarter of a century ago.

Choosing a Child-Care Center

It is important to choose a quality child-care setting for your infant. The following suggestions may help you in making that choice. Many communities now have early childhood referral services that can provide the names and numbers of qualified child-care facilities in the community. Check to see if there is such an organization in your town or city. These organizations will help you find a child-care arrangement in your neighborhood that is affordable and of good quality.

If such a facility is not available, talk to other mothers for leads to child-care they have used and been happy with. Although word of mouth is useful in providing leads, do not take it on faith; visit the center and talk to the child-care workers before making a decision. The same is true if you have to resort to the yellow pages to find child-care facilities.

In checking out a center, there are a number of things you should keep in mind. Is the center located in a safe area away from traffic and business or factory activities? Walk through the building. Are the rooms clean and well kept? Is the equipment in good condition, or is it in disrepair? Is the room bright and airy, and is there direct access to a protected out-of-doors area? Look at the materials to see if they are in ample supply. Are there enough blocks, dolls, books, etc., to keep all of the children occupied? Well-organized facilities have interest areas with materials grouped by activities, such as a reading center, a dramatic play area, and a block corner. I like to see plants and animals in a center, too; living things make the center more attractive and more homelike.

After checking out the physical facility, you need to inquire about the staff. It is not an insult to ask the director and the other workers about their educational backgrounds. Many are proud to say that they have degrees in early childhood education. Others may have Child Development Associate (CDA) Certificates, evidence that they have been trained by professionals on the job. The National Association for the Education of Young Children now certifies centers that have attained a high level of excellence. Ask whether the center has been certified or is in the process of being accredited. If it is certified or in the process of being certified, you can be assured of its high quality.

The last matter to be concerned with is the teacher-to-child ratio. In most states, the allowed ratios are often higher than that which most professionals would regard as optimum. As a rule of thumb, an optimum caregiver-to-child ratio would be one to three times the child's age. That is to say, for children one year old and younger, an optimum ratio would be 3 to 1; for two-year-olds, the optimum ratio would be 6 to 1; for three-year-olds, 9 to 1, and so on. These are optimum ratios, and slightly higher levels ordinarily are manageable. If the ratios go up to one caregiver to six times the child's age, the quality of care has to suffer.

Once you have decided on a center (and it is a reassuring precaution to pass your choice by friends and neighbors as a kind of validation by consensus), you need to prepare your child for the experience. In general, the younger your child is, the more time you need to spend in getting him ready for the child-care experience. If you are going to leave a one-year-old, for example, you will need to give him a chance to get over his stranger anxiety. That may mean staying with him for a while over the first few days or weeks. You can help prepare an older child by taking him to the center, walking him through the rooms, showing him the equipment and materials, and, of course, introducing him to the teachers. In addition, you need to talk to your child, even when he is very young, about the center, about the fact that he will be there for a while every day, and the fact that you will take him in the morning and take him home in the afternoon. It is important to emphasize that you are taking him to the center and taking him home rather than leaving him at the center and bringing him home. The term *taking* tells the child (and you) that you are in charge and are neither abandoning him nor bringing him home like a sack of groceries! With adequate preparation, most youngsters, with the exception of those who are insecurely attached or difficult, will usually adapt to the child-care routine.

Parents should expect certain consequences as a result of their child's enrollment in a child-care setting. First, your child is more likely to catch cold and other communicable diseases because of his greater exposure. However, he may also develop immunities earlier. Fights and quarrels are also to be expected when young children are together for long periods of time. On the other hand, your child may develop friendships with other children in the center. There is evidence that even infants seek to make social contact with other infants. Peer attachments start early. Parents, too, who have their children in the same center over a period of time may become friends and form a community of parents that can be the start of lifelong friendships.

Your child may also develop an attachment to a particular teacher or an aide, but this is healthy and in no way means that your child no longer loves you. Children, no less than adults, can care for more than one other person at a time. Sometimes, however, it is not easy to appreciate this. I recall spending a day at a child-care center in connection with a research project. It had been one of those days with one crisis after another. One child had come in upset over a new sibling who had just been brought home; another found that her cherished truck had been broken by another child. One of the aides called in sick, and the telephone was ringing like a fire alarm. Through it all, one three-year-old girl went about her business, seemingly unaware of the emotional chaos around her.

Her circumstances were special. She was being raised by a single father whose wife had abandoned him and left him with two small children. Like so many single parents, he worked long hours and then spent time in child care, cooking, and cleaning once he got home. This afternoon, when he came to fetch his daughter, she was playing with a child-care worker. As soon as she saw her father, the tears poured out and she clung to the child-care worker as if she were about to fall into an abyss. Her father was crestfallen. I could see his face crumble as he took in the scene. Fortunately, I was able to explain to him how controlled his daughter had been all day and that only when she saw him was she at last able to show her feelings. As if to support my words, she suddenly left the child-care worker and rushed to her father with joy and happiness.

So far, I have not said anything about the type of program offered by the center. In general, if the center has many of the components described above, the program will be developmentally appropriate for the child. If, however, you see anything like workbooks, ditto sheets, and other materials usually found in classrooms for older children, bells should go off in your head.

There are a variety of programs for children from traditional to Montessori to Waldorf, all of which speak to young children's need to work with things, not with symbols. If you see a program where work with symbols predominates, you are well advised, in my opinion, to find another program.

General Characteristics of Infancy

Perhaps the most outstanding characteristics of the infancy period are the young child's relative dependence and helplessness. Despite the gigantic strides made in two years, a child at the age of two is really unable to fend for himself in the world. The dependency and helplessness of the infant have both positive and negative consequences.

The smallness, the needfulness, and the dependence of the infant call out our protective and loving impulses. Because infants cause little damage, do not challenge adult authority, or make outrageous demands, they tend to be enjoyed and catered to. Furthermore, all babies are cute (the so-called cuteness factor), and all babies seem to invite favorable comments, even from strange adults. Consequently, parents are likely to get unanimous approval for their infant. Strange adults are, in general, more critical and less accepting of children than they are of infants. Parents of older children are, of necessity, a little more defensive.

The negative side of the infant's dependence and helplessness is that this combination of traits sometimes excites the anger of immature parents. In recent years, we have come to appreciate that child abuse is much more widespread than was commonly thought. Our failure to fully appreciate the extent of child abuse came from several directions. Our belief in instinctive parental love made it appear impossible that mothers or fathers would intentionally harm their children. Moreover, Freudian psychology argued that the older child's recollection of sexual abuse was a "screen memory" created to cover up the child's incestuous wishes toward the parent of the opposite sex. Today, we appreciate that many young children repress the abuse they experienced in childhood and only become aware of it in adolescence.

There are many forms of child abuse. In addition to sexual and physical abuse, there is also verbal abuse and neglect. During the infancy period, physical abuse is the most common. It often derives from attributing to the infant motives he could not have. One young mother who had beaten her infant said, "I came home with a wicked headache and he kept crying and I knew he was doing it just to get me, so I hit him." Parents who perpetrate these acts upon the young are troubled individuals. More often than not, they themselves have been abused and are repeating what was done to them. This does not excuse their behavior, but it does mean that to stop the cycle of abuse, we must intervene at an early age.

Although dependency and helplessness are clearly major aspects of the infancy period, it is necessary to stress the other side of the picture as well. Infants often take the initiative in many activities, such as in their "conversations" with their parents. They also prompt their parents to engage in repetitive games, such as retrieving objects dropped from the crib. In these ways they act so as to promote their own linguistic and mental development. We also have some recent research evidence that infants will initiate friendly social contact with other infants. In other words, although dependency and helplessness in an adult are generally associated with a passive attitude toward life, this is not true for the infant. Although he is passive and helpless in some respects, the infant is also a fully active participant in the interpersonal world in which he lives and grows.

The World of Self, Home, and Community

During the first and second years of life, the infant elaborates a basic component of his self-concept. This is the conception of the self as an object. This self-conception is but one evidence of the infant's major developmental task, to be described in more detail in the next chapter: that of coming to understand the world of permanent objects. At birth, the infant does not clearly distinguish between himself and the outer world. He cannot tell the difference between sensations that come from within or from without his body. If something touches his skin that he does not like, he cries but does not try to move the object away. Likewise, the young infant does not yet grasp that objects are permanent and that they continue to exist when he is not looking at them. If a young infant is happily playing with a rattle and you cover the rattle with a napkin, he will not cry. At this early stage, out of sight is literally out of mind. If you repeat this experiment a few months later, the infant will cry but not lift the napkin to regain his rattle. Only toward the end of the first year will the infant actively uncover an object he has seen hidden.

There is some controversy among professionals regarding the exact age at which the infant constructs the idea of objects as existing outside of his immediate experience. However, there is agreement that this idea of object permanence is constructed and that it is neither inherited and present at birth nor a learned copy of reality. The infant constructs the concept of the object by repeatedly looking at, touching, tasting, and tapping the object and then coordinating these perceptions into an inner representation of the object as a whole. It is this inner representation of the object that enables the infant to appreciate that objects continue to exist when they are outside of his immediate sensory awareness.

Just as the infant gradually constructs a representation of objects outside himself, so does he also begin to build a concept of self as an enduring object in space and time. One evidence of this budding sense of self as object is the fear of strangers that he manifests toward the end of the first year of life and into the second. The infant's fear of strangers reflects the ability to tell the difference between familiar and unfamiliar faces, but it also gives evidence of the infant's first awareness of danger to the self. The child will show fear only after he has a concept of himself as an object that can be injured or destroyed. The concept of self as an object is the foundation upon which all later components of the self-concept are built and about which they are all organized.

The extent to which an infant will display fear of strangers will also depend upon the quality of his attachment to his parents. A child who shows *secure attachment* to his parent will explore his surroundings even in his parent's absence. An infant who shows *avoidance attachment* does not cry when the parent leaves the room but will avoid the parent on his or her return. These avoidant attached infants do not reach out to their parents when they are unhappy, and they do tend to be angry and unhappy. The infant who has *ambivalent attachment* will cry even before the parent leaves the room. Although he will reach out for contact with the parent on his or her return, he will also show his ambivalence by kicking and squirming. In part, these differences reflect inborn differences in temperament, and in part, they reflect the quality of the parent-child relationship.

Some infants are temperamentally *easy*. These children are, from the very first days of life, adaptable in their biological functions. They quickly develop regular patterns of eating and sleeping, take easily to new foods, and react to strangers with little or no fuss. Such children laugh and smile, enjoy bodily contact, and actively engage others in social interchange. To their parents, their grandparents, their pediatrician, and some-times, their child-care workers, these children are a joy to be with. The only concern parents have about such babies is that their ready adaptability may make them too friendly with strang-ers. In any case, these infants are the ones most likely to be se-curely attached to parents. In a population of middle- and upper-class children, temperamentally easy youngsters make up about 40 percent of the total group.

At the opposite end of the adaptability scale are tem-peramentally *difficult* children. These youngsters are very un-even in their biological patterns. From birth onward they have difficulty sleeping and are finicky eaters. They are easily upset by new situations and by strangers, and their overall emotional tone tends to be negative. In these children, crying is much more frequent than laughing. When these children do laugh, it is very loud, almost exaggerated, as if expressing positive emotions takes a special effort. Everyone—parents, pediatri-cians, grandparents, child-care workers—finds these children can be a handful and a half. In the same population as de-scribed above, temperamentally difficult children make up about 10 percent of the youngsters. These youngsters are also likely to be ambivalently attached.

A third temperament type found among infants is a group that has been called *slow-to-warm-up*. In some respects, these temperamentally slow-to-warm-up children resemble the difficult infants but are less extreme. They show initial difficulty in eating and sleeping but eventually establish regular routines. When faced with strange situations, these children are more likely to withdraw and become subdued, in contrast to the dif-ficult children who, in similar circumstances, are more likely to explode. Slow-to-warm-up children are shy in the sense of needing time to warm up to people and to new situations. These children are likely to be avoidant in their attachment behavior.

In general, the easy, securely attached infant is likely to have a generally positive concept of himself as an object, thanks to the positive social responses his behavior elicits. In contrast, the difficult, ambivalently attached child is likely to have a negative concept of himself, reflecting the frustrating reactions his behavior tends to bring out in caregivers. The self-concept of the avoidant attached, slow-to-warm-up child is likely to be somewhere in the middle. Again, this concept of self as object is the product of both the infant's inborn temperament and the quality of the parenting that he receives and encourages.

Long-term follow-up studies suggest that these individual differences in adaptability and self-concept persist well into childhood and into adolescence. When children who have difficulty adapting are recognized early, there are a number of things we can do to make their lives easier. Most important is that we train ourselves not to expect too much or demand too much of these youngsters at one time. When we appreciate that a child's difficulty is largely biological, we will not blame him for laziness or touchiness, and we will give him tasks he can accomplish and the time he needs to complete them. It is not that we should have *no* expectations for such children—of course we must—but we need to tailor our expectations to who the child is, not who we might wish him to be.

Infant-Adult Relationships

We have already touched upon some facets of infant-adult relationships in the discussion of the infant's dependency and helplessness. There are, however, some additional aspects of the infant-adult relationship that require comment. First of all, for many mothers, the birth of a child comes as a kind of earthquake or volcanic eruption. Suddenly, the mother is in love all over again and finds it a real wrench to separate from her child. When she is away from her baby, she thinks about him constantly. Many life priorities are suddenly reassessed, and being with the child now often ranks at the very top. On a recent plane trip, I sat next to a biologist traveling to a scientific meeting at which she was presenting. She was returning that night because she was breast-feeding her infant! She told me that though she loved her work, she also had an overwhelming desire to be with her infant.

Although many mothers do indeed fall in love with their infants, it is usually not until we begin to make eye contact that we really experience the infant as a unique person. This usually does not happen until the infant is about a month old. This eye contact seems to promote a peculiar "chemistry" that makes us feel that we are relating and communicating to another individual. Once we establish eye contact, our child-rearing moves to a higher, more interactive level.

Another facet of infant-adult relationships is the one that we have already touched upon, namely the interaction between the infant's temperament and attachment type and the mother's personality. For a long time, it was thought that if children were not well behaved or if they had emotional problems, it was entirely the parents' fault. More recently, however, we have come to recognize that such an ascription of blame is probably unjust. In fact, some infants often provoke certain negative behaviors on the part of even the most patient and devoted parents. Indeed, it is now recognized that a child can sometimes be as much a factor in the emotional disturbance of his parents as the parents can be in the emotional disturbance of their offspring!

The two-way impact of parent personality on the child and vice versa is illustrated in the following case. The mother was a warm, affectionate, outgoing person who loved to touch and fondle her baby. The infant was difficult and insecurely attached and showed displeasure and annoyance when his mother attempted to cuddle him, but he also fussed when she stopped! Although she wanted to nurse her baby, he rejected the nipple. After months of frustration, of yearning to touch and cuddle her baby but being foiled in the attempt, she became dispirited, passive, and resigned. At a deeper level, she felt that her child had rejected an essential part of her as a person, and this left her feeling chronically inadequate and depressed. If you saw this depressed, apathetic mother at the end of the first year, as I did, it would be easy to blame the child's unresponsiveness on the mother. In fact, of course, just the reverse was true.

The point of this illustration is that it is fruitless to blame either parents or children when emotional disturbance appears.

Without investigation, it is often difficult to assess what the real origins of the problem are. At such times, it is best to get professional help. Many pediatricians now work closely with psychologists and psychiatrists to provide a full screening of problems that are both medical and psychological. In the above illustration, for example, once we took a full history and noted the infant's temperament type, we could reassure the mother that she was not responsible for her infant's behavior. Once she felt better about herself, she began to deal realistically with her child's temperamental orientation.

In summary, we need to remember that a child can shape the parents' behavior every bit as much as the parents can shape the behavior of their offspring.

Selected Readings

Brazelton, T.B. *On Becoming a Family.* Reading, MA: Addison-Wesley. A thoughtful, sensitive discussion of parenting in the early years.

Leach, P. (1983). *Babyhood,* 2nd ed. New York: Knopf. A well-written, factually based description of the neonatal period and first years of life.

Maurer, D., & Maurer, C. *The World of the Newborn.* New York: Basic Books. Presents the growth of the infant from the infant's point of view and describes what the world looks, feels, sounds, and tastes like to a newborn.

Worth, C. (1988). *The Birth of a Father.* New York: McGraw-Hill. A helpful book that uses interviews with fathers as a basis for dealing with questions new fathers have about their role.

2

Mental Development
in the Infant

As adults, we are in the habit of judging an individual's intellectual ability by his or her verbal skills. Because the infant has learned only a few words during the first two years of life, it is easy for us to miss the enormous gains he makes in his intellectual ability. Although this ability is less powerful than it will be later, it is still very significant. We can get some understanding of this prowess by following intellectual growth in three domains: language, the understanding of object permanence, and sensorimotor reasoning.

Language

The infant's ability to produce sounds is in part anatomical. Initially, the infant's larynx (voice box) is positioned high in his throat, which permits him to breath and ingest milk from a nipple at the same time. Yet this high placement of the larynx also makes it impossible for the infant to articulate the range of sounds found in human languages. (The high placement of the larynx is characteristic of the higher apes and explains why researchers have been able to teach these animals to sign but not to vocalize.) During the first year, the larynx descends into the throat, and the infant is able to progressively articulate more sounds.

Because of the initial high placement of the larynx, the infant's initial sounds are often mewing and throaty. Between the ages of three and nine months, the *k* and *g* sounds are very common. This helps to explain why adults, in imitation, often say *coo* or *goo* to our babies. Later in the first year of life, as babbling comes into play, the early *g* and *k* sounds are less prominent as the larynx drops and these sounds become less easy to produce. Once the larynx has moved down into the throat, the infant begins to babble. In the course of this babbling, the infant is likely to produce all of the phonemes—the basic sounds—of his language.

The importance of this early babbling for language acquisition has been demonstrated by recent studies of children who have had their vocal apparatus obstructed by the necessity of a breathing tube in their throats. Their inability to babble during the early months of life delayed not only their acquisition of correct articulation, but also their mastery of other expressive language skills. Because babbling is often a repetitive, rhythmic activity, it has been related to motor development. That is to say, some investigators have found that there is a correlation between motor development and linguistic development. The earlier a child walks, the earlier he is likely to talk. Other investigators, however, find that *compensation,* not correlation, is the rule. They report that children who walk early, talk late, and vice versa.

Current neurological research suggests that the relation between motor development and language development is more complex than the notion of either correlation or compensation suggests. Brain function is extraordinarily diversified and intricate. Many highly specialized functions combine to form more general functions in a number of different ways. Both language and motor development are linked to brain development, but the interconnections between these developments remain obscure. Put differently, there is no simple relation between motor development and language development, and all sorts of combinations can and do occur.

We can, however, describe the general course of language development. This development involves not only the growing ability to articulate sounds, but also the ability to express meaning and to comprehend the language of others. The babbling that infants engage in during the second half of the first year of life contributes to both of these achievements. First of all, infant babbling is a way of practicing and perfecting the production of speech sounds. Initially, the infant produces many more sounds than those of his native language. Gradually, through hearing adult speech and through being rewarded for making certain sounds that elate parents (like *mama* or *dada*), he begins to limit speech production to the sounds of his particular language environment.

Babbling, however, also serves a social function. Children differ in the extent to which they engage in babbling. Some infants babble to adults—any adults—whereas others are more discriminating. Likewise, some children stop babbling as soon as they start to speak, whereas others continue babbling long after they have a spoken vocabulary of several dozen words. Even before they have a spoken vocabulary, while they are still babbling, most infants already have a passive vocabulary of several dozen words. They demonstrate this passive vocabulary, for example, by pointing to a picture in a book when they hear the name of the depicted object.

By the end of the first year of life, most children begin speaking recognizable words. The process is different for different children. For some, the first words may simply be reproductions of words the child has heard over and over again. One child who loved the record *Puff the Magic Dragon* uttered *Puff* as his first word. Other children's first words may come from reinforcement by the parents. If a child says *duh*, an easy sound for the child, the parents may rejoice and say aloud, "He said 'Daddy.' Say 'Daddy' again for Daddy." Through this reinforcement and modeling the child may acquire his first recognizable words.

For some children, the understanding that words carry meaning, that they stand for something, comes as kind of a sudden "aha" experience. When this happens, the child's vocabulary explodes from dozens to hundreds of words. For other children, the understanding that words have meaning comes more gradually, an increasing awareness of the linkage between words and things. For these children, vocabulary growth is much more gradual than it is for those who gain sudden insight into the meaning of words.

Toward the second year, the child gives evidence of our truly unique human capacity: the ability to create words of our own. This ability separates us from all other animals, including the higher apes. Although it has been possible to teach higher animals to use sign language and tokens and to respond to computer symbols, it remains doubtful that they can create new symbols on their own. Yet children do this with ease. When one of my sons was young, he began talking about "stocks." I foresaw a glorious future for him on Wall Street and had his business school selected. He soon indicated, however, that he was using *stocks* as a word for both his mother's stockings and his father's socks.

By the age of two, children show other evidence that their language is but one facet of a broader, *symbolic* capacity. For example, it is only after the age of two that children begin to report dreams and night terrors. These reports coincide with the appearance of REM brain wave patterns, which are usually associated with dreaming. After the age of two, children demonstrate their new symbolic abilities in other ways. They engage in *dramatic play* and dress up like Mommy or Daddy or teacher or firefighter. They also display *deferred imitation*, the ability to observe a behavior at one time and to imitate it at another. A child who visits the doctor, for example, may return home and deploy a tongue depressor (given to him by the nurse) into the mouth of a younger sibling. In general, as children progressively represent their world internally (symbolize it), they can increasingly manipulate it internally.

In our interaction with infants and young children it is natural and enjoyable to enrich their language experience. While feeding or changing an infant, we can talk to him about everything and anything. Many infants will nod their heads as if totally absorbed in the discussion. Singing to infants and young children and reciting rhymes to them is also very beneficial to their language development. Infants and toddlers love the sounds and rhythms of songs and rhymes and are often soothed by them. By talking to infants and young children while we engage in routine activities and in play, we help them learn the all-important auditory discriminations they require to speak their language.

When you talk to your infant, do so as if he really understands what you are saying. If you do this, you will use natural language and your tone will be truly conversational. Also, talk in a way that feels comfortable to you, and don't worry about how you may sound to other adults. You will feel and sound more in tune with your infant if you do what comes naturally when conversing with your baby than if you are trying to create some impression on other adults. Finally, don't overdo the use of pacifiers. Children who are clamping down on pacifiers much of the time are less likely to babble and vocalize as much as they might otherwise.

The World of Permanent Objects

As adults, we have amnesia for much of the first five years of our lives. This is true because to remember something we have to locate it within a time-space framework. If I say to you, "Remember," you are most likely to reply, "What? Where? When?" Until about the age of six or seven, however, we have no unit concepts of space and time. Accordingly, although we may retain a few affective memories of these years, little systematic memory is possible. It is because of this amnesia for our early years that we are likely to overestimate how much knowledge is inborn or given at birth. Because we don't remember learning it, we just assume that it was there from the start.

It was Jean Piaget, the famed Swiss psychologist, who first challenged many of our beliefs regarding the knowledge children bring with them into the world. Through painstaking experiments with his own three infants—experiments that have now been replicated by researchers all over the world—Piaget demonstrated that although children come into the world with some reflexes, most of their knowledge about the world is acquired by a slow and laborious process of construction. The infant neither copies a preexisting external world nor projects inborn ideas. Rather he creates and re-creates his world out of his experiences with the environment.

It is not that the infant has no understanding of the world, only that his first constructions of it are minimal. Infants create limited, situation-bound notions of time, space, causality, and number. As he matures, the child will successively reconstruct these ideas in accord with his growing mental abilities and educational experience. From this perspective, learning about the world involves *unlearning* earlier concepts and *relearning* them at more general and more abstract levels. Intellectual growth, then, is best pictured as an expanding spiral and not as a vertical ladder.

A good example of how the infant constructs reality out of his actions upon and experiences with the environment is the attainment of the concept of the *permanent object,* which was touched upon in the first chapter. During the first month or two of life, the infant behaves as if he could make objects appear and disappear. After the bottle is removed, he may continue sucking as if the sucking would restore the bottle. He might continue looking at the place where his mother has disappeared as if the looking might cause his mother to reappear. Between the third and seventh month of life, the infant gradually begins to separate the object from his actions upon it. He begins to behave as if he thought objects had movements of their own. At this stage, an infant will look at where a dropped object hit the ground, rather than fixate upon the point where it was released. During this period, too, the infant can look away and then back at the same object. This suggests that he is acquiring a sense that objects have permanence independent of his actions.

Between the ages of eight and ten months, the young child begins to look for hidden objects. What he does now—and did not do before—is actively remove barriers (say a blanket or a pillow) that has been placed over an object so that he can see it again. That is to say, he now begins to coordinate his own actions with those of the object's actions that are recognized as different from his own. Nonetheless, at this stage the child shows a kind of perseveration and acts as if the object always remains in the place where he found it. If he finds his ball behind a chair and then sees it roll behind the couch, he crawls to the chair, not to the couch, in search of the ball.

During the second year of life, the young child makes good progress in dealing with hidden objects, and by the end of the second year, he can find a toy that has been displaced several times. He will now also retrieve a toy that was first placed behind a chair and then put into a closet. At the age of two, the child understands that the object is not only independent of his own actions but that it is also independent of particular places and of other objects. It means, too, that the child has elaborated an elementary conception of space in which he and other objects are located. He can also follow the successive displacement of objects and thus indicates a beginning sense of temporal order. Finally, by removing objects in the way of attaining a desired object, he displays an early sense of causal relationships.

A number of investigators have attempted to show that infants attain concepts such as object permanence earlier than Piaget claimed. Usually, however, these experiments require quite elaborate equipment, in contrast to the Piagetian experiments, which are quite simple. In one experiment using trick lighting and mirrors, infants of four months looked longer at an impossible event—a board swinging through the place where a box had been—than at a possible event—the board missing the absent box. This suggests that, even at four months, the infant has some notion of an object's solidity and existence even in its physical absence.

One might argue, however, that this experiment, like many others that demonstrate early competence on the part of the infant, have only made the task easier. That is to say, it may be easier for a child to give visual signs of having attained object permanence than it is for him to act as if objects are permanent. Children will succeed on cognitively easier tasks earlier than they will on cognitively more difficult tasks. That is to say, with the Piagetian tasks, children still do not give evidence of object permanence until the end of the first year of life. Making a task easier for a child does not accelerate his development.

However that may be, these studies should not distract us from Piaget's most important point. What he has argued and spent his long career documenting is that the construction of reality is extraordinarily complex and exceedingly difficult. The real danger of an overemphasis on infant competence is that it may lead us to regard as an inborn or easy attainment that which is achieved only by unrelenting effort on the part of the infant and young child.

The Emergence of Reason

Since ancient times, the Catholic Church has described the age of six or seven as the age of reason. It is certainly true that explicit verbal reasoning, of the syllogistic variety, appears during that age period. By the end of the second year of life, however, we can already observe an implicit logic and reasoning in the actions of the child.

A child's logic and reasoning are perhaps best illustrated in his attempts to solve problems, to attain a goal that is blocked in some way. In one experiment, infants and young children were presented with a balance beam that, when moved appropriately, would make a bell ring. There were several variations of this connection between bell and balance beam. In one variation, pushing down on one end of the beam would make it touch and ring the bell. By the age of four to eight months, children who observed the experimenter push down the balance beam and make the bell ring responded by performing the same action themselves. In another variation, children observed the experimenter push down on one side of the balance beam to make the other end rise and strike the bell hung above it. Twelve- to eighteen-month-old children could imitate this action and make the bell ring. By $2\frac{1}{2}$ to three years, children could figure out how to make the bell ring without the experimenter's example.

In another study, infants and young children were shown a more complex problem. They were presented with a jar containing a pellet, which they were to retrieve. At fifteen months of age, most children tried to retrieve the pellet by shaking the bottle. When this was unsuccessful, the children inserted their hand into the bottle and tried to "hook" the pellet with their fingertips. By age two, however, the children immediately turned the bottle over to retrieve the pellet. When children turn the bottle over, they give evidence of an elementary notion of gravity, spatial orientation, and implicit reasoning.

Piaget demonstrated the implicit reasoning of the young child in still another way. He showed a two-year-old a piece of candy in his hand, which he then closed and placed under a hat on the table. While his hand was under the hat, Piaget released the candy but closed his fist again before he withdrew it from beneath the hat. When the child was encouraged to find the candy, he first opened Piaget's hand and, finding nothing there, proceeded to search beneath the hat, where he found the hidden sweet. The child then unwrapped the candy and put it in his mouth to ensure its permanent disappearance.

It is important to recognize that the child could not have solved this problem by simply looking and seeing what Piaget did. In fact, the child never actually saw Piaget put the candy under the hat. To realize that he had to look under the hat for the candy, the child had to reason as follows: Candy in the hand, hand under the hat, candy not in the hand, candy under the hat. This is not a trivial achievement.

It marks an important advance in the child's intellectual development. The child is now capable of systemic inference and deduction, at least with concrete materials.

The Zone of Proximal Development

Piaget's descripition of the child's mental development suggests that the infant realizes his full intellectual potential pretty much on his own and without adult intervention. A somewhat different position was taken by Russian psychologist Lev Vygotsky. In his work, Vygotsky argued that a child may well realize a part of his intellectual potential on his own, but he is unlikely to maximize his achievements by himself. Vygotsky postulated a zone of potential development (*the zone of proximal development*) that would be realized only through the intervention of adult teaching and instruction.

In learning language, for example, our talking to the child is necessary, from the Vygotsky standpoint, for the child to maximize his language potential. We see the important role of our teaching and instruction in other areas as well. When we help our child to hold a spoon, we may bring him to a level of proficiency that he might not attain on his own. In our own work on perceptual development with children at later age levels, we found that children's spontaneous level of perceptual development could be improved with training. We also found that although children at all age levels did better as a result of the training, the older children made the most improvement with the least training.

This concept of the zone of proximal development is a very important one for parents. It emphasizes the importance of our interactions with our infants and young children. As parents, we are important mediators of the child's learning. In the language we use, the games we play, and the tasks we set, we encourage the child to fully realize his abilities. That is why it is so important that we provide good language models and age-appropriate play materials for the child to utilize and to build upon.

By the age of two, therefore, the child has (1) attained the basics of language and representation; (2) gone far toward constructing a world of permanent objects and of himself as a discrete entity within that world; (3) demonstrated an implicit logic of actions—a forerunner of the more explicit reasoning powers that he will acquire at later stages of development; and (4) given evidence of a zone of proximal development that can be fully realized with the aid of adult teaching and instruction.

Over the next few years, the child will progressively coordinate language, objects, and reasoning to arrive at a more integrated system of thinking about himself and his world. To be sure, the infant's view of reality is still far different than that of the older child and adults. It is nonetheless a huge advance over the impermanent world of the young infant. Although children accomplish a great deal on their own, parents and teachers also play a significant role in helping them realize their abilities.

Selected Readings

Barron, N. (1992). *Growing Up with Language*. Reading; MA: Addison-Wesley. An in-depth look at language growth and development with the aid of three case studies.

Green, B. (1984). *Good Morning Mary Sunshine*. New York: Atheneum. A warm, charming account of a daughter's progress through the first year of her life.

Maxim, G.W. (1990). *The Sourcebook: Activities for Infants and Young Children*, 2nd ed. Columbus, OH: Merrill. A very useful and practical compilation of activities and materials for use by parents of infants and toddlers.

Powell, D.R. (1989). Families and *Early Childhood Programs*. Washington, D.C.: NAEYC Publications. An important review and discussion of the literature on the relations between families and the early childhood programs that serve their children.

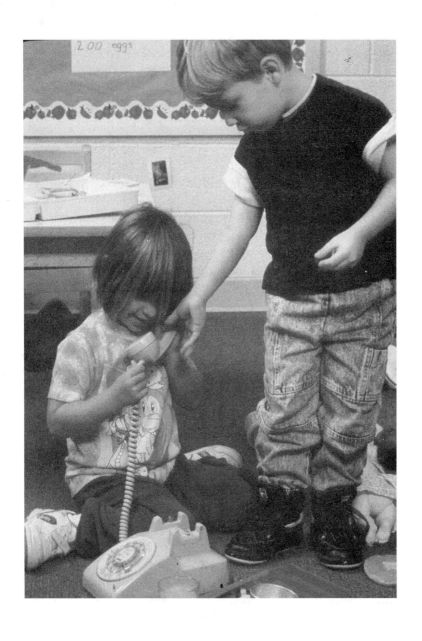

3

Personal and Social Development in the Young Child

Facets of Growth and Development

Children between the ages of two and five years demonstrate many new abilities and powers not given to infants and toddlers. Nonetheless, they also sometimes reveal carryovers from their recent past. Although toilet training is usually complete by age 2½ or three, even four- and five-year-olds occasionally have accidents. Such accidents are most likely to occur at times of stress, such as the introduction of a new baby into the home or the first day of attendance at a child-care center. Likewise, crying fits and tantrums common to the infancy period are not unusual among children of preschool age. Many young children continue to sleep for several hours in the afternoon and may still require a quiet or nap time when they enter kindergarten.

Just as there are continuities between infancy and early childhood, there are some quite obvious discontinuities as well. Although infants show some willingness to socialize with other infants, this usually amounts to little more than smiling and babbling at the other infant. By three or four, however, children are engaging in true social give-and-take. They may play a game together, take turns, help one another with a task. In the same way, while the infant is busy producing and separating out the speech sounds of her language, three- and four-year-olds are already making up their own words. One three-year-old, for example, remarked to her mother, "I'm sick; I think I have diaperiah!" It is also the age at which children's symbolic play comes into full flower. Preschoolers are often engaged in playing house, playing doctor, or emulating Superman™ or Batman™.

Individual differences, which were already evident in infancy, become more pronounced in early childhood as youngsters take on more recognizable personalities. During early childhood, children give many clues as to whether they will be aggressive, shy and quiet, loud and outgoing, or secretive and conspiratorial. Although not all children continue to follow the personality paths they pursue in early childhood, many do. Long-term studies suggest that many personality traits that appear during early childhood are still present in adulthood. Such long-standing dispositions are probably the result of genetic potential actualized by a particular pattern of social experience. Once in place, however, these patterns seem to be self-reinforcing and self- perpetuating through the whole life cycle.

Young children grow rapidly in many different but related directions. They make growth gains in height and weight, display changes in body proportions, exhibit increases in muscular control, show heightened self-awareness, demonstrate greatly enhanced mental and language powers, and evidence expanded capacities of social awareness and for social interaction. The following sections describe a limited sampling of the sweeping new achievements and attainments of the early childhood period.

Physical Development

During the preschool years, physical growth slows down somewhat from the frantic pace of infancy. In contrast to the 7 or 8 inches in height gained by the infant during the first and second years of life, the preschool child gains only 3 to 4 inches a year in stature. Height during the preschool years provides a rough index of the child's eventual adult height. At 2$\frac{1}{2}$ years, for example, a child has attained about 50 percent of her final stature as an adult. A girl who is 33 inches tall at age 2$\frac{1}{2}$ will likely be 5 feet 6 inches tall when she is fully grown. In contrast, a child does not attain half of her adult weight until about age ten. Generally, females tend to be somewhat smaller and lighter than males throughout early childhood, as they will be in adulthood.

There is a growing body of evidence supporting the importance of sound nutrition for healthy growth and development. Pregnant women who were undernourished and did not eat enough protein were found to have infants with lower brain size than children of pregnant women who were adequately nourished. Likewise, pregnant women who smoked or drank to excess put their babies at risk for a variety of serious defects and ailments. Once children are born, sound nutrition continues to be very important. For example, children who are overweight are likely to develop more fat cells than children who are not. Children with more than their inborn number of fat cells are predisposed to obesity in adolescence and adulthood.

Children can learn healthy food habits. For example, if children are given fruit and vegetables for snacks, they will be less likely to snack on junk food. This is important because children are subject to the same problems as adults when they overindulge in fats and sugars. Although children need, and burn, more fat than do adults, too much fat can raise their blood cholesterol. Likewise, children who ingest too much sugar and salt may be predisposed to conditions such as diabetes and high blood pressure.

Children can learn good food habits if we ensure that meals are well balanced and include all the food groups. Children should have free access to all of the food in the house. If there are foods we don't want our children to eat, we should not buy them or bring them into our homes. Likewise, if there are things we don't want our children to eat, they should not be on the dinner table. Once food is set out, children should make the decisions about how much and what foods to eat. Our job is to provide them with healthy choices; their job is to decide how much of what kinds of food they want at mealtime. Many battles over food can be eliminated by following the simple rule of not bringing home any food you do not want your child to eat.

At about age five, the termination of the preschool period, the average boy is about 43 to 44 inches in height and weighs about 43 pounds. Girls are close behind in both height and weight. By age five, the child's body proportions have changed as well. The preschool child's head is about one-fourth her body size and reflects the fact that the brain has reached 90 percent of its adult weight at age five. At age five, however, the top heaviness of the toddler is beginning to give way to the scrawny, scarecrowlike body configuration characteristic of the elementary school years.

While the preschool child is growing in size and weight, she is also becoming more skillful in both large- and small-motor activities. Not only can the two-year-old walk, but she can also open doors and cupboards, pick things up, and drop them. By the age of five, she has developed many other small-motor skills and and can handle spoons and forks, pencils and paintbrushes. She is usually able to get at least partly dressed by herself with the exception, perhaps, of not being able to button buttons, zip zippers, or tie her shoes. Modern technology, in the form of Velcro™, has solved some of these problems! There are many other achievements. She can pour drinks from a large container and unwrap candy bars. Large-muscle skills have also developed apace, and many four- and five-year-old children can ride bicycles as well as tricycles. At this age, children also climb jungle gyms with ease and with considerable enjoyment.

The activity level of young children always amazes adults, who marvel at how they keep it up. Within a short period of time, a four-year-old will go up and down a slide, ride a tricycle, get into a fight, grab something to eat, and be off to the jungle gym. In part, this high activity level is made possible by the child's rapid metabolism and heart rate, which pumps proportionately more oxygen into her blood than is true for adults. Hence, children tire less easily and recover more quickly. The relatively faster metabolism and heart rate of preschoolers also explains why they are less sensitive to temperature extremes than are adults. Preschoolers will play in the snow with glee while adults stand shivering nearby. It is no wonder, then, that preschool children often wear out both their parents and their teachers.

A negative consequence of the preschool child's high activity level is that she may get into dangerous situations. Running into the street, eating pills from the medicine closet, and pushing a wire into a wall socket are some of the dangerous situations to which young children are prone. Toys that may be appropriate for older children may be dangerous in the hands of young children. Balloons, for example, are the most frequent cause of asphyxiation among preschool children. It is very important to ensure the early childhood setting is childproofed and that there are no "attractive nuisances" that are potentially dangerous for curious, active preschoolers.

Sex Differences

"Girls, ugh" is a frequent expression among elementary school boys who are at great pains to show their distaste for the opposite sex. Although some of these attitudes filter down to young children, they are much less in evidence among pre-school youngsters than they will be later. At the preschool level, boys and girls play together without constraint and will often model adult behavior. In the preschool it is not unusual to see a girl bedecked in an apron call out to a boy dressed in a fire hat, "Come to the table and have your dinner, honey."

It is generally accepted today that many of the behaviors that distinguish boys from girls are learned and do not reflect innate, genetic, or physiological differences. Until recently, girls were taught that fighting, climbing, and rough games were not ladylike. Boys, in contrast, were taught that sewing, cooking, and dancing were things that only girls do. Although there is much greater awareness of such sex role stereotyping today, it still goes on. Research indicates that children from fifteen to thirty-six months of age in a child-care center already displayed clear preferences for "gender-appropriate" toys. Girls, however, conform less to sex role stereotypes than do boys. A girl is more likely to play with a truck than a boy is to dress a doll. This may reflect the fact that, in our society, male activities are much more clearly defined than are female activities.

Although it is important to be aware of the extent to which sexual differentiation is culturally imposed, it is also necessary to recognize the biologically linked differences between the sexes. Girls are smaller and lighter and have proportionally more fat than muscle than do boys. Girls, however, are less vulnerable than boys to all sorts of physiological and environmental risks. Boys are more likely than girls to be miscarried, to die in infancy, and to contract heritable diseases.

Girls' greater invulnerability extends to environmental risks as girls get older. For example, during the Second World War, European girls suffered less from concentration camp experiences than did European boys. Their growth was less stunted as a result of malnutrition, and they recovered more quickly from deprivation. Likewise, four times as many boys as girls suffer from early childhood autism, a schizophrenia-like disorder in which absence of emotional attachments is a dominant symptom. Finally, many more boys than girls are likely to be diagnosed as having Attention Deficit Hyperactivity Disorder (ADHD), a condition that affects children's learning ability.

In other domains, the differences are less clear cut and long lasting. Girls are initially superior to boys in language, including vocabulary size, reading comprehension, and verbal creativity. Interestingly, in verbal interactions girls are more likely to engage in face-to-face exchanges, whereas boys are more likely to engage in side-by-side exchanges. Preschool girls, too, are more ready to enter into one-on-one verbal interactions than are boys. These differences diminish, however, by the time boys and girls reach the later elementary and secondary grades.

At the same time, whereas there are few differences initially in visual and spatial abilities, boys begin to surpass girls in these domains by about the age of ten, and this superiority persists until adulthood. You can see this difference most dramatically with computer games. Such games require good visual-motor coordination, and boys excel at them.

Beginning at ages ten and eleven, boys also excel in mathematics. This difference may, in part, have an experiential base. A solid foundation in mathematics is best established by young children who engage in a great deal of manipulative play with materials such as blocks. Girls are less likely to engage in this form of activity than are boys. As a consequence, they may not develop as sound a grounding in math fundamentals as boys. It is also true, however, that in early adolescence it is socially less acceptable for girls to excel at mathematics. Even girls who are mathematically gifted may, as adolescents, forgo taking higher order math courses for reasons of social acceptance.

In the social/emotional domain, boys are more aggressive than girls. They are more frequently the initiators of aggression and also more often the victims of aggression than are girls. Boys are more likely to choose or to make guns as playthings than are girls. Boys also tend to be less compliant to adult authority. With peers, however, there appears to be no sex difference in regard to compliance. Girls may be as resistant to compliance with their peers as are boys. Finally, girls tend to be more nurturant, protective, and giving, with respect to children younger than themselves, than is true for boys.

In talking about boy-girl differences, it is important to emphasize that these are not absolute and that there is much overlapping between the sexes. Many boys, for example, can be warm and nurturant to young children, and some young girls can be rather mean to those who are younger. Likewise, some girls are gifted in math, and some boys are better at verbal skills than at spatial skills. Although it is necessary to generalize about sex differences, it is also important to remember that the variability within the sexes may be as great or even greater than the variability between the sexes.

Psychological Development

"Let me do it myself" is in many ways the central theme of early childhood. It is often difficult for adults, who have been self-sufficient for as long as they can remember, to fully appreciate the child's feelings in such matters. The urge to do things by herself reflects the child's newly acquired motor abilities and, even more, her newfound sense of self and of personal initiative. She is busy discovering that "I am me," and one way to find out who you are is to do things for yourself. Indeed, the young child's positive sense of self is very much determined by her ability to take the initiative. It is for this reason that parents and teachers are well advised not to do for a young child what she can do for herself. Waiting a few moments for a child to button herself up or pull up her own zipper is well worth the wait in the support it provides for the child's budding sense of being able to initiate and to complete a task on her own.

One of famed Italian educator Maria Montessori's most important contributions to early childhood education was based on her insight into young children's need to do for themselves. Montessori found that when she changed the environment, children could do much more for themselves than adults had assumed they could accomplish. She placed a stool by the wash basin so children could reach it by themselves. She hung a small towel nearby so young children could wash and dry their own hands. Child-sized tables, chairs, dishes, cups, glasses, and silver made it possible for children to set the table and to feed themselves easily and without mess. Montessori made it clear that many of the young child's difficulties in self-help derive from the fact that the environment is structured for people of adult size and strength. When the environment is downsized, children can succeed in many more self-help activities than they can in an adult-sized environment.

Despite her eagerness to be independent and self-sufficient, the preschool child, like the elementary school child and the adolescent, experiences that basic conflict that she will confront throughout the process of growing to maturity. This is the conflict between the wish to grow up, to be independent, and the wish to remain a dependent child. The preschool youngster may fall back on earlier patterns when a new baby is brought home or when she is tired or frustrated. Such backsliding is entirely natural and happens to all young children. If we accept it for what it is, a momentary hesitation, a pause in the rapid pace of growth, the child will rapidly regain her momentum and initiative.

Parents and teachers can, however, engender a sense of guilt in the young child if they treat her momentary lapses as malicious actions. Although there are many effective ways to handle such backsliding, depending upon the cause, the important thing is to regard it as a normal part of growth and not as an intentional challenge to adult authority. If we accept such backsliding without fuss, children will get back on track quickly.

Young children often begin to experience fears and night terrors associated with their new capacities for mental representation and their tendency to project their fears onto objects in the environment. Although these fears may seem foolish and unreasonable to us, they are a serious business for the child. The following example illustrates some strategies that do and do not work in such situations. Imagine a four-year-old who wakes up crying, "Mommy! Mommy! There is a bear in my room!" One way to handle this is to go into the child's room, turn on the lights, open the closet, and look under the bed. "No bear here!" you might say and turn off the light and return to bed. Moments later, the child is likely to cry, "Mommy! Mommy! Now there are two bears in my room!"

Another way of handling this situation is to say, "Oh yes, I see the bear. What nice brown fur and what pretty black eyes he has! He wouldn't hurt anybody." Our child is apt to look at us as if we had suddenly gone mad. Nonetheless, moments later, the child is likely to call out, "Mommy! Mommy! That nice bear is back!" A third option is to turn on the lights, go into the room, put our arms around our child, and say with confidence, "I won't let anything hurt you!" When we do this, we let the child know that although we may not see the bear, we accept that it is very real for the child, and we will be there to protect her. This is really what the child was asking for, and she is not likely to call out again.

One of the great charms of the preschool child is her wonderful creativity. At every turn, the child's verbal creations give voice to her fresh view of the world about her. One youngster, looking up at some wispy clouds, cried out, "Look, Daddy! I can see God's fingers." Another preschooler, whose lusty baritone had to be stilled so that the other children could keep the melody, lamented, "I used to sing pretty good until they invented tunes."

The preschool child is also capable of rather straight-forward reasoning and empathy. At four, one of my sons asked, "Dad, why don't you get rid of this old car?" I asked in return, "Well, I'm pretty old, older than the car anyway. Would you like to get rid of me?" To which he replied, "Well, no, not yet. You still work pretty good!"

It would be easy to fill these pages with more examples. The preschool years are, in a very real sense, the magic years. The young child is so charming in her eagerness for life and in her creative approach to it that this period is by far the favorite stage of childhood as far as most adults are concerned. Another quality of young children should be mentioned: their lack of vengefulness. Young children fight and then play together; they do not bear a grudge. Perhaps it was this quality that Jesus had in mind when he said, "Only as ye. . . become like young children shall ye enter the gates of heaven."

Social Development

In the center of a sandbox in a nursery school stood a steam shovel. Two boys were looking at the shovel when the teacher told them to "share" it and to "take turns." Within moments, the boys were fighting, and each one claimed that it was his turn. Although sharing and taking turns are familiar concepts to older children and adults, they are foreign to the young child.

The truth is that young children often regard toys as an extension of themselves. Asking them to share is like asking them to give away part of themselves. It is because children regard objects as parts of themselves that they get into such violent fights over toys. One of the achievements of the pre-school years is the gradual separation of the self from things. This separation also helps the child appreciate objects in their own right and not simply as an extension of herself or of another child.

This process of separation is gradual, and we can help it along. We must begin by recognizing how important possessions are to children. Offering rewards for sharing, although a natural reaction, is not always helpful. It ignores the child's investment in the object. A more successful procedure is to acknowledge ownership or temporary possession. If your child, say, has a friend over who wants to play with her truck, it is helpful to clearly label it with her name, perhaps with a placard that reads, "Mary's truck." When the toy is labeled in this way, your child is much more willing to share because it is clear that the truck is hers and will be returned. (You should, however, explain to the other child's mother why you are labeling the truck in this way!) Often underlying a child's unwillingness to share is the very public loss of what she regards as part of herself.

When my children were young, I spent a lot of time teaching them to share, to help them separate the self from things. When they got older, however, I found myself encouraging them *not* to share! One son was characteristically too generous. He sometimes loaned his toys to other children and did not ask for them back. One friend often borrowed his bike and then returned it scratched and dirty. As my children grew older, I tried to teach them that they had to be discriminating about whom they shared with. Learning about sharing, like so much in child development, must necessarily be relearned at older ages.

Another facet of socialization during this age period is the progressive overcoming of a form of *egocentrism*. Because of intellectual limitations, the young child cannot easily place herself in another person's position (when it is different from her own) and see things from that person's point of view. Accordingly, the young child tends to think that everyone sees the world as she does. The young child's egocentrism helps to explain many otherwise puzzling behaviors. For example, when one of my sons was at this age he complained of a toothache. I asked him if it hurt very much, and he replied, "Yes. Can't you feel it?" He did not appreciate that I could not feel his toothache! Likewise, a young child may know her own right and left hands but not the right and left hands of a person standing opposite her.

Egocentrism can also be observed in children's play. Preschool children often engage in parallel play and tend to talk *at* rather than *to* one another. One says, "My dog is going to the hospital to get fixed," and the other says, "Grandma sent me five dollars for my birthday." True communication involves taking the other's point of view, and young children are limited in this regard. On the other hand, when a preschooler has some perceptual cues, she can sometimes take the view of others. For example, young children will sometimes "change registers" in their language and engage in "baby talk" with a baby or younger child. Likewise, a preschool child may also comfort another child who is visibly upset or crying. A young child *can* overcome her egocentrism if she has perceptual clues to help her take the other person's position.

When young children deal with adults, another aspect of egocentrism may come into play. Consider the following incident. A young mother told her son, who was busily banging on a drum and enjoying the great din he was making, that she had a headache and would appreciate it if he played the drum a little less loudly. The child paid little attention and continued to pound away at his drum. Because a headache is invisible, the child had no clues to his mother's distress and so was unable to take her point of view. Fortunately, his mother intuitively understood this and said, "It makes my head hurt when you play your drums so loud." By giving the child a term he could relate to, namely the word *hurt*, he was able to take her point of view and to stop banging. This mother recognized that her child was not being insensitive but simply had no perceptual clues to her distress.

Learning to take the other person's point of view, to attend to and follow instructions, to share and to take turns, and to start a task and bring it to completion are some of the skills a young child has to accomplish before she begins her formal education. In addition, she must be able to control her feelings and emotions so that she can verbalize her anger and disappointment rather than act them out against her peers. When a frustrated child says to another, "You give me back my doll or I'll. . . I'll explain it to you," she has made the transition from expressing her feelings through action to expressing them with words. These social accomplishments, not the learning of letters and numbers, are the true prerequisites for a successful transition to formal education.

The change in attitude toward the education and rearing of young children over the past three decades is a telling example of the extent to which our perception of children and their education is a reflection of the prevailing sociocultural ethos. Prior to the social upheavals of the 1960s, early childhood education, as embodied in the nursery school, was regarded as a luxury, a form of enrichment for well-to-do young children. Only about one in ten preschool children participated in such early childhood programs. Today, however, more than 85 percent of children under the age of five are enrolled in some form of early childhood program. Private and public child-care centers, home care programs, preschools, and full-day kindergartens are but some of the programs now available for young children.

The rapid expansion of out-of-home care for young children has raised a number of questions that researchers are attempting to answer. Perhaps the most important question has to do with the effect on children of being in out-of-home care for many hours of the day on a regular basis. The answer to that question depends very much upon the quality of the program. When children are in programs with low teacher-to-child ratios, when the teachers are trained early childhood professionals, when the setting is roomy, attractive, and well outfitted with age-appropriate play and learning materials, young children can do very well indeed. When programs are below minimum standards, however, the results may be less salutary.

Another question has to do with the difference between preschool and child-care programs. Today, this difference is more one of history than of practice. The child-care center was initially introduced to provide child care for poor working mothers or for problem families. It was thus tainted with a social welfare label. Preschools, on the other hand, were introduced as a form of enrichment for the children of middle-income families. Unlike child care, which was a full-day affair, preschool was often a half-day program. Ordinarily, three-year-olds attended for only three days, four-year-olds for four days, and five-year-olds for five days.

Today, however, there is often little difference between the programs offered in good child-care programs and those provided by quality preschools. Moreover, many preschools now operate full-day programs for children as young as six months. We have come to recognize that the principles of sound early childhood education are the same for all early childhood programs, no matter what the funding sources or the physical settings. Early childhood education is now recognized as a form of education, like elementary and secondary education, that has its own curriculum and requires trained professionals to carry it out effectively.

What to Look for in a Quality Early Childhood Program

A complete description of quality early childhood education is beyond the scope of this book, but some general characteristics of such education need to be described.

This is important because there is a strong tendency in our society to ignore the special quality of early childhood education and to make it a "size smaller" first or second grade. From this perspective, early childhood is simply a little less of elementary education. It is as if education were a kind of medicine, and if you give an elementary school child a full teaspoon, then you had better give young children a half teaspoon. The medicine is the same; only the dosage is different!

Early childhood education is different from elementary school education because young children learn best from interaction with concrete materials rather than from books and workbooks. A good early childhood education program, therefore, provides an environment rich in materials that children can manipulate and explore. It is often organized according to interest areas where small groups of children can work for extended periods of time. Over the day or week, children can rotate through one or more of these areas. Group activities and opportunities to go out of doors help make up the daily program of the early childhood center.

One interest area to look for is the science center. This area is usually outfitted with a water table that lets children observe which things sink and which things float. Other materials might include magnets that let children determine which objects are attracted and which are not. A balance scale permits children to get a beginning sense of measurement even before they can grasp unit quantities of weight. A dramatic play area should also be available. This area should be the repository of discarded adult clothing that encourages children to play house, school, or office.

It is important for an early childhood program to have a nature area with plants and animals, which offer a variety of wonderful learning experiences. For example, children can learn responsibility from tending plants and animals. In addition, children can observe them and learn about how things grow and change. Children can also measure the plants and animals and draw them and write about them. In the nature area, children are thus learning science, math, and language as well as enjoying the satisfaction that comes from growing and caring for living things.

An early childhood classroom should also have a comfortable, quiet reading corner. Such a corner can be outfitted with large comfortable pillows, a rocker, even an old carpet-covered bathtub! Racks of well-choosen books of stories, poems, and rhymes should be part of this corner. Sometimes teachers have old record players or tape decks with records or tapes of songs or children's stories. The reading corner can be a place for children to go on their own and for the whole group to congregate when the teacher is telling or reading a story.

Some early childhood teachers play the piano or the guitar or the recorder, and this can be the focal point of a music area. Simple instruments for children to play—such as triangles, symbols, and recorders—are fun for children and can be placed in the music area.

An art area, outfitted with a couple of easels, finger paints, watercolors, crayons, and abundant newsprint, provides a place for children to engage in the graphic arts. In their drawings and paintings, children can also express some of the feelings and concerns that they may not yet be able to verbalize.

In addition to interest areas, a quality early childhood classroom is adjacent to an outdoor area so that children can move easily from the classroom to the outside. A facilitative play area will have a safe, splinter-proof climbing apparatus, swings and slides, a sandbox, and a path for trikes. It should be surrounded by a high fence and be away from the street and traffic. In addition to the play area, there should be opportunities for the children to make excursions into the neighborhood and to explore their immediate world. Sometimes this can be a trip to a library or to see what goes on behind the scenes at a restaurant, a fire station, a cemetery, or a railway depot.

Before leaving this issue of early childhood education programs, let me underscore the importance of play for young children. When parents come to visit our Children's School at Tufts University, they sometimes complain that children spend too much time in play. I have to explain to parents how important play is in young children's education and that, in fact, it is a very important form of learning. When a child is playing at being a bus driver, what is he doing? He has been on a bus, and he has observed the bus driver at work. Now he is doing the same thing in the preschool in an imaginative and inventive way. In fact, he is transferring what he learned in one situation to a very different situation. This is what the educational psychologists call *transfer of training.* It is one of the most important outcomes of education. When children are engaged in dramatic play, one of the things they are learning is how to transfer what they learned in one setting and apply it in another. One could hardly wish for a better learning activity than that!

Other forms of play are also highly educative and pleasurable at the same time. Where is it written that learning cannot be fun? For example, consider a group of children who are joining the teacher in making vegetable soup for lunch. As the children help to prepare the vegetables, they learn their names (vocabulary) and their shapes (geometry). After the vegetables are cut up, they need to be measured so that the proper quantities are added (math). Then the water and vegetables have to be boiled, and children learn about things that get soft when they are boiled, such as vegetables, unlike those that get hard when they are boiled, such as eggs (chemistry). When making vegetable soup, children acquire a lot of information in an enjoyable way and with a consumable and tasty end product.

No discussion of early childhood education would be complete without talking about early childhood educators. The quality of training around the country has improved enormously as our knowledge about early childhood has grown and as job opportunities have expanded. Many universities and colleges now have early childhood majors, and many states now certify early childhood teachers. Unfortunately, salaries have not kept pace with the high level of training and responsibility now demanded of early childhood teachers. However, this too is changing. Eventually we will come to appreciate that early childhood education demands as much or more in the way of knowledge, skill, training, and art as does any other level of education.

In many respects, the early childhood educator must be better prepared than teachers at later levels. Not only must the preschool teacher know the curriculum, but he or she must also be able to scoop up the weary youngster who announces, "I need a lap." On the other hand, the teacher must also be ready to let the child go a few minutes later when she decides to leave the lap and join her friends. At times, the teacher needs to demonstrate age-appropriate expectations for the children. When it comes to putting on coats, for example, the teacher should expect children to do this for themselves. The teacher should usually not do for the child what she is capable of doing for herself.

Able early childhood educators also recognize that preschool children are less able to control their emotions than are school-age youngsters. They get angry quickly and are likely to express their anger in physical action. One boy who was upset by the presence of a new baby brother in his house needed only the slightest provocation to bite through the sleeve of a friend's jacket. With most young children, fortunately, anger abates as rapidly as it develops; preschool children rarely engage in vengeful actions. However, the emotional vulnerability of preschool children makes them particularly sensitive to the moods of others, and it takes only one child who is out of sorts to set the whole group on edge. Able teachers must possess good management skills to deal with young children who sometimes lose control.

General Characteristics of Early Childhood

"Daddy, how come you have those lines around your eyes? I don't like them. They are scary." Young children are, if any-thing, frank and outspoken but sensitive realists. They usually call the shots as they see them and will say that somebody is ugly or smells bad if that is what they perceive. Young children are also not fooled by adult facades. They see through the syrupy, sweet gushing of the woman who really hates children. They can also sense the positive feeling of a quiet, retiring man who has a genuine affection for little people. Young children have no mystical abilities in this regard; they probably just respond to cues that adults have been trained to ignore.

It is the young child's sensitivity to adult moods and feelings that makes her both a vulnerable and a very difficult opponent. Because she is sensitive, she can experience rejection and dislike even when the adult tries to cover these up. At the same time, she can also discern when the grown-up can be pushed just a hair's breadth further. Of course, sometimes young children get too sure of themselves and push the adult too far, but for the most part, young children gauge adult intentions with considerable skill.

Just as the young child is at times a realist, she is also a visionary. The two traits are really not that discrepant and often go together in adults. The individual who does not blink from reality in all of its harshness, bleakness, and cruelty can also envision a world of kindness and compassion. Great government leaders, like great religious leaders, share the young child's unflinching appreciation of the real world, but also her capacity for seeing what is good in human nature and her desire to encourage that better nature to take charge. There is a difference, however. The adult envisions a better world on the order of the present one, but improved. The better world of the young child is the fairy-tale world of princes and princesses and of wondrous miracles.

A young child therefore believes in Santa Claus and in the good fairy who will bring her a quarter if she puts her tooth under a pillow. Young children believe in fairy godmothers, in magic wands, and in never-never lands. The existence of an old woman who lives in a shoe, a ginger-bread man who runs, and a candy house in the forest are not outside the range of possibility for the preschool child. To be sure, even young children would be surprised if Santa Claus really did come down the chimney! Fantasy for young children is like a good drama for adults. While watching a good drama, we are able to believe in the characters and in the story even though we know, at a different level, that they are just actors on the stage. At a certain level, young children, too, understand that fantasy is fantasy, but they enjoy the suspension of judgment and the exercise of imagination just as much as adults do.

Some parents and teachers wonder whether fantasy, as it appears in fairy tales, is good for young children. Some fairy tales are indeed grim. Moreover, so this argument goes, when we tell children about Santa Claus and the tooth fairy we are really lying to them. When they get older and discover the truth, won't they resent the fact that we have not been honest with them? Wouldn't it be better, for the child and our relationship, to be honest from the very beginning? Not really. Children will be no more angry at us for telling them about Santa Claus than they might be angry at us for taking them to a good play.

For children, as well as for adults, fantasy is enjoyable while it lasts, and that is the important thing. In addition, when children discover the truth about Santa Claus or the Easter Bunny (which they really knew all along), it gives them a marker of having attained a new level of maturity and intellectual ability. While visiting an elementary school around Easter time, I observed a third grader putting up an Easter display on the bulletin board. He noticed me watching him and said over his shoulder to me with considerable pride, "I don't believe in the Easter Bunny anymore!"

The World of Self, Home, and Community

I and *me* are among the most frequently employed terms of the young child's vocabulary. Early in the history of child psychology, German investigators spoke of this age period as the *Trotzalter,* literally the age of pride or defiance. This defiance often involves the young child's resisting adult authority and demanding to have her own way. The young child also shows pride in her ability to make and do. She comes home from preschool eager to show her artwork and hear it praised by her parents. At school she tugs her parents into the play area to show them block towers, garages, and well-set child-sized tea tables. In her defiance and her need for approval, the young child shows the two sides of her emerging self; personal autonomy and social interdependence.

Although the child's self is an organizing force at all stages of development, it functions differently at different age levels. During early childhood, particularly ages three to five, the self organizes itself and the world symbolically with words and images. For example, the child at this stage organizes much of her sense of self around her name and around words such as *me* and *mine*. This is one reason for teachers to learn young children's names very quickly and to get them right! No one likes to be called by the wrong name, but young children are particularly sensitive in this regard. Knowing a child's name and using it to identify and label her drawings and models ("Mary's drawing," "Mary's clay dog") are rewarding to the young child and reinforce her symbolic sense of self.

Supporting the young child's symbolic sense of self can be done in other ways as well. For example, when two children in the same play group have the same name it is thoughtful to call them by their full names. Likewise, it is necessary to learn what name the child prefers. Some children have nicknames or diminutives such as "Meg" for Margaret or "Bobby" for Robert. One young child, called "Robert" by his friend's mother, told her immediately, "not Robert, Bobby." We need to support and reinforce the child's symbolic sense of self in every way that we can.

Within the home, the young child is a constant source of amusement, exasperation, and amazement. She is amusing in her body size and proportions and in the contrast between these and her adultlike verbal pronouncements. We don't really expect these little people to come up with expressions like, "You do that again, and you are history!" At the same time, she can be exasperating in her demands for time and attention, for food, for help with her clothes, the television, or the VCR. The next moment, however, she will insist on doing things by herself and vigorously resist the very help she had just called for in the most urgent way. It becomes clear that her demands for help are as much, or more, demands for attention and social recognition.

Sometimes the young child amazes us with her feats of memory, of motor skill, or of psychological acumen. It comes as a complete surprise when a four-year-old says, "Hello Harry," to a man she saw only once a year earlier. And it is a minor miracle when we see those tiny hands, which could once merely clutch, now wield a pencil or a paintbrush with considerable skill and accuracy. It is touching, too, when our young child senses our moods and tries to comfort us when we are unhappy. More than anything else, however, the young child is a source of great personal satisfaction because she is so verbally and physically open in her expression of love and affection for her parents.

As far as the community is concerned, it was, until the last few decades, little concerned with preschool-aged children. That is no longer the case. Over the last several decades there has been a discovery of the importance of the early years of childhood, not just for the child's long-term mental health, but also for her mental development. The importance of the early years for giving children the intellectual wherewithal to do well later has been the impetus for programs such as Head Start, which now serves more than 500,000 low-income preschool children. It has also been the rationale for TV programs, such as "Sesame Street," aimed at helping young children acquire basic skills.

The Action for Better Childcare (ABC) bill, passed by the Congress in 1992, provides support for community child-care services. This bill allocates funds to enhance training, raise standards for child-care workers, and upgrade child-care facilities and equipment. In addition, more than 4,000 businesses now provide child-care services for children at or near the workplace. This enables employees to drop their children off on the way to work, visit them at lunchtime, and pick them up as they leave for home. In this and a number of other ways, the government and local communities are taking a greater part in providing for the care and education of young children.

The Child in Relation to Adults

Giants frequently appear in fairy tales for children, and one encounters them in stories such as "Jack and the Beanstalk" and "The Brave Little Tailor." To the young child, who stands barely three feet tall, adults do appear to be giants. They are giants, moreover, who can give out punishment, who can roar with outrage, and who can, at times, be childish in their pettiness. Not only does the young child's world abound in giants, it is also replete with giant-sized chairs, tables, dishes, doors, and drinking fountains. For the young child, the world is made to adult measure such that it often excludes her active participation. One reason young children, particularly boys, identify with superheroes such as Superman or Batman is to feel empowered to cope with and to master the seemingly invincible adult world.

Thanks to their level of mental ability, young children also tend to see adults as unidimensional: as good or bad, clever or stupid, kind or mean. Gifted writers for young children understand this mode of thought. In fairy tales, for example, characters such as the Fairy Godmother or the Wicked Ogre are either all good or all bad. In addition, young children may have difficulty recognizing their teacher when they meet him or her in the supermarket! (To the young child, you cannot be a teacher and simultaneously a person who shops.) One consequence of this mode of thought is that children also relate to adults as being all good or all bad. If children take a dislike to someone, it is difficult to disabuse them of this attitude. On the other hand, when children sense a gentle spirit, they may be too willing to give that person a hug.

The young child's tendency to see her parents and her teachers as all good has some interesting side effects. The child often attributes the "bad" motives, qualities, and actions she encounters in her parents to other people and to animals. Many of the preschooler's fears of monsters or wolves or tigers reflect her tendency to project "bad' parental qualities onto other creatures. This type of projection enables the young child to persist in her belief that her parents are all good and have no bad personality traits.

Young children also believe that parents are all-powerful and all-knowing. It seems to them that everything in the world is made by and for grown-ups to suit their convenience. Parents can therefore do anything. Likewise, because parents have answers to all the child's questions and can operate so many different appliances and gadgets, they must be all-knowing as well. In brief, to the young child, parents take on godlike qualities of omnipotence and omniscience, and negative parental qualities get projected onto other people and animals.

This orientation toward adults has some negative consequences that we need to recognize. For example, if something bad happens to a family member or if parents separate, the young child is likely to blame herself. Inasmuch as parents are perfect, they cannot have done anything wrong, so it must be the young child's fault. At such times, the young child may sacrifice her favorite toy or forego some special treat to atone for her imagined "sin" and to make things all right again. It is important to reassure children engaging in these activities that they are loved and that they have done nothing wrong.

In schools, this orientation toward the teacher as all-wise and all-knowing can also have negative consequences. This is particularly true in schools where academics are pushed too early. A young child who is confronted with phonics, for example, may not be able to understand that one and the same letter, say the letter *a*, can be sounded in two ways: the long *ay* and the short *ah*. The child's difficulty is the same one that she encounters in appreciating that one and the same person can have both bad and good qualities. Although the child's difficulty derives from being presented with an age-inappropriate task, the child is not aware of that fact. She thinks, "This teacher is all-wise and all-knowing and says I must learn this. But I can't; I don't understand. It must be me. I must be dumb."

The early years are critical for children's budding symbolic sense of self. It is of vital importance that we do everything we can to ensure that children leave the early years feeling good about themselves, about school, and about learning. The best way to achieve this is to make age-appropriate educational demands upon young children. If we do not, as in the above example, we run the risk of producing children who feel badly about themselves, hate school, and are turned off to learning. Young children put not only their trust, but also their sense of competence, in our hands. We must not abuse that trust nor injure that sense of self-worth.

Adults in Relation to Children

Most adults—whether or not they are parents—like young children. This is true not just because young children are charming and amusing, but also because of their mode of thinking. Young children, who believe in the omniscience of adults, flatter the adult ego. The small size of the young child brings out our protective feelings. In addition, young children do not threaten us either physically or intellectually because there is virtually no contest on either score. Finally, it has been argued (by Sigmund Freud) that because adults have renounced their own narcissism or self-centeredness, we find the self-centeredness of the young child charming and wish to protect it. Young children thus not only do not threaten us, but reawaken in us the sense of paradise lost and the wish to prolong the stay for those who have not yet left it

Obviously, the unthreatening quality and self-centeredness of the young child are only some of the attributes that make her appealing to adults. Her openness and creativity, her love of life, and her abundant energy and exuberance are a joy to observe and are rewarding in and of themselves. However, the deeper understanding of the adult's liking for the young child must also acknowledge that the young child, in neither thought nor deed, poses any kind of challenge to the adult ego. On the contrary, she appears to bolster that ego on every count.

Selected Readings

Fraiburg, S. (1949). *The Magic Years.* New York: Harpers. A classic, written from a pscyhoanalytic perspective, that affords wonderful insights into the thoughts and feelings of the young child.

Garvey, C. (1977). *Play.* Cambridge, MA: Harvard University Press. Provides a developmental overview of play from peekaboo with infants to the games with rules of school children.

Joffe, C.E. (1979). *Friendly Intruders.* Berkeley, CA: University of California Press. A frank discussion of what parents expect from early childhood programs and what early childhood educators expect from parents and some of the conflicts and contradictions these expectations engender.

Tizard, B., & Hughes, M. (1984). *Young Children Learning.* Cambridge, MA: Harvard University Press. Presents the results of a study dealing with the conversations of four-year-old children and their mothers and teachers. Demonstrates how much children can learn from everyday conversations.

All I really need
to know I learned in
kindergarten

hamster

4

Mental Development
in the Young Child

In young children, as in infants, mental abilities are much less independent from one another and from the emotions than they will be in later childhood. A school-age child who is unhappy may still be able to function and participate in learning activities. The young child, however, is so beset by distress that it dominates her intellectual as well as her emotional outlook. This observation is relative, of course. Adults, upset by severe emotional distress, may also be unable to go about their normal affairs. It is simply that older children and adults are usually better able to distance themselves from their emotions than are young children.

The Development of Mental Abilities

Young children think differently than do older children and adults. Such thinking is not wrong, simply different and age-appropriate. When a preschooler asks, "If I eat spaghetti, will I become Italian?" she reflects, in an original and amusing way, her belief that "you are what you eat." Rather than "correct" the child, we might ask, "What do you think?" Children usually have answers to the questions they ask and are very happy to share these with us. The child might reply, "I think so, because my friend Robert eats spaghetti, and he's Italian."

Transductive Reasoning

The foregoing example illustrates a form of reasoning that is characteristic of young children. This *transductive reasoning* is from concrete event to concrete event, as opposed to *deductive reasoning,* which is from a general principle

to a specific conclusion. If the child were reasoning deduc-
tively, she might think

People who eat spaghetti become Italian [major premise].

I eat spaghetti [minor premise].

Therefore, I will become Italian [conclusion].

In fact, though, her reasoning is transductive, and she thinks

Robert eats spaghetti, and he's Italian.

If I eat spaghetti, I will become Italian too.

What is missing in transductive reasoning is the major premise, the overriding rule from which a particular conclusion can be deduced. Instead the child reasons from case to case.

Transductive reasoning helps us to understand a number of otherwise puzzling features of young children's behavior. For example, young children often believe that when two events occur in succession, the first causes the second. A child who crosses her fingers before going to the doctor and does *not* get a shot will henceforth cross her fingers whenever she goes to the doctor. Transductive reasoning thus underlies what often appears to be superstitious behavior in young children (as well as in older children and adults!).

We can observe this transductive approach to causality in many other ways as well. For example, it helps to explain why children label things the way they do. When a mother and her preschool children were walking on an icy sidewalk, the mother slipped and fell. From then on, her children called the outfit she was wearing that day her "sliding clothes" because they saw the clothes as having made their mother slip and slide. Likewise, a child who was always served just one slice of pizza had trouble understanding that the whole round pie was a pizza. For this child, a pizza was triangular and not round.

Transductive reasoning also plays a part in the child's adoption of *transitional objects*. In the cartoon "Peanuts," Linus's blanket is a transitional object. Such objects help us to bridge the time interval between the loss of one source of gratification and the attainment of another. Once weaned, some children need a transitional object to carry them over until they find another form of gratification that is equally satisfying. At that point, the transitional object can be discarded. Transductive reasoning operates in the choice of the transitional object. A young child believes that if a blanket gave her comfort once, it will do so always.

Transitional objects are very important to young children, particularly those who are going through a difficult time in their lives, such as the divorce of their parents. If we recognize that the child needs this object to help deal with the separation and loss of gratification from parents, we can better accommodate to the object (blanket, doll, and so on) and encourage other children not to tease or joke about it. It is important to point out that adults use transitional objects as well. We sometimes rush into a new relationship after an old one is broken, simply to bridge the time period until we have regained our emotional balance. Young children use transitional objects in the same way.

Physiognomic Perception

Other facets of young children's thinking also relate to its transductive quality. Because young children tend to think on the concrete, observational level, they are apt to be more attentive to perceptual clues than are adults. This tendency appears in what has been called *physiognomic perception*. Such perception is not unknown among adults. When we visit an art gallery, some paintings make us feel happy and uplifted; others make us feel sad and depressed. These emotional reactions to what we see are examples of physiognomic perception.

Physiognomic perception helps account for the young child's fearfulness in strange situations. The waving of a branch or the flitting of a shadow can take on a frightening quality if it is perceived as reflecting angry forces. The frequent but transient phobias of young children are, in part, attributable to such physiognomic perception. A three-year-old of my acquaintance became frightened whenever he saw a broken object. This was a display of physiognomic perception. The broken object seemed to the child to betoken a disembodied anger that could be unleashed against him. In some cases, physiognomic perception in the young child reflects a tendency to project onto inanimate objects the angry impulses she senses within herself or in her parents.

Closely related to the young child's transductive reasoning is her tendency to engage in *magical thinking,* the belief in the efficacy of her own thoughts and wishes. Such thinking is a direct product of transductive reasoning. If a child wishes for something to happen that does indeed occur, she will believe that her wish made it happen. Parents unwittingly reinforce this magical thinking when they tell their child not to say certain words. This gives the child the impression that if she says the forbidden word, something terrible will happen. Nonetheless, many young children tempt fate by saying forbidden words in the privacy of their own rooms while they wait, in fear and trembling, for the inevitable clap of thunder and flash of lightning.

Magical thinking also accounts for some of the emotional disturbances we see in young children. If a child secretly wishes that a younger brother or sister would be injured or go away and something does indeed happen to that sibling, the child may believe that the wish caused the event. Such a child will be very distressed and will try to undo the wish by giving away treasured possessions or promising to be good forever and ever. A similar dynamic is at work when a young child feels responsible for parental separation and divorce. A young child may want to possess one parent and wish that the other would disappear. When this happens in reality, the child believes that she is the cause, and she suffers great guilt and remorse. Children to whom this has happened often become highly accident-prone.

To be sure, magical thinking, like the other forms of thinking we observe in young children, is not unknown among adults. I recall a game we played in high school. We would not allow ourselves to think that we might get a good grade in a difficult subject. Our fear was that if we thought we might get a good grade, this very thought would magically prevent us from getting the desired grade! Instead, we tried to convince ourselves we would get a bad grade to counter the power of the wish for a good grade. At a certain level, however, we knew that we were playing mind games and did not really believe that our thoughts would affect our grades. Young children, however, are much more likely to truly believe in the magical efficacy of their thoughts.

Concepts are all important tools of thought. Once we have a concept of, say, dogs, we can talk about these animals in general without specifying their color, shape, the sounds they make, and so on. Young children form concepts, but their concepts are less general and distinctive than those of older children and adults. This again relates to the transductive, single-level nature of young children's thought. For example, young children often have trouble distinguishing between the "one" and the "many." When a three-year-old calls a strange man "Daddy," she is not really being disloyal. She does not yet clearly distinguish between the one Daddy and the many men.

Young children may also experience difficulty in *nesting* classes. If you ask a preschool child of four or five years of age how many boys and how many girls are in the class, the child can often answer correctly. She might say, for example, seven boys and ten girls. Teachers usually take roll and the children are accustomed to hearing how many boys and girls are in the class. However, if you ask the child whether there are more girls or more children in the class, she is likely to reply that there are more girls than boys. To nest the classes of boys and girls within the larger class of children requires the mental abilities that usually appear at ages six or seven and that Piaget calls *concrete operations.*

Likewise, young children also experience difficulty in nesting (seriating) size-graded materials. A child of four or five can copy a "stairway" made of sticks of different sizes aligned side by side. If, however, you give the child some additional sticks that are intermediate in size to those making up the stairway, the child usually cannot correctly insert or nest them within the series. To do so, the child would have to understand that the stick to be inserted is both larger than the stick on one side of it and smaller than the stick on the other side. The ability to appreciate that one stick can be both smaller and larger than other sticks must wait for the attainment of concrete operations that allows the child to grasp that one object can be in two relationships at the same time.

A number of investigators have shown that children can nest classes and series earlier than Piaget observed. These investigators, however, use different tasks that often make it possible for the child to nest classes or series by means of visual cues. Although the child's ability to accomplish these feats is interesting, it does not invalidate the limitations described above. It is the child's ability to nest classes and relations at the intellectual, rather than the perceptual, level that Piaget was interested in. The evidence is still consistent that perceptually unassisted classification and seriation must wait for the attainment of concrete operations.

The same argument can be made for children's concepts of number. Piaget demonstrated that children do not usually have a *unit* concept of number until they attain concrete operations. Young children can use *nominal* number, the use of number like a name. Numbers on football or baseball jerseys are nominal numbers that do not stand for quantities but for individuals. Likewise, young children can grasp *ordinal* number wherein the number stands for a rank order. When judges use numbers to rate the performance of ice skaters, for example, those numbers simply stand for ranks, not units. A skater who gets a ranking of 7.0 is not 0.5 units better than a skater who is given a score of 6.5. There are no units of skating performance, and the numbers are simply used by the judges to objectify their subjective rankings.

It is only when children attain concrete operations that they can form a true unit concept of number. When a child achieves a unit concept of number, she grasps that a number is like every other number in that it is a number, but different from other numbers in its order of enumeration. The number 4, for example, is like every other number in the sense that it is a number. It is also different from every other number in the sense that it is the only number that comes after 3 and before 5. It is only when the child can coordinate sameness and difference that she can arrive at the notion of unit quantities.

Piaget assessed the child's understanding of number by means of the *conservation task*. These tasks always offer the child a choice between reason and perception. In the case of number, a commonly used conservation task presents the child with a row of six or seven pennies. The child must first construct a similar row from a pile of pennies on the side. Four-year-old children often have trouble copying the row and may match the length and ignore the interval size or may match the interval size and ignore the length. Five-year-old children are often able to copy the row of pennies correctly. Many children at this age are often able to count the pennies correctly as well. If one row of pennies is now spaced out much farther than the other, however, young children are likely to judge the longer row as having more. They are basing their judgment on the appearance of one row being longer than the other rather than upon the rational understanding that if both have the same number they will be the same despite appearances. Concrete operational children do judge the two rows to be the same.

Other investigators have shown, however, that when you use only three or four pennies, young children do recognize that they are the same, even when one row is spread out. With small numbers, however, the child can solve the problem perceptually, by overall size of the array, and does not need to employ reasoning. So, although it is interesting that children can understand numerical sameness with small numbers, it is still no indication that they have a true number concept. Indeed, once children show a true number concept, they can engage in the simple operations of arithmetic. This is something that children who can see the sameness between three or four elements spread out and three or four elements together cannot do.

It is important to point out that in emphasizing that young children do not yet have a true concept of number, my intent is not to minimize or belittle their intellectual powers. Quite the contrary. What must be emphasized, and what is underplayed by those attempting to show how much young children can do, is the extraordinary complexity of concept formation and of mental processing generally. We are beginning to appreciate how difficult it is to program a computer to mimic the human brain. The difficulty arises because brain processes are very complex. A child's thinking mirrors that complexity. We do young children a disservice when we underestimate the enormity of the intellectual tasks they confront in constructing concepts in general and the concept of number in particular.

Language

Language growth is very rapid during the preschool years. From a vocabulary of no words at about one year of age, the two-year-old may have a vocabulary of two or three hundred words and can even form two- or three-word sentences.

By the age of five, children can construct simple sentences and may use past and future as well as present tenses correctly. By this age, children also demonstrate considerable mastery of possessives and of definite and indefinite articles and may have an active vocabulary of about 2,500 words. Their passive vocabulary—the words they can hear and understand but do not usually use—is much higher and may be as large as 14,000 words. Averaged over the child's lifetime, she has acquired nine words a day since birth!

Although language growth is relatively easy to describe, it is more difficult to explain. Indeed, there are at least three different types of explanation of language growth, and there is some evidence to support each one.

One explanation of language development starts from the assumption that the language system is present from birth and follows its own path of development quite independently of the development of thought. This is the position of famed linguist Noam Chomsky. Those who look at language development from this perspective try to map the progress of the child's linguistic structures in relation to the child's experience and point to the fact that experience cannot account for the observed achievements in the evolution of language.

Young children's earliest words are often *holophrases*, or single-word utterances that are meant to convey as much meaning as a full sentence. A child who says "Car" may mean, "I see a car" or "I want to be in the car" or "Where is the car?" As children become more proficient they may use *telegraphic* speech in which they evidence their understanding of word order by the ways in which they combine two or more words, such as "All gone," "Baby up," and "Daddy go bye-bye." Since children do not learn these combinations directly from adults, it is argued that they are evidence of an independently emerging language system.

Other language phenomena during early childhood also support this position. One of these is *overregularization*. A child may understand a grammatical rule but not its exceptions. For example, a child may say, "The boy runned home." Here the child is generalizing from the past progressive rule—add *ed*—to all verbs, but she does not appreciate that the verb *to run* is irregular. The understanding of grammatical rules but not their exceptions suggests that language acquisition is not simply a matter of copying adult speech. Adults, children's presumed language role models, do not make such errors.

Another evidence for the independence of language development is the creativity of children's language. Children are always coming up with original speech utterances that are not copies of adult verbalizations. Parents do not say, "All gone milk" when they have finished their drink or "Mommy, sleep time" when they are ready for bed. Moreover, parents tend to reinforce the truth value of children's statements, not their grammatical correctness. A child who says, "Mommy dress red," is likely to be told "Yes" if she is correct factually if not grammatically. On the other hand, if the child says, "Mommy's dress is blue" she is likely to be told "no" even though she is grammatically correct. That children learn grammar even though it is not rewarded by parents is another evidence of its, independence from adult instruction.

A different position with respect to language development is that of Piaget and his colleagues. According to this view, language development is regulated by intellectual development. The child's language limitations always reflect her cognitive limitations. In one study preoperational and concrete operational children were asked to describe three blocks of different sizes. Preoperational children often described them in nonquantitative ways, such as "the baby block, the mommy block, and the daddy block." Concrete operational children, in contrast, described the blocks in quantitative terms: "This one is taller and wider. That one is shorter and thinner."

Sometimes children's failures on the conservation tasks are attributed to verbal misunderstanding. A child who says that six pennies in a line next to one another is less than six pennies spaced apart simply does not understand the term *less*. Piaget's reply is that "verbal misunderstanding" begs the question. The real question that must be asked is why the preschool child does not understand the term *less* in the accepted sense while the older child does. The answer, according to Piaget, is that the older child now has the requisite mental abilities to understand the term while the young child does not.

A third position with respect to language development is that of Russian psychologist Lev Vygotsky. In his view, thought is determined by language—and not language by thought as Piaget contends. According to Vygotsky, language is progressively internalized, and whispering is a stage along the way. When language is completely internalized, it is the tool of our thinking. Inasmuch as language is, in part at least, learned, so too must be our thinking, and because language varies from society to society, thought must vary from society to society as well.

Evidence for the language determination of mental development comes from observations of how children use language when they go about their everyday activities. Children often talk out loud as they are engaged in building or in making something. At such times, their language seems to be a necessary guide to their action. This directive use of language has been called *verbal mediation.* Children often use verbal mediation as a memory strategy. If, for example, something is hidden in front of them, they may say "It is under the blue cup" as a way of remembering where the hidden object is until they are permitted to actually look for it.

Language development is so complex that no one of these theories can encompass it all. In fact, there seems to be a little truth in all three. Language structure does seem to follow its own course, quite independent of experience. On the other hand, the use of conceptual terms does seem to be related to conceptual development. Finally, language does sometimes enable young children to bridge delays and regulate their actions. In fact we all use language in this way. If we are doing something very delicate, we may walk ourselves through the task: "Okay, now just move this lever a little to the left." Language is directed by thought, but thought is also directed by language.

Despite these differences, researchers generally agree that adults play a very important role in the child's language development. First, adults provide a linguistic model from which children learn vocabulary, expressions, articulation, and so on. Second, from the earliest days of life, adults and children engage in a variety of verbal dialogues that teach children not only language skills, but also social interaction patterns. Finally, by reading to children, parents give children some of the requisite skills and interests that promote their later literacy.

I have already emphasized the importance of parents and other adults talking to and reading to young children as an essential part of their linguistic growth. Such interaction helps build the child's auditory, or listening, skills. These are critical for learning to read. When young children watch too much television, more than an hour or two a day, they may not develop the necessary auditory discrimination skills that are critical to learning to read. This is true because when young children watch television, they often do not listen. It is easier for them to get the information visually. We all take the path of least effort, but this path will cost children dearly when they set out to attach printed words to sounds that they cannot clearly discriminate. Limiting young children's television watching is essential if we wish them to develop the listening skills needed to become accomplished readers.

Young children, then, make enormous progress in intellectual and language development. Despite these enormous accomplishments, they still have a long way to go before they can fully comprehend the language and thought of the adult reality. This is in no way a negative description of young children, but only a realistic statement regarding the extraordinary complexity of the cognitive and linguistic world that the child must master and a recognition of the large amount of time and effort that is required to get a better understanding of our world.

Selected Readings

Elkind, D. (1987). *Miseducation: Preschoolers at Risk.* New York: Knopf. Details some of the ways parents and the schools are placing inappropriate educational demands upon young children and describes the resulting stresses these demands engender.

Kaye, E. (1979). *The ACT Guide to Children's Television.* Boston: Beacon Press. A thoughtful discussion and review of the literature about the effects of television on children. Provides useful guidelines for parents.

Siegel-Gorelick, B. (1983). *The Working Parents' Guide to Child Care.* Boston: Little, Brown. Provides thoughtful and helpful answers to the many questions and concerns parents have about out-of-home child care.

5

Age Profiles

In the last edition of this book, I suggested that even though age profiles were out of style, psychologically speaking, they are still useful as rough guidelines to development. Today, more than a decade later, age profiles are even less fashionable than they were at that time. To be sure, age profiles ignore the wide individual differences among children of the same age. Nor do they take sufficient account of cultural and ethnic group differences.

That said, it is still true that children are growing organisms whose development shows an organization, pattern, and direction that is characteristic of the species. This pattern becomes even more apparent when we look at children year by year rather than over longer time spans, such as early childhood, childhood, and adolescence. Indeed, when we look at development in smaller units, we can observe short-term growth patterns that are lost when longer time units are employed.

The rationale I gave for using the year as a unit for the profiles seems equally sound today. The use of the year as the unit of observation is justified by the fact that it is the unit that is consensually validated by home and school. We celebrate the child's birthday annually, and the school curriculum is calibrated on a yearlong course of study. Accordingly, while using the year as a unit of observation has some drawbacks—we might miss changes that are better observed at half-year or two-year intervals, for example—it remains the most reasonable and acceptable one to use.

Cautions are in order. The description of the unique features of children at different age levels must be taken as an abstraction, a rough prototype if you will, to which no child will conform in every detail. That is to say, the profiles must not be taken too literally as the master pattern from which all children of an age are cloned. In addition, it is very important not to see these profiles as assigning good and bad labels to children's behavior. The profiles are descriptive and not prescriptive; they tell us what is, not what should, in any moral sense, be.

Finally, neither parents nor teachers should use the profiles in a competitive fashion to boast of how their child or their class is at a more advanced level than that suggested by the profile for the age group. Being ahead of the prototypes is not necessarily good, and being behind is not necessarily bad. The growth rates for ability and talent are quite variable, and a child who may be behind today, may be well ahead tomorrow.

Despite the risks outlined above, I still believe that the advantages of age profiles considerably outweigh their disadvantages. One of the advantages is that age profiles provide parents and teachers with some guides as to what to expect from children at certain age levels. For example, if we know that most six-year-olds take things from schools and doctor's offices, we can deal with these actions more objectively than if we perceived them as unique to a particular child and evidence of her bad character. On the other hand, if we know that most six-year-olds no longer wet the bed and we have a six-year-old who does not have a dry night, we may be motivated to seek professional help.

It is with such considerations in mind that I offer the following age descriptions. If you will keep in mind that these are prototypical descriptions and not ideal types, I think they will provide useful ideas around which to gear your observations and interventions with your child.

The One-Year-Old

Although chronological age is a convenient reference point, it by no means always, if ever, signals the completion of particular achievements and the undertaking of fresh ones. At one year of age, the infant is very much in transition, and there is nothing new and entirely complete to mark his first birthday. Many of the motor, intellectual, social, and linguistic skills that he will master later can only be glimpsed at this way station.

Motorically, the one-year-old is just beginning to give hints of his future accomplishments. He is just starting to pull himself up to an erect position and inch himself along using the crib or playpen frame to maintain his balance. In a few more months, he will be able to get up and walk without support. He is beginning to grasp for a spoon, push blocks, and clutch crayons. These efforts will later be elaborated into effective self-feeding, block play, and drawing.

All facets of the child's growth are interwoven. This is particularly true for his motor and intellectual growth. For example, as he becomes more mobile, he is beginning to have a sense of himself and of other objects in space. He has a better sense of how far things are from him and how far he has to go to get them. In addition, his new muscle coordination allows him to turn a bottle to insert his fingers into it and attain a desired object. Motor skill thus facilitates problem solving. Sometimes he will use his new motor skills to put several objects—such as a rattle, a ball, and a small doll—in a row. With this activity, his motor skills enable him to attain a preliminary notion of a series.

Motor skill also helps advance the one-year-old's social interactions. For example, he is developing the motor ability to let go, and he delights in dropping a rattle out of the crib and in seeing mommy or daddy fetch it back. This new motor skill allows him to elaborate a form of social play. He is also very conscious of adults in his presence and will repeat motor actions that won him parental approval or surprised laughter. By the end of the first year, the child gives evidence of all of the basic emotions: fear, rage, love, anger, and jealousy. He may also show a fear of strangers and may cry if his parents leave him with a babysitter.

There are also signs of beginning social independence. The one-year-old wants to feed himself—with his fingers to be sure!—and is annoyed when we try to help him do something he has chosen to do himself. On the other hand, he is also more cooperative while being dressed than he was as a young infant. At one year of age, he already seems sensitive to our moods and feelings and will even modulate his own reactions in accord with these perceptions.

Language growth is also very much in transition at one year of age. The one-year-old listens intently when adults talk to or around him and often mimics words that he likes or finds interesting. His passive vocabulary is quite large, and he can respond to commands such as "Give it to me." He also tries to use language socially to attract attention and sometimes, or so it appears, to evoke smiles in admiring adults. Much of his language, however, is still expressive jargon, or incomprehensible speech production that serves as a kind of vocal accompaniment to his actions.

In summary, at one year of age the child's motor, intellectual, social, and language skills are at the swelled bud stage and give wonderful hints of the full flowering that is to come.

The Eighteen-Month-Old

Growth is so rapid during the second year that it would do an injustice to this development to merely summarize it at the end of a full year. So I will make one exception to the year-by-year age profile presentation and talk about what has been achieved by the age of 1½.

Physical growth is exceedingly rapid during the early months and years of life. In six months, the eighteen-month-old has gained several inches in height and is now between 30 and 33 inches tall. He has made similar gains in weight and now weighs between 20 and 27 pounds—about triple his birth weight. In six months he has also added a comparable number of teeth and sports a respectable dozen. The child can now bite and chew a wide variety of solid foods. Although he still sleeps some thirteen hours a day, he now takes only one nap, during the afternoon.

Motor control has increased apace. At eighteen months, the now-ambulatory toddler puffs along at a rapid flat-footed pace, reminiscent of the movements and gait of long-distance walkers. Other skills attest to his new muscular development and coordination. He can aim his backside at a chair and get it there with reasonable accuracy. Stairs have a magnetlike attraction for him, and he loves to crawl up them without assistance and to bump down them all on his own. The problem at this age is often to keep the toddler away from the stairs.

Small-motor control is also better than it was at age one, but the child's performance is not consistent. With some effort he can get one block to sit atop another one, but he is likely to knock them all over if he attempts to go higher and build a three-block tower. The eighteen-month-old can now use his thumb and opposed forefinger to pick up a piece of paper and even turn the pages of a book with a sweeping motion that often turns a bunch of pages at a time. Well-coordinated small-motor movements will have to wait for a bit more growth.

At eighteen months, new intellectual feats are apparent. The child's sense of space is such that he now knows where treasured toys are and can retrieve them from where they are usually kept. In addition, he begins to understand *frames*, or repetitive patterns of social interaction, such as eating and sleeping. Frames have a beginning, middle, and end as well as their own emotional rhythm. Frames are the building blocks of socialization, and the attainment of some frames is well along by age eighteen months. For example, while eating, the child puts down his spoon to signal the end of the eating frame, saying in effect, "I have had enough." Likewise, he now uses the phrases "bye-bye" and "all gone" as general sign-off terms to signal the end of a completed social frame. The world of the eighteen-month-old is no longer merely episodic. Rather, it is now made up of predictable, recurring frames.

The eighteen-month-old has also begun to use language to express his wants and desires. Language and action are still a unitary pattern, and every *no* is accompanied by vigorous head shaking. Likewise, *eat* is usually said to the tune of some pounding and banging. The child's passive vocabulary and comprehension have also progressed at a leapfrog pace, and he can now understand involved commands such as "Put the ball on the chair." At this stage, however, he still uses a lot of contextual clues, such as his parent's intonation and gestures, to decipher these complicated requests for action.

The eighteen-month-old's self-concept is more distinct than it was a scant six months before. At 1½ years, he distinguishes between "you" and "me" and makes claims about things being "mine." Emotionally, however, he is still a bit unstable and is likely to show distress and unhappiness with tantrumlike behavior—lying down, kicking, flailing the air. At the same time, he is also making progress toward greater self-control by imitating adult actions. This miming, however, is often of parental actions, such as talking on the phone, rather than of facial expressions or verbal intonations. These more complex imitations will come later.

What is important about this imitation is that the eighteen-month-old has discovered a useful technique of social learning that will, along with his acquisition of frames, enable him to meet the many demands for socialization that are visited upon all young children.

The Two-Year-Old

At age two, the average child stands between 32 and 35 inches tall and weighs anywhere from 23 to 30 pounds. He still sleeps more than twelve hours, and he requires a nap of one or two hours during the afternoon. When he is awake, however, the two-year-old is going all the time. He has much more motor control than he had a scant six months before, and anything that can be climbed on or jumped from has an almost irresistible attraction for him. Indeed, he often makes his parents nervous when he appears at the top of the stairs and starts coming down as if he were being chased by demons. Language growth is also exponential and competes with physical exuberance as the major theme of this age period.

Motorically, the two-year-old is expansive and expressive. Now that he can walk and climb without assistance, he takes great pleasure in his mastery of these skills, and he uses his newfound control over his body to express his emotions. The two-year-old jumps up and down, laughs and chortles when he is happy, and cries, yells, and screams when he is unhappy. Small-muscle control is also much advanced over what it was but a few months earlier. He now can hold a small glass of juice with one hand (a feat his parents often watch with fearful anticipation that the juice will spill). The two-year-old can also succeed at other small-motor tasks, such as stacking a number of blocks and stringing wooden beads. Effective artwork, such as drawing and painting, does not usually become fully operative for another year.

Motor, intellectual, and language activity are still all of a piece in the two-year-old. For example, he likes to hold and examine things he is learning to name. In contrast to the eighteen-month-old, the two-year-old looks for hidden toys and shows that he has begun mentally to represent external objects and to let the inner representation guide his actions. We can also observe this new capacity for internal representation in the two-year-old's ability to recall events that happened earlier in the day and in his ability to anticipate events that will occur later in the day. In this regard, the two-year-old's time/space world has begun to expand beyond the immediate here and now to events that are occurring at somewhat greater temporal and spatial distances.

The two-year-old's goal-seeking actions reflect this new expansion of his time/space world. If a two-year-old sees a ball roll behind one chair and then behind another, he goes immediately to the second chair in search of the ball. At an earlier age, he would have gone to the chair where the ball first disappeared and, not finding it there, would have given up. The two-year-old can even engage in an early version of transductive reasoning. If we hide a piece of candy in a box that we then place in a cupboard with other boxes, the child will search all of the boxes until he finds the one with the candy. He reasoned transductively that if the candy was not in one container, it will be in the next.

Memory is another facet of intellectual ability in which the two-year-old demonstrates quite remarkable gains since the age of eighteen months. Not only does the child learn the names of many different objects, but he retains them and uses them correctly. He also recalls where he left toys and where desirable treats are most likely to be found. We can also note this new memory ability in the two-year-old's use of deferred imitation—the ability to observe an action at one point in time (say a mother pushing a baby carriage) and to imitate that behavior at a later point in time. The two-year-old's memory skills are both a cause and an effect of his growing abilities to extend his spatial and temporal boundaries.

It is the two-year-old's progress in language, however, that is perhaps his most remarkable achievement. By the age of two, most children have an active vocabulary of as many as three hundred words and have a passive vocabulary of as many as a thousand words. The two-year-old is mastering words and grammatical forms at an enormous rate and has already acquired the basic pronouns for talking about himself: *I*, *me*, and *mine*. He also produces two- and three-word utterances that reflect a beginning grammatical understanding. Multiple-word combinations such as "Peter fall down" or "Bobby eat candy" are quite common.

Nonetheless, for two-year-old children, words lack the specificity of meaning and separateness they have for adults. "Peter up" may mean "Pick me up" or "Peter wants to pick it up," or "Peter is up in the chair" and so on. For children at this age, language is still very bound up with action, and it is the child's actions that provide the best clue as to the most probable meaning of his utterances. At this stage, too, children very much enjoy the rhythmic pattern and musical qualities of language as much as they do its meaning. One reason two-year-olds like to hear the same story over and over again—often to our dismay—is that they take as much or more pleasure from the music of the story's language as they do from its content. In this respect, young children are no different than adults who never tire of hearing favorite musical compositions.

Within the social sphere, the two-year-old shows mounting evidence of independence from adult assistance and increased interest in children his own age. The two-year-old will often object to his mother's help and will insist on doing things for himself, such as putting his arms in his jacket or using his spoon to eat pudding. With other children he is still quite self-centered, but he will sit next to another child and play alongside him or her for a while. He seems to enjoy the companionship of people his own size. When he plays alone, the two-year-old is apt to dramatize the caregiver-baby relationship, perhaps as a way of working through his mixed feelings about growing up and becoming more independent.

The two-year-old shows his budding socialization in other ways. When he does something wrong, he tends to look sheepish as if he were beginning to experience guilt about his misbehavior. His many negativisms, his refusal to follow adult directions, and his frequent demands show that he is beginning to distinguish clearly between himself and others. Indeed, his negativism has to be understood as an important tool of setting himself apart from his parents and other caregivers. What appears to be willfulness in the two-year-old is, in fact, his growing ability to assert himself and to establish his individuality.

The Three-Year-Old

The transition between ages two and three, as between all age epochs, is gradual rather than abrupt. The three-year-old is more motorically adept, more verbal, and more social than the two-year-old. Yet, although the differences in each dominion of growth are only quantitative, when they are all put together, the three-year-old seems almost qualitatively different than she was but a few scant months earlier.

In the motor realm, the three-year-old still enjoys motor play as she did at two. Now, however, she persists for longer periods in such play and prefers much more complex activities. When she succeeds in getting a ball out of a box with a lid, she may drop the ball in the box again, close the lid, and repeat the process of opening the lid and retrieving the ball. In contrast, the two-year-old would simply play with the ball. Although she still cannot draw stick figures, the lines that she does draw have definite direction and are less repetitive than they were at age two.

Large-motor development is also more advanced. At three, the child can ride a tricycle and push a wagon. When she runs, her stoppings and startings are controlled, and she does not often bump into people or things in the course of her trajectory. In jumping and climbing, she has also gained more control than was evident at age two. We don't wince when we watch a three-year-old climb a ladder to go down a slide because she seems to do it so well. In contrast, watching a two-year-old climb will put us on edge for fear he will topple.

Visual-motor coordination is more advanced than it was at age two. In her block play, her drawings, and her imitations, the three-year-old shows more order and direction than she did a year before. In the process of separating herself from other people and things, she gains a better perception and understanding of both. There is a reciprocity, too, in her comfort with motor activities and the comfort adults experience in watching her perform. That is to say, our greater relaxation about her motor behavior supports and encourages her own self-confidence in her actions.

Arnold Gesell wrote that there is "jargon at eighteen months, words at two years, sentences at three years." As Gesell was quick to point out, however, this guideline is a vast oversimplification of what the three-year-old has accomplished in the way of language. The three-year-old's language is truly phenomenal. At this age, young people come out with expressions that often dumbfound us. I heard one three-year-old say to his father, "Well, Dad, what do you think we should do next?" Sometimes they mimic us with almost exact intonation: "Don't you do that anymore!" Although some of this may be imitation, much of it is not. It reflects a wondrous capacity to generate unique linguistic expressions.

At the same time, the three-year-old's language is still more circumscribed than it will be later. Young children talk to themselves while they are playing, eating, or engaging in activities with other children. The three-year-old's language is more than an accompaniment to action, however. It is also a form of practice. In her incessant vocalizing, the three-year-old is practicing pronunciation, grammatical structure, and inflection. For adults, however, this constant talk can be a nuisance. When she was an infant we could not wait for her to be able to talk. Now that she is three, we cannot wait for her to be still.

In her active and persistent vocalizing, the three-year-old is also beginning to coordinate words and actions. Words are slowly gaining some executive control over her behavior. With a verbal command we can now interrupt a three-year-old's actions. But she is also beginning to use language to regulate her own behavior as well. At three, the child can retrieve a toy hidden under a cover by saying to herself the color of the cover. Language is beginning to serve as a mediator between actions and things. Now the child, by means of language, can delay reaching for something she wants by saying to herself, "No touch." In her use of language as a mediator of action, we see evidence for the Vygotsky position that language serves to regulate behavior.

By the time a child is three, she no longer needs to assert her individuality to the extent that she did at two. She accepts her separateness as she does that of others. Now she wants to be accepted and liked by other people and tries her hardest to please. In part, these efforts may reflect her delight in understanding verbal commands and the pleasure she derives from matching words to actions. At any rate, the three-year-old takes great pride in doing little errands or in fetching her parent's slippers or sweaters.

The three-year-old's social orientation is shown in other ways as well. She laughs when adults laugh, as if she really understood what the joke was all about. She even tries to make adults laugh by laughing herself. At this age the child is more reticent with age-mates than she is with adults. If she spends time at a preschool or child-care center, for example, she does not immediately relate to the other children. It takes several months for three-year-old children to learn each other's names and to feel comfortable enough with each other to engage in joint activities.

To be sure, the three-old-old is not all obedience, deference, and seeking to be liked. She sometimes throws tantrums and may get angry and destroy toys or puzzles that she cannot manage. She may experience night terrors and animal phobias. On occasion, she exhibits jealousy and willfulness that are reminiscent of the two-year-old. At the same time, however, she begins to use language as well as action to express her displeasure. In general, the three-year-old is beginning to coordinate thought, language, and emotion so that she appears much more stable, both socially and emotionally, than she did at two. Nonetheless, her world is still largely limited to the immediate here and now and to the immediate persons about her. Her adaptations are adequate to this encapsulated world, but she has much to learn about the larger world of school and community.

The Four-Year-Old

The four-year-old has consolidated many of the social, emotional, and linguistic gains that she made during the previous year. She appears more at ease in social situations, and her use of language is quite sophisticated. Thanks to her wonderful powers of verbal imitation, the four-year-old can use words and verbal expressions that are far beyond her level of comprehension. This verbal sophistication can be, and often is, mistaken for conceptual understanding by grown-ups. As a result, adults often talk at too abstract a level for the four-year-old's level of understanding. Nevertheless, the four-year-old manages to cope very well with misguided adults as well as with her peers.

With regard to motor development, the four-year-old shows a new confidence in her motor abilities and a new willingness to try new tricks and stunts. She will jump off a low embankment or a couch and will try climbing up a slide the wrong way. Her bold willingness to try new and exciting motor feats reflects her recently achieved coordination of leg and arm muscles. It also reflects the four-year-old's budding sense of *initiative,* her readiness to undertake tasks on her own and bring them to completion. The four-year-old has learned the joys of success and mastery and is always on the lookout for new worlds to conquer.

In her drawings, the child reflects both her improved perceptual-motor skills and her intellectual limitations. When she draws a man, it usually consists of a head, arms, legs, and eyes—with the torso omitted. The child at this stage draws what she knows or thinks is important rather than what she sees. In other perceptual-motor activities, the four-year-old can copy single features of an arrangement of objects, but she cannot coordinate the features. To illustrate, when she attempts to construct an evenly spaced row of six pennies to match another such row, she does one of two things. Either she matches the space between the pennies but neglects the length of the row (and puts in too many pennies) or she matches the length of the row but neglects spacing (and again puts in too many pennies). Likewise, when a four-year-old is asked whether two pictures of houses are alike or different, she makes her judgment by comparing only the windows or the doors and may come to different conclusions depending upon which features of the houses she chooses to compare.

Perhaps the major characteristic of the four-year-old is her curiosity. This reflects the sense of initiative so characteristic of this age period. Adults encounter this curiosity in the seemingly endless "Why" questions asked by children at this stage: "Why do the birds sing?" or "Why is the grass green and the sky blue?" Writers for this age group have built this curiosity into their stories. "How the Elephant Got His Trunk" and "How the Zebra Got His Stripes" are stories that anticipate some of the questions asked by four-year-olds.

In answering these questions, it is important to remember that the queries of a young child are not the same as questions asked by an older child. First of all, these questions are often intended to get the adult's attention as much as to get a meaningful answer. Indeed, the child's questions are often rhetorical and asked in hopes that the adult will ask the child for an opinion. One of our options is to ask the child to answer her own question by saying something like, "What do you think?" If we do this, the four-year-old is quick to provide an answer to her own question. She has lots of opinions and is most eager to share them.

If we choose to try and answer a four-year-old's "why" questions, it is important to recall that she believes that everything in the whole world has a purpose, a reason for being there. When she asks why the grass is green, she expects a reply such as, "To hide the green caterpillars so they won't be eaten by the birds." If we answer the question in a more scientific way and talk about photosynthesis, we have missed the intent of the child's question. We have also given her an unintelligible answer. We really don't have to worry about giving simple, purposive answers to the young child's questions. Children will learn the more socially acceptable answers eventually. What is more important is that the child has the comfort and assurance that we understand her way of seeing the world.

Perhaps because she believes that everything has a purpose, the four-year-old is often quite verbose. When replying to a question, she often goes on and on, as if each thought that came to her mind was the cause of the next. Transductive thinking is thus reflected in her language in keeping with the Piagetian position regarding language and thought. in the same way, the four-year-old's commentaries on the passing scene are also frequently prolix. Here is an example quoted from Gesell: "I don't even know that. You almost hit him. Now I will make something else. They are like one another, but that one is bigger. That one too." This example also illustrates how elaborate the child's language has become within the space of two short years.

At four, the child also manifests considerable consolidation of her social skills. Internal control over her behavior is quite advanced, and she can refrain from certain actions she would like to undertake by subvocal talking to herself. She also shows a nice balance between comfort with being on her own and enjoyment of the company of other children and adults. Because of her enhanced perceptual motor skills, she is more self-reliant than ever before and can dress herself (even do her shoes if they are closed with Velcro!) and feed herself (with the exception of cutting meat). Now the four-year-old enjoys playing with other children as much as or more than she likes playing by herself. Four-year-old boys and girls have no hesitation playing with one another, as long as the influence of older siblings is not there to disrupt the pattern.

Although the four-year-old shows much more independence than she did at three, she also often displays what appear to be unreasonable fears. These may be fears of the dark, of dogs, of birds, and so on. Such fears are not rooted in any actual traumatic experiences but are more likely projections onto external objects of the child's own unacceptable anger and frustration with her parents or her caregivers. Accordingly, reasoning with the child about such fears and telling her that there is nothing to be afraid of has little value. A more effective strategy is to accept the child's fear as real for her and to assure her that we will not let anyone or anything hurt her.

The four-year-old not only has fears, she also makes up stories, rationalizes and alibis her "accidents," and often plays the social clown. All of these words and deeds bespeak her growing awareness of the social world about her and of the importance of adult approval for her emerging sense of self as a social creature. Nonetheless, the extent and the complexities of the social world into which she is moving are not always easy for her to deal with. Some of the four-year-old's gaucheries have to be forgiven in the light of her social immaturity and the intricacies of the social world into which she is trying to integrate herself.

The Five-Year-Old

In many ways, the attainment of age five marks the completion of the early childhood period. Small- and large-muscle control and coordination are quite advanced. Many independence skills, such as toileting, dressing herself, and feeding herself are now well-established habits. Socialization is also well advanced, and the five-year-old has mastered most of the eating, sleeping, visiting, playing with other children, and other social frames she will need to move into schooling. The five-year-old enjoys companions of her own age and may have one or more close friends. Although she is still not ready for formal education involving the inculcation of rules, she can enjoy a kindergarten experience and engage in a number of manipulative learning activities that will promote her math, language, science, and artistic skills.

With her new motor coordination, the five-year-old can do such things as ride a two-wheeler and learn simple dance steps. In her movements, actions, and posturing, the five-year-old shows a new grace and coordination that is a pleasure to watch. Her small-motor control is a little less advanced, but she can effectively manage utensils, such as a toothbrush, and tools, such as a hammer. She can now complete some picture puzzles and do simple weaving and basket making. Her small-motor achievements prepare her for such skills as writing and table games that involve spinners and moving tokens.

In her intellectual development, the five-year-old is in a kind of transition stage. When she attempts to construct a row of six pennies to match a model row, she is now able to do so, but she succeeds by a process of trial and error. That is, she first makes a row that is the right length but has too many pennies. Once she has got the proper length, she then removes the extra pennies to arrive at the proper density. If, however, we spread the model row of pennies such that it is now longer than her row at both ends, she believes that the longer row contains more pennies than the shorter row. Sometimes she is even able to count both rows correctly but still says that the longer row has more. The higher order coordination of row length and interval size—which involves the recognition that what the row gained in length it lost in density—will not usually appear until the age of six or seven.

In other arenas of growth, the five-year-old gives evidence that she is moving toward the self-direction and self-control required of the school-age child. She persists longer at tasks and works until she completes a project. She has a more differentiated conception of time and space than she did at four, and she can talk meaningfully about tomorrow and about yesterday as well as about distant places, such as a farm or a fire station. In many ways, the five-year-old seems more painstaking than she was at four. She is more careful, more persevering, and more concerned with accuracy than she was only a year earlier.

By the age of five, most children have conquered many of their speech difficulties. Some children celebrate their overcoming of these limitations as did the boy who could not pronounce the letter *l* until one day he found himself saying "love" and "yellow" with ease. At that happy discovery, he made up a song, which he sang to himself Pooh-fashion: " Yellow, yellow, yellow, it is so easy to say yellow." The questions asked by five-year-olds are less general and rhetorical and more to the point—"Where does this go?"—than they were a year earlier. As adults, we find these questions a little easier, if less interesting, to answer.

Her specific questions are indicative of the five-year-old's general practical orientation. She wants to know what things are for and what to do with them. This orientation is reflected in her definition of words: "A horse is to ride, a fork is to eat, a hole is to dig." The five-year-old is beginning to move away from enjoying fairy-tale fantasy, but she will still sit and listen when a story of this kind is being read to a younger child. Her preferences, however, are moving toward realism and comedy and away from fantasy and magic.

The language proficiency of the five-year-old is truly remarkable, and the conversations held by children at this age are a delight to hear. As suggested earlier, children at this age can even shift their language registers when talking to younger children. Naomi Baron provides this example:

> Five-year-old Sara was telling the story of "Goldilocks and the Three Bears" to her three year old brother. She had gotten to the part where each of the bears asks in turn, "Who's been sitting in my chair?" With a deep voice, she echoed the words of the father bear and the mother bear, and then launched into the baby bear's line with the same basso voice. Half way through she switched to falsetto:
> "Who's been sitting in my chair?" she squeaked, correcting her earlier intonations in order to match the voice of a baby.*

The five-year-old attempts to make sense out of everything she hears and sometimes comes up with amusing interpretations. For example, there was the Connecticut youngster who sang out in church, "Our father who art in New Haven, Harold be thy name." And many a child goes to church wondering whether she will ever see the "cross-eyed bear" (the Cross, I'd bear).

In her social behavior, the five-year-old has clearly completed the social learnings of the early childhood period. She has now mastered most of the frames she will need

---

* Barron, N. (1992). *Growing Up with Language. Reading, MA.*

to move successfully into formal education. She is quite self-sufficient in so many different domains that she can easily be taken for a miniature adult. She enjoys her own friends with whom she may exchange visits. Her well-developed preferences are shown in her unequivocal selection of toys, clothes, and TV programs. She is relatively undemanding of parental time and attention. Moreover, she is able to handle stress in a much more calm and matter-of-fact way than she was at earlier ages. If she gets separated from her parents at the mall, she will tell the security official her name and address and may even enjoy hearing her name on the public-address system!

The five-year-old thus reflects, in many ways, the benefits of five years of socialization within the family and in out-of-home child-care arrangements. At the end of the early childhood period, she has a sense of herself as a person, of who she is, and of what she can do that will stand her in good stead as she moves toward the ever wider world of school and community.

II

The Child

6

Personal and Social
Development

The elementary school years, roughly from age six through age eleven, are in many ways a developmental intermezzo between the rapid advancement of the preschool years and the accelerated growth pace of adolescence. It would be a mistake, however, to view middle childhood as nothing but a period of marking time until adolescence. In fact, much is happening that flows from experiences in the preschool period and that prepares the young person for the onset of the next season of rapid growth. By his appearance, the elementary school child reminds us of his past and suggests his future. Nonetheless, we must understand middle childhood as a stage of life to be valued in its own right, not simply as a time of preparation.

In general, childhood tends to involve a solidification and refinement of the social frames and skills that the child attained during the years of early childhood. There is individual continuity. The child who is active and social and is an initiator of activities in preschool or child care is likely to continue his leadership ways in elementary school. He becomes captain of his team, president of his class, and so on. Likewise, the child who is on the sideline of activities in the early childhood program tends to perpetuate this role after he begins elementary school.

Remarkable individual personality changes can and do, of course, occur. Some children "find" themselves in school and blossom out socially in a manner that would have been hard to predict from their preschool shyness. On the other hand, because of unseen circumstances, such as a death or a divorce in the family, a sociable child's interaction patterns may change for the worse. As a rule, however, we are much more likely to observe continuity rather than discontinuity in a child's social behavior between the early childhood and elementary school years.

The same is likely to be the case for the child's intellectual attainments. We can get a fairly reliable assessment of the child's IQ by the age of four and can make reasonably accurate predictions as to what his mental attainment will be at age eighteen. A child who is bright and alert in the early childhood program will continue to be so in the elementary school setting. The same will be true for children who have more of a struggle with intellectual demands. Once again, we must be open to wide individual differences in these respects. Some children will make phenomenal gains in intellectual ability when they enter school, whereas other children who seemed bright and to have promise begin to show a gradual decline in intellectual achievement. By and large, however, continuity rather than discontinuity is the rule with regard to intellectual attainment across the early childhood and elementary school years.

Finally, continuity is also the rule for physical attainments. Children who are well coordinated and who will be good at sports give hints of their talents in the preschool years. They demonstrate early facility in eye-hand coordination and can catch balls, ride their bikes, skate, ski, or swim at a young age. During the preschool years, the less athletically adept will also show their athletic limitations by the difficulty they encounter when trying to keep pace with their more adept peers. Individual exceptions do occur. Some children who seem clumsy as preschoolers may become quite athletic as children and the reverse may sometimes also occur. Although athletic prowess is to some extent a matter of physical endowment, it can be improved with coaching and practice and with the elimination of fear.

Facets of Growth and Development

Growth during the elementary school years is of many different kinds and includes growth in height, weight, and strength; increased sexual differentiation; enhanced intellectual powers for learning and problem solving; and vastly expanded social awareness and participation. Each of these facets of growth is described in detail.

Physical Development

In contrast to the rapid increase in weight and height during the first months and years of life, height and weight increase much more slowly and evenly during middle and late childhood. On the average, most elementary school children gain two to three inches in height each year. Although boys are generally taller than girls at most age levels, there is an exception. There is apparently some relationship between the onset of puberty (sexual maturity) and height. Girls, who commonly begin puberty at age eleven, have an average height of 58.0 inches at that age, whereas boys, who do not begin puberty until a year later, have an average height of 57.7 inches. Put differently, there is a period toward the end of childhood when girls are taller and more physically mature than boys of the same age.

Individual differences in height are most closely related to parental height, although there can be significant deviations. In general, tall parents will have tall children, and short parents will have short children. We also have some evidence that height is related to such attributes as weight and intelligence. Thin boys are likely to be shorter than boys of the same age who are of average weight. Likewise, bright children are likely to be taller than children who are average or below average in mental ability. These relationships, however, are much less solid than, say, the continuity of individual growth patterns. Many thin children grow to be quite tall, and a good number of short children are exceptionally bright. Although the general trends need to be remembered, the frequent exceptions should not be forgotten.

Just as growth in height maintains a more steady pace in childhood, so too does growth in weight. At the age of six years, the child is about seven times his birth weight. To illustrate, a child who weighed seven pounds at birth would be expected to weigh about 49 pounds at age six. The average birth weight for girls is a little less than that for boys, and their average weight at six years is a little less as well. Girls average about 48.5 pounds at age six while boys average about 49 pounds. By the end of the elementary school period (grade six), the average girl weighs about 85.5 pounds, whereas the average boy weighs about 96 pounds. Here again it must be emphasized that these figures are averages and that wide individual differences in growth rates—hence in height and weight at each age—are as much the rule as the exception.

At the ages of five and six, children often are finicky and faddish when it comes to food. One child of this age would only eat chicken noodle soup! Fortunately, this tendency declines during the elementary school years, when healthy appetites for a variety of foods are the rule. Some children—because of unhappiness, unfortunate parental models, or simply from sitting in front of television for long hours eating junk food—may become obese. Obesity not only makes the child the butt of jokes and ridicule, it also interferes with active play and the attainment of some of the social skills that are acquired interacting as a team member.

In addition to the changes in height and weight during the elementary school years, there are also changes in body proportions. Like the preschool child, the elementary school child has a head that is too large for his body. Our adult head is about one-seventh our total size, whereas the toddler's head is about one-fourth of his body size. This disproportion decreases gradually during the middle and late childhood years. In addition, the eruption of the permanent teeth and the enlargement of the lower part of the face change the proportions of the face and make it appear less top heavy in childhood than it was during the preschool years.

Changes in the child's trunk and limbs occur as well. The trunk becomes slimmer and more elongated in contrast to the chunkiness of the preschooler. The chest tends to become broader and flatter, which permits shoulders to droop. The school-age child's arms and legs become long and spindly, with little evidence of musculature. It is the thinning out of the trunk and the elongation of the spindly arms and legs that give the older elementary school child the "all arms and legs" appearance. The young person's hands and feet grow more slowly than his arms and legs. It is the different rates of growth of the different body parts that accounts for the awkwardness and clumsiness of the young person in the late childhood years.

Because of the rapid changes in their bodies, children are particularly concerned about physical appearance. Perhaps because of their concern about their own bodies, children are quick to tease and make fun of a homely child or one with some physical anomaly. Even children who, out of choice or necessity, dress differently from their peers can be the butt of jokes and ridicule. Although prejudice in the true sense has not yet emerged, children tend to be hostile to those youngsters who deviate from the norm of dress and appearance. Parents and teachers can help children be more sensitive to the feelings of other children by not reinforcing this negative behavior and by setting an example of tolerance and acceptance.

Sexual Differentiation

Although some sex differences can be observed during the early childhood period, these differences become more pronounced during childhood proper. Boys tend to be more aggressive than girls and engage in more fighting and in more warlike play than do girls. This difference emerges in early childhood and persists into the elementary school years. During the primary school years, boys tend to engage in vigorous active play and highly organized games that require sensorimotor coordination and that involve competition between teams. Girls tend to participate in more cooperative, more sedentary, and less competitive motor activities, such as jumping rope and playing hopscotch.

To some extent, the activities boys and girls engage in are culturally conditioned. Today, there are many more opportunities for girls to engage in competitive team sports than was true in the past. Nonetheless, even now, many more boys than girls are involved in soccer, Little League, Peewee Hockey, and Pop Warner football. Girls are more likely to participate in such sports as tennis, ice skating, and gymnastics. In general, athletic girls are more likely to engage in individual, rather than team, competitive sports than are athletic boys.

As noted earlier, although the experts are not always in agreement as to the reasons, there are boy-girl differences in academic achievement that appear during the elementary school years. Girls are superior to boys in verbal skills, such as vocabulary and reading. Boys tend to excel in mathematics and spatial tasks. It should be said, however, that sex differences in math do not usually appear until adolescence. During the elementary school years, girls get as good or better grades than boys in mathematics. Boys are, however, more likely than girls to have reading problems.

An interesting sex difference between boys and girls centers around achievement motivation and intellectual

curiosity. Boys tend to be higher in achievement motivation than girls, but girls are higher in intellectual curiosity
than boys. School achievement is more closely correlated
with intellectual curiosity than it is with achievement motivation. This may account for the finding that, on the average, girls get better grades than do boys all through the
school years. However, this finding may be confounded by
the fact that elementary school teachers value quiet, cooperative, and helpful behavior. Thanks to differences in socialization, girls are more likely to exhibit these traits than
are boys. Boys may thus be less likely to win teacher approval and get good grades.

Although some sex differences may be linked to genetic
factors, these differences are also heavily overlaid by cultural conditioning and learned sex role expectations.

Psychological Attainments

Perhaps the major issue of the middle to late childhood years
is the conflict between the child's desire to grow up and
his desire to remain a child forever (a fantasy embodied in
J.M. Barrie's *Peter Pan*). The child wants to grow up so that
he can enjoy the prerogatives of adult life: the right to stay
up late, to go on trips, to drive the car, to have money to
buy the things he wants. More than that, the child wants
to be big and to live in a world adapted to his size rather
than in the world he does inhabit, wherein door handles
and chair seats and cupboards are all too high for easy and
comfortable access. Finally, he wants to know all the adult
"secrets"—the answers to his many questions about the
physical world, about sexuality, and about the interpersonal
relations that adults tell him he cannot yet understand. He
wants to be able to laugh at the jokes his parents laugh at
and, most of all, to be accepted into their confidence and
their secret discussions.

On the other hand, he also wants to be a child and
to retain the many prerogatives of childhood. Quarreling,
fighting, and roughhousing are accepted boy behavior, whereas
they are regarded as rowdyism in adolescence. Likewise,
the girl who puts on her mother's makeup and dons her
mother's clothing is merely amusing, whereas similar behavior on the part of her young adolescent sister may be

cause for alarm. A child is given toys as gifts, not just money or useful things (such as clothing). And the child is still permitted affectional extravagances (climbing into his parents' bed) that will later be forbidden.

In addition to the positive features of staying small, children are also put off by some of the negative features of physical maturity. Children's acute sense of smell makes them sensitive to adult body odors (children do not have sweat glands and do not have body odor) as well as to the smells of alcohol and tobacco. Beards feel scratchy, and the enlarged adult skin pores often seem enormous to the acute and critical vision of the young. Pot bellies, double chins, liver spots, and wrinkled skin all run afoul of children's natural aesthetic sense. Likewise, although children are eager to assume adult roles and become privy to adult secrets, these roles and secrets also seem more than a little scary.

Other psychological features of this age period include fears and anxieties about academic achievement and social acceptance. While the preschool child fears animals and imaginary creatures, the school-age child fears school failure and rejection by his peers. It is because academic achievement is so valued by parents and teachers that it comes to be such a focus of concern and preoccupation of children. Too often, the child gets the impression that the grades he earns are more important than what he learns or knows. Likewise, as the peer group begins to play an increasingly important role in his sphere of activities, particularly after grade three, acceptance by the group becomes an increasingly potent source of anxiety and stress. Fears of failure and of rejection thus emerge as prominent components of the elementary school child's experience and behavior.

Social Development

There is a culture of childhood that is tremendously viable even though it is passed on solely by oral tradition. Children's games—such as hopscotch, marbles, kick-the-can, and blindman's bluff—are passed down verbally from generation to generation. All manner of jokes, riddles, and sayings with significant timely modifications are also transmitted from generation to generation. In contrast to the culture of adolescence, the culture of childhood has considerable stability.

The culture of childhood is less prominent today than it was a quarter century ago. The culture of childhood was passed on naturally when children played out-of-doors by themselves. Today, it is often not safe for children to "go out and play," and as a result, much of children's playtime is spent in adult-organized activities, such as soccer. Consequently, while children's games, such as marbles, are still played, these are often engaged in primarily in the school yard, one of the few remaining places that are safe and reserved for children. On school playgrounds, we can still hear the jump rope songs and witness the tag and marble games that children have played for hundreds of years.

We can also hear some of the characteristic gibes that have to do with intelligence and appearance:

You make as much sense as an ejection seat on a helicopter.
When you were born, the doctor spanked your face.

When they are called names, children today may respond as they did centuries ago:

Sticks and stones will break my bones, but names will never hurt me.
When I am dead and in my grave, you'll be sorry for what you called me.

Like nicknames, superstitions of children are passed on by oral tradition. On seeing an ambulance, a child may chant

Cross my fingers
Cross my toes
Hope I don't go
In one of those.

Or, on seeing a ladybird:

Ladybird, ladybird, fly away home!
Your house is on fire, your children are gone.
Except the little one under the stone.
Ladybird, ladybird, fly away home!

And when the rain interferes with play, children still chant:

Rain, rain, go away.
Come again, another day.

One final illustration of traditional child lore: A child says to another, "Do, Re, and Mi went to the monkey house. Do and Re came out. Who was inside?" The other child replies, "Mi," to which the first retorts, "Oh, I didn't know you were a monkey!"

The variety and scope of children's language and lore seem to have shrunk in today's society. In addition to participation in organized sports, children play many more adult-prepared board games with printed instructions. Increasingly, computer games take up much of children's playtime. Boys, in particular, like games such as Nintendo™ that require good eye-hand coordination. Many of these computer games require the child to learn certain visual-motor patterns. In general, much of the play of today's children involves either participation in adult sports or playing video games produced by adults. As a result, children today have much less opportunity to experience and reconstruct the culture of childhood.

Children's friendships undergo a change during childhood. From about the age of six to nine, children are learning to take the other child's point of view. Nonetheless, friendship is often based upon whether or not the other child will go along with what the first wants to do: "He's not my friend anymore. He didn't want to play GI Joe™." Children of six and seven tend to think of friendship as a matter of playing together and sharing: "She plays dress up with me. She always shares her candy with me."

As children get older, they come to see friendship as mutually beneficial, but they do not yet see it as based on shared values and goals. By age eight or nine, children say that another child is a friend if "We do things for each other." The emphasis is upon shared activities and equalities: "We all like to collect baseball cards. We trade them and give doubles to our friends who are missing some. No one brags." Toward the end of childhood, children are beginning to appreciate that friendship is founded upon getting along with each other and upon shared and valued interests and activities. Only toward the end of childhood do children begin to view friendship as a long-term commitment that goes beyond shared activities and interests.

Sociocultural Change

Over the past quarter century, sociocultural change has had a tremendous impact upon children and upon childhood. Around midcentury we saw children as innocent and in need of adult-provided protection and security. This view of childhood innocence was reflected and reinforced by the schools, the media, and the legal profession. Childhood was seen as a very special period of life, to be savored and enjoyed before moving on to the next stage. Stories such as *Tom Sawyer, Peter Pan, Penrod Schofield, The Wind in the Willows, Winnie the Pooh,* and *Pinnochio* all celebrated childhood as a special and indeed, magical, period.

This view of childhood was reinforced by the schools. Up until midcentury, our schools were "progressive" in the sense that they were designed to be in keeping with children's developing interests and abilities. Precocity was seen as abnormal: "Early ripe, early rot." Portrayals of children in the media—such as those depicted in the movie *It's a Wonderful Life* and those conveyed in early television series such as "Ozzie and Harriet"—reflected this childhood innocence. Children's literature was protective as well, and stories reflected nuclear family values. The legal system also operated to protect children, and child labor laws and compulsory schooling laws were passed to ensure that children were not exploited and that they were educated.

Since the sixties, however, our social perception of children has changed. We no longer see children as innocent, but rather as competent, ready and able to deal with life's many vicissitudes. This new perception has come about for many different reasons, but not because of any new information about child growth and development. In fact, adult society has changed, and the new perception of children has more to do with the change in adult life-style than it does with any change in the nature of childhood. In effect, we can no longer protect and secure children the way we were able to in the past. As a result, we *need* to see children as competent and able to deal with the many demands for maturity we and society have placed upon them. This new perception of competence is reinforced by the schools, the media, and the legal system.

When children are perceived as competent, the adult demands for adaptation are overwhelming. The schools, for example, are no longer child-centered, but rather curriculum-centered. It is the curriculum, rather than children's developing interests and abilities, that determines what is taught and when it is taught. For example, in some communities, as many as 10 to 20 percent of kindergarten children are retained or placed in transition classes. The demands for achievement have become so uniform that many children are held back or retained simply because they are younger or have a slower growth rate than their peers.

The media has also begun to depict children as competent. In movies and television shows, children dress like adults, outwit adults, and even help adults with their life problems. The literature for children is replete with stories about relatives with AIDS, children who have been sexually abused, and parents who are alcoholics. These stories are meant to be therapeutic, but they may inadvertently expose young people to problems they might otherwise never have encountered. The legal system today protects children's rights, rather than children, and, as a result, sometimes neglects the fact that children need to be protected from themselves.

These changes have affected children of all backgrounds and from all walks of life. Children in the suburbs are as affected as children in our inner cities. Children living in small rural towns are as affected as children living in large urban centers. There are differences, of course. The quality of schooling varies tremendously from community to community, but the curriculum emphasis often undermines effective schooling in even the best schools. Likewise, divorce knows no social class, ethnic, or racial boundaries. Although divorce is more common today than in the past, it does not hurt the individual child any less. No matter how many other people break their legs, when you break yours, it still hurts.

Likewise, the range of normality has also been narrowed for all children. Whereas we once accepted a young child, whose curiosity and high spirits sometimes got him into trouble, as "all boy," we may now label him as having an attention deficit disorder. Children are being labeled at ever younger ages, and labels stick. Whereas our programs for special-needs and gifted children are commendable, they are often provided in such a way as to accentuate rather than minimize differences. As we see the average child as competent and as we narrow the limits of what we regard as competent, an increasing number of children fall outside these limits. Our new conception of childhood thus has the effect of labeling large numbers of children as incompetent.

To be sure, children are probably more competent than we gave them credit for being in the first half of this century. However, they are less competent than we might

like them to be. We need to recognize children's many limitations as well as their many strengths and powers.

General Characteristics of Middle and Late Childhood

The child is, by nature, a pragmatist. He is concerned with *how*
things work, rather than with *why* they work or *how well* they
work. It is an age at which doing, making, and building are all
important. Now that young people have good small- as well as
large-muscle control, they are beset by the urge to sew, cook,
and bake; they want to build things, make things, and put things
together. Although children still engage in these activities to
some extent, such activities have to compete with less challenging pastimes, such as computer games, television watching, and
organized group activities. Although some children still engage
in craft activities today, children are more often involved in
more adultlike pursuits.

The child tends to be an optimist as well as a pragmatist. Children have a tendency to deny unpleasant realities
and to have a cheerful outlook on life. The world is a new
and exciting place full of things to experience and learn about.
Because the child lives in the here and now, every activity is important, and the most important activity is the one
in which he is presently engaged. That is why it is often so
difficult to disengage children from their play or computer
games. Children also look forward to growing up, and they
look forward to birthdays as evidence of their growing maturity
and independence.

To be sure, children are not always happy. Particularly
today, we see a phenomenon that was rarely seen in the
past, namely, school-age children with depression. Some
children have chronic low moods, apathy, and self-derogatory
ideas. Sometimes this depression is merely a reflection of
parental depression, but for some children, it arises from
their difficult life circumstances. Although most children retain
a sense of hope, even under the worst conditions, for some
young people the stress is just too overwhelming.

Fortunately, for most children, their optimism is
undaunted. They are excited about what they would like
to become and are not bothered by the real and many hurdles
that lie in the path of the desired goal. In fantasy, children

can move away from the family, leave school, sail around the world, and become a beachcomber or continue their studies and become a doctor or a lawyer. At its base, children's optimism rests in their belief that they have an almost unlimited number of years to attain their goals.

The pragmatic attitude of children is very important for personality development and is a prerequisite for the personality integration that is the task of adolescence. By engaging in all sorts of activities, children are discovering themselves. It is a psychological truism that we are what we do. The child must discover what sort of pupil, athlete, musician, peer, and friend he really is, and these discoveries can be made only through his classroom work, his participation in sports, his efforts to play an instrument, and his interactions and friendships with peers. By engaging in these many activities, the child evokes reactions in others that give him the information he needs to find out about himself.

Childhood, then, is a period of self-discovery in which the child learns about himself in the course of engaging in a variety of academic, extracurricular, and recreational activities and in relating to other people. These various aspects of the child are, however, not yet coordinated into a general scheme of self as a functioning totality. The child is more or less unaware of the many discontinuities in his behavior and in his self-evaluations. For example, he may be a perfect gentleman at his friend's house but a demon at home, or vice versa, without being aware of the contradictions in his behavior. The adolescent may show similar contradictions, but he is aware of these discrepancies and tries to rationalize them, at least to himself.

In addition to finding out about himself, the child is also discovering the larger social world about him, the world of entertainers, politicians, scientists, and athletes. Often children choose individuals from these professions as persons to idealize and emulate, particularly as they discover that their parents are not as all-knowing and as wise as they had thought. By the age of seven or eight, the child has dethroned his parents from the once-exalted position they held for the child during the preschool years. Now, new gods are introduced into the pantheon of childhood. However, it is often the glamour of the entertainer or athlete, rather than his or her character or accomplishments, that attracts the child.

This does not mean that the child no longer loves his parents or that he denies the authority of the family. His family is still the center of his life. It is just that other forms of authority and other adult figures now begin to have an influence upon him, namely the peer group and his new nonparental adult idols. The child's attitude toward authority is not entirely subservient, for he does express negative feelings toward adult constraint. He does so, however, in a manner peculiar to childhood—a manner that is often missed by adults. If we listen closely to children's rhymes and riddles, we notice that they often poke fun at important adults and at adult practices and institutions. Take a recently overheard example:

Jingle bells, Bush smells,
And Reagan ran away.
Oh what fun it is to ride
In a Clinton Chevrolet."

Such gibes, it is important to add, are shared by the group so that no child takes individual responsibility for them. In this way, the child can participate in hostile bantering of the adult world without fear of reprisal.

The dominant characteristics of middle to late childhood, then, are its traditionalism, pragmatism, and optimism. The elementary school years are devoted to discovering the self through repeated encounters with others and to discovering the world through incessant activity. Although the child is generally subservient to authority, he nonetheless expresses his underlying defiance in concert with the peer group. In this way he avoids taking individual responsibility for being disrespectful to those who maintain the balance of power.

The World of Self, Home, and Community

The child's discovery of the various facets of himself leads to an increasingly accurate picture of himself and his traits. Children acknowledge their stubbornness, noisiness, and so on. In general, however, they often admit only to those negative traits, such as stubbornness, that are regarded with resigned amusement by adults. Traits that are regarded as being very negative are much less frequently admitted to, even though the child may believe they hold true for him.

Children's attitudes toward their parents vary considerably with the family structure. In general, children prefer parents who work together and cooperate in their child-rearing activities. They dislike parents who are arbitrary and who will not listen to their side of the story. Although children appreciate parents who set rules and limits, they do not care for parents who are overly strict or overly lenient. Children interpret such extreme behavior, and often quite rightly, as a sign that parents do not care enough about them. These findings reinforce other data to the effect that the most effective parents are authoritative (show firmness with warmth).

Within the home, the child's perception of himself and of his siblings is, in part, determined by his birth order. It is a well-established finding that firstborn children are usually high academic achievers even though their intelligence may be no greater than that of children born later. Parents are least experienced with their first child and often have high expectations for him. They also expect him to take responsibility for his younger siblings. In part, the high achievement and competitiveness of firstborns probably derive from the high expectations and demands for maturity that were placed on them from an early age. The oldest child is more likely than later-born children to identify with authority and to adopt maternalistic or paternalistic attitudes toward siblings.

The effect of birth order on the self-perceptions of later-born children depends upon a number of factors. It depends, for example, upon the age separation between the births, upon the sex of the children, and upon their relative intelligence. Apparently, the optimal spacing of children is about two years. This amount of time gives the oldest child an opportunity to experience being the only and youngest child of his parents, without getting too entrenched in this perception. When a child comes after only a year, the older sibling is likely to be more jealous than if the baby came a year later. Not only did the older sibling not have the mother to himself for very long, but during much of the time he did have her to himself, she was carrying the baby and was often distracted.

In the same way, a sibling who comes three or four years after the first child is likely to be resented. The new baby displaces the older youngster from a very comfortable and satisfying position in the family circle. Obviously, there are great variations. In many cases, the older child may be happy to have a playmate after all those years, or the parents may still favor the older child. It makes a difference, too, whether the oldest sibling is a boy and the next child is a girl, or vice versa. Like so many other generalizations, those with respect to the effects of the age spread between siblings has to be qualified by consideration of the possible variations and by the exceptions and special cases.

The middle child usually has the most problems because he has none of the special benefits that accrue to being either first or last. Moreover, his position is the most difficult to conceptualize. He is both younger than some siblings and older than others. In contrast, the oldest and the youngest are one or the other, not both at the same time. If, in addition, the oldest and youngest side against him, as sometimes happens, his plight is even more serious. This is likely to happen if there are only three children in the family. In general, three is a bad number, sociologically speaking. Whether it be children in the family or students in a dorm room, when there are three together, there is often a two-against-one alignment. Why this happens is not easy to explain, but that it does happen is quite easy to demonstrate. The middle child in a three-child family is thus also likely to be deprived of the support of his two siblings.

As a rule, the youngest child has the best of all possible worlds. First, his parents are much more experienced than they were with his older siblings and thus can be more relaxed and less inappropriately demanding. Second, the youngest child is never displaced by still another child and thus retains a very special position. Finally, the last born has the care not only of the parents but of the older siblings as well. Not surprisingly, last-born children tend to be the most well rounded, happy, and psychologically sound of any of the age positions.

The child's position in the family, then, plays an important role in how he sees himself and how he is perceived by others. It may well determine lifelong reaction patterns as well. Firstborn children are likely to be "take charge" people, both as children and as adults. Middle-born children may be rebellious and antiestablishment as an expression of their resentment against their anomalous position in the family hierarchy. Youngest children may often be overly trusting and expect others to look out for their welfare as their parents and siblings were wont to do.

The structure of the family can also color the child's perceptions of himself. A child in a single-parent home, for example, may be expected to take more responsibility than might have been the case were he growing up in a two-parent home. Although many single parents do a superb job, it is often tempting to expect the child to be more than a child and to share in equal measure the issues of finance, friendship, dating, and so on that preoccupy the single parent. Some children even pass judgment on their parent's dates. In such circumstances, the child may come to see himself as having to take on serious responsibilities and to make important decisions. Although this is flattering to the ego, it is also very stressful to a youngster who would sometimes prefer to be just a child.

Children in two-parent working families also may see themselves as taking on more responsibility than children in homes where one parent is always present. These children may have to be in some form of before-and-after school program to cover the time period until their parents come home from work. Generally, children like to have a parent home when they arrive from school, but that is not always possible in today's world. Children in these circumstances tend to see themselves as grown-up and able to assume adult responsibilities. Although they are responsible and can manage, it is always important to sometimes do for them what they could do for themselves. If they always make their own breakfast, it is a real treat for them if we occasionally make their breakfast for them—to show we love them, care for them, and appreciate the responsibilities they have assumed.

Another family structure issue is the age of the parents. Over the last few decades, couples have been delaying having children until both are well into their thirties. From the child's point of view, this is sometimes advantageous. Older parents are often more financially and occupationally secure and more emotionally and psychologically mature. They can thus provide the child with a comfortable home and a relaxed atmosphere. It does not always work out this way, however, and some older parents have less patience with young children than they might have had when they were younger. In addition, although some older parents are quite laid back in their child rearing, others are quite educationally demanding. For the child, there are thus potential pluses and minuses to having older parents.

The family's religion also colors the child's self-perception. Catholic children soon learn of the long-standing prejudices in American society against members of their religion. Jewish children are also likely to discover not only that they do not celebrate Christmas but also that they may be seen as "Christ killers" and "money lovers." In our contemporary valuation of cultural diversity, these attributions are fortunately less common than they once were. At the same time, it must be admitted that there has also been a rise of religious extremism, which helps keep these prejudices alive.

Other salient determinants of a child's self-perception are his ethnic background and his socioeconomic class. Within any particular school or neighborhood, research suggests that it is the minority group—whichever group that might be—that experiences lower self-esteem than the majority group. This is true whether it is black children who are a minority in a white school or Jewish children in a predominantly Christian school or Catholics in a largely Protestant school. Black children growing up in largely black communities in the South, for example, have higher self-esteem than do black children growing up in northern urban communities where they are a minority. It is minority status, rather than race or ethnicity as such, that has a lowering effect upon self-esteem.

Social class differences also tend to shape the child's conception of himself and the world. Basil Bernstein, the English sociolinguist, observed that the language of low socioeconomic groups is *restricted* in the sense that communication is as much by way of gesture, inflection, and intonation as by the words themselves. Among higher socioeconomic groups, language is more *elaborated,* and a plenitude of words minimize the need for gesture, inflection, and intonation.

These language differences also affect the child's socialization inasmuch as language is the means whereby children acquire the basic units of socialization, namely, *frames.* In teaching children frame rules, for example, lower socioeconomic parents use many fewer words than do middle-income parents. When these lower-income children attend school taught by middle-income teachers, they may not understand the frame rules that are in play. Some lower-income children may be labeled as rowdy and disruptive when, in fact, their understanding of frame rules is dependent upon gestures and intonations absent from the middle income teacher's language repertoire.

In addition to the direct effects of racial, ethnic, and economic status influences upon the child's self-conceptions, there are equally significant indirect effects. The values, expectations, and social frames of parents vary greatly between socioeconomic groups. These values, expectations, and frames affect the child's school performance and hence his self-perception as a student. As suggested above, our schools are largely middle class in orientation, and children from other backgrounds may be handicapped, not by intellectual limitations, but rather by ethnic values, expectations, and frames that differ from those prevalent in the school.

Studies have shown that when economically disadvantaged mothers attempt to help their children solve problems, they often direct them to do the correct thing without explaining why they should perform as the mother directed. Economically advantaged mothers, in contrast, are likely to offer lengthy verbal explanations, such as "This goes in here because this is the box for the white buttons. Now, where does this button go?" The low-income mother is more likely to say: "Put these in here and those in there."

Children who come from low socioeconomic backgrounds, therefore, may lack experience in labeling, classifying, ordering, and comparing material and are likely to fail because the school assumes that the child comes to school with these skills already well in hand. The child who fails in school because he was not adequately prepared may acquire a negative self-concept that will be difficult to change. The situation is compounded by the fact that schools have become more demanding at earlier ages so these children are doubly disadvantaged, not only by the home, but also by the school.

Fortunately, programs such as Head Start and Parents as Teachers are providing large numbers of lower-income children with the early childhood education they need to succeed in our public schools. The Parents as Teachers program, now in some fourteen states in the Midwest, involves home visits by parent educators who help parents to interact more effectively with their children. Parent educators teach parents how to provide their children with enriching experiences that will further their social, intellectual, and emotional development. As more and more of our children have quality early childhood education, many of the educational handicaps of low-income children will be minimized.

The child's perception of his home also changes as a function of going to school. He learns the social status of his family from other children and not infrequently from teachers. He soon becomes aware of how his parents stand in the occupational status hierarchy. Children from homes in which parents have high status (parents who are in the professions, who own their own businesses, or who are in high managerial positions) tend to have comparable high status among their peers. On the other hand, children whose parents are blue-collar workers or skilled laborers tend to have relatively low status among the other children. These variations in self-perception are particularly noticeable when the school has children from a wide range of socioeconomic levels.

In considering the child's perception of the school and himself within it, a factor in addition to ethnic and socioeconomic status must also be taken into account. This factor is age. The young child who is just entering school is, in most cases, excited at the prospect. For one thing, going to school is a sign of growing up and evidence of increased independence. In addition, the child has heard a great deal about school and has high expectations about what he will do there. Unfortunately, this early enthusiasm for school is relatively short-lived. By the time children reach fifth grade, more than 50 percent dislike school.

There are many reasons for this mounting dislike of school among so many schoolchildren. An important reason is the peer group. Some of these groups take an increasingly negative attitude toward school and impose this attitude upon all of their members. In addition, there are individual experiences of failure, the inevitable personality clashes between particular children and teachers, and the interference of homework with other more attractive activities. In recent years, large classes, the pushing of the curriculum downward, and the cutting back on recess and art programs have further contributed to children's negative attitudes toward schooling.

Another factor contributing to children's dissatisfaction with school is technology. Although many schools now have computers, they have not been fully integrated within the curriculum, and many teachers remain computer-illiterate. Children are often aware of the technological lag between what is in school and what is outside it. Moreover, thanks to television, children have a great deal of information about a lot of subjects that are ignored, rather than built upon, by the school curriculum. With new interactive technologies with which children can interact with text material, computers will necessarily play a larger role in the education of the future than they do today. Children, however, are more ready for this than are the schools.

Accordingly, for a variety of reasons, the child's perception of the school changes from extremely positive to lukewarm or negative as he advances up the grades. Although this does not hold true for all children, it holds true for a sufficient number of them to constitute a significant educational problem. Motivation is the single most important factor in learning, and dislike of school could well be one of the major hindrances to effectively educating our children.

By and large, the child has only a limited perception of the community as a whole. He knows parts of the community, such as its parks, zoos, museums, movie theaters, and shopping malls as well as some of its police, mail, and fire protection services. On the other hand, the child has little awareness of the more intricate functions of the local government and its politics. The child's perception of the community will vary with his social class. A lower-class child may be very well acquainted with the welfare agencies and with hospital clinics. The middle-class child, on the other hand, is acquainted with private physicians and dentists but may have no direct acquaintance with government agencies. It is only toward the end of the elementary school period that the child begins to get a better understanding of community, state, and local government.

In contrast to the adolescent, who often sees at least part of his community in a negative light, most of the child's experiences in the larger community tend to be positive. Fire fighters enjoy taking him through the firehouse and letting him climb on the engine. Because he is usually accompanied by parents while shopping, he is generally well received by sales clerks in stores and by caretaking personnel at parks and places of amusement. Children's museums, planetariums, and aquariums are also welcoming places for children in large cities. Walt Disney World and Disneyland are particularly appropriate for this age group. During the elementary school years, therefore, the child's perception of the community is incomplete but generally quite positive.

The Child in Relation to Adults

Although we have changed our perception of children from innocence to competence, some underlying dimensions of these relationships have not changed. What is most prominent in these interactions is the inequality. Not only is the adult bigger and smarter, he or she also has all of the power and the authority in the relationship. It is the adult who sets the rules and limits for the child, and not the reverse. Children, in turn, need these rules and limits, frames if you will, to become socialized and effective citizens within society. Unfortunately, however, the new perception of childhood competence has sometimes brought parents to deny the inequality of the relationship and to treat their children as equals. In so doing they abrogate their responsibilities with regard to teaching their children frame rules. Undisciplined behavior at home and at school is often the result.

Although children want and need to have parents set limits and rules as well as example values and standards, it is paradoxically human for children to resist this authority as an infringement on their autonomy. When parents do exercise their authority, children often attempt to redress the balance by what amounts to guerrilla tactics. We have already noted the hostile gibes and parodies on prominent adults and respected institutions. More than that, however, children become quite astute psychologists. They look for the adult's weak points and attack him or her at just those points. For example, parents who are overly concerned about their children's eating habits are likely to have children who make food an issue for conflict.

When parents do not exercise appropriate authority, children see this as an opportunity to take charge and can do this in an infinite number of ways. Some children throw tantrums or get ill and dominate parents who are afraid to set firm limits for fear of another episode. These children have their parents at their mercy and know how to manipulate their parents to get whatever they want. They are learning that manipulating people is what gets results. It is easy to project what sort of adults such children will become. Other devices, such as failing to wash or take care of clothes, are characteristic of most children and reflect more healthy, expectable, and necessary reactions to the proper exercise of adult authority. Children's resistance to adult authority is appropriate, but their assumption of adult authority is not.

Another way children have of getting at their parents is by fighting among themselves. Of all child behaviors, fights between siblings is perhaps the most universally distressing to parents. We want so much for our children to get along and love one another as we love each of them that it is frightening to see them attack one another with such vigor. Nonetheless, the fact that such fighting usually occurs when we are around is a good clue to its dynamics. Our children want us to take sides and in so doing show the other child which child the parents really favor! That is why it is so important to be impartial—and not to automatically assume, say, that the older sibling is at fault. Each child should have a chance to "explain" what happened. What the children have to say is perhaps less important than that, in their eagerness to explain verbally, they forget about fighting. Asking for explanations can usually diffuse the situation. By treating children's fighting in a "no-fault" manner, we tell children that we will not take sides and that their fighting will not make us do so.

In summary, then, the relation between children and adults is one that is characterized by inequality of authority and power. Many of the disruptive and anxiety-provoking features of child behavior are either a reaction to this authority or a usurpation of it. When parents do exercise appropriate authority, children assert their individuality and autonomy by attacking parents on their most sensitive concerns. Such self-assertions provide children with a healthy outlet for their resistance to the proper exercise of adult authority.

However, when adults do not exercise appropriate authority, children's resistance to authority takes on a very different visage. Children will take charge if adults allow them to do this. They will dominate their parents and get whatever they think they want. This authority is not earned, however, and it teaches children all the wrong lessons about the use of power. At a deeper level, children do not really enjoy this power and find it frightening. Nonetheless, they feel they must take charge if no one else will. So, although children should be expected to act against the inequality of the adult-child relationship, they should not be permitted to change the fact of that inequality, which is both necessary and appropriate.

Adults in Relation to Children

I noted above that the most general characteristic of the adult-child relationship is one of inequality. For the child in such a relationship, the problem is mainly one of how to redress the balance. In the preceding section, we saw some of the means by which children redress this imbalance. For adults, on the other hand, the problem is of a different order. We must learn how best to use the power and authority that is invested in us by our children. Unlike other forms of authority, however, that which we exercise over children is not earned but thrust upon us by virtue of our role as parents.

How then are we to handle our power and authority over children? There is no simple answer to that question. To be sure, we can say that authoritative parenting is more effective than either permissive or authoritarian parenting. However, we differ so greatly in personality and style that the way to exercise authoritative parenting within the confines of our personalities and styles is not self-evident. What is important is that we appreciate that children do need us to set standards and limits and that we cannot abrogate our authority because of the erroneous perception of child competence.

A few principles for authoritative parenting may provide guidelines for tailoring the exercise of this authority to your particular parenting style. One general rule is to *start tough* and ease up later. It is when children are young that we, as parents, have to insist upon rules, limits, and frame behavior. If we do that consistently, by the time they are adolescents they will have incorporated these rules, and we can ease up on our rules and limit setting. Too often we do the opposite. We start off easy with our children and then try to get tough when they are adolescents. It just doesn't work. You can believe in the tough drill sergeant who turns out to be a softy at the end of the movie, but you cannot believe in a softy at the beginning of a film becoming the tough sergeant at the end. We know that it never works that way, and children do too.

A second rule of authoritative parenting is to *allow children a voice in decision making.* Even when we have the final say, it is important to hear children's opinions about rule making and breaking, say, and the appropriate punishments. Whenever possible, it is important to incorporate the children's ideas into the rule and limit setting. Otherwise, just listening to children's views becomes an empty exercise, and they know it. Likewise, when there are conflicts, everyone who is a party to it must be given an opportunity to have their say. If possible, setting a regular time for family meetings is a useful way to ensure that children have a regular time to talk and to be heard.

The third and final rule for authoritative parenting is to try and *take the child's point of view* when he tells us that our rules or limits are too oppressive or demanding. When we take a trip to visit relatives, it is important to ask our child where he would like to stop and have lunch. He may not have had much choice in going on the trip, but he can be given a choice as to where to eat. We have to look for opportunities to involve children in decision making when they are involved in the activity.

Regardless of our personalities and styles, therefore, we can still employ the rules of authoritative parenting. If we start tough, give children a voice in decision making, and attempt to take their point of view, we can exercise our authority with warmth and compassion.

Parent-Child Contracts

In the foregoing paragraphs, I described the child's position in relation to adults and the adult's position in relation to children. Here I want to describe a more general model of reciprocal parent-child interactions.

We can look at the development of parent-child relations as a set of higher order frames, repetitive patterns of social interaction that change in the course of child and parent development. These higher order frames I call *parent-child contracts*. A parent-child contract consists in the often-unverbalized expectations and demands made by parents and children upon one another. The transformation of these contracts over the course of development reflects the changes that occur in both children and parents as the family itself matures.

Because contracts are mostly implicit and are often unverbalized, their existence often comes to the surface in the breach. That is to say, the existence of contracts usually becomes evident when either the parent or the child violates the contract. A mother whose children have all moved away, for example, may complain, "I don't even get a phone call, and after all I have done for them!" She thus reveals that she believes she was operating according to a contract that she has fulfilled but her children have not. Likewise, the teenager who says, "No matter how much I do around the house it is never enough," also voices a sense of a contract that has been violated. Such remarks, with which we are familiar, attest to the all-pervasive nature of implicit contractual arrangements between parents and children in our society.

The contracts between children and parents have three invariant clauses: the freedom-responsibility clause, the achievement-support clause, and the loyalty-commitment clause. Although these contracts remain the same during the course of development, their content changes as children mature. Indeed, when the content does not change in accord with the child's growing powers and abilities, interfamilial conflicts can occur. We need to look at how these contracts are played out at successive levels of development.

Freedom and Responsibility

During each of the major periods of development, parents demand that the child demonstrate particular responsibilities before they will allow him corresponding freedoms. Parents generally require very little in the way of responsibility from an infant. The infant, in turn, demands little in the way of freedom from his parents. Nonetheless, the responsibility-freedom clause is already in evidence. An infant of a year or so may insist upon feeding himself and holding his own cup of milk. If he manages to get some food into his mouth and does not spill all of his milk, parents will usually allow him the freedom to continue to eat without assistance. If, however, the food is thrown around or the milk is spilled as a joke, the infant will not be allowed to feed himself until he "cleans up his act."

During the preschool period, parents demand more responsibilities and allocate more freedoms than they did during the infancy period. Parents expect that the child will now take responsibility for toileting, dressing, and feeding himself and for a number of other behaviors. For example, parents may expect children to use their crayons on paper, not on the walls. If children demonstrate that they can assume these responsibilities, they are given the freedom to engage in them. As he moves into childhood proper, the child demands new freedoms, and his parents in turn expect fresh demonstrations of responsibility. A child may be allowed to ride his bike to a friend's house if he demonstrates that he wears his helmet and is careful when crossing streets. In adolescence, the contract is rewritten again and young people are allowed to drive the car if they have taken driver's ed, and they are allowed to go out at night if they have been responsible about calling if they will be late.

Achievement and Support

A similar developmental course is taken with respect to achievement and support. Parents demand little in the way of achievement on the part of the infant other than that he walk and talk at about the right time. In return, parents provide abundant emotional support. For example, there is a big to-do when the child takes his first step or says his first word. During the preschool period, parents begin to demand achievement in bowel and bladder control, verbal comprehension, and social behavior. For her part, the child asks that parents praise her accomplishments and devote time to supervising and instructing her.

When the child begins formal schooling, parental demands for achievement begin to center upon the three major areas of academic achievement, athletic performance, and social acceptance and popularity. In return, children make complementary demands for material, intellectual, and emotional support in these areas. For example, children expect their parents to support them with what they need in the way of materials for schoolwork, sports equipment, and peer-appropriate clothing. Likewise, children expect that parents will support demands made for academic achievement with help on homework and research papers. Finally, they may expect parents to support their social life by driving them to their friend's house, to games, and to other events.

When young people reach adolescence, the content of the achievement-support contract is once again rewritten. Parents now intensify their demands for academic, athletic, and social achievements. Young people correspondingly escalate their demands for material, emotional, and intellectual support. Parents are sometimes fooled by what seems to be the preeminence of monetary demands for support to the exclusion of all others. Yet teenagers still need a hug (in private, please, and never in front of peers!), still need to be told that they are loved, and still need parental attendance when they are in a play, giving a concert, or playing in a game.

Finally, in the contractual domain of loyalty and commitment, a developmental progression is equally discernible. Parents usually demand little in the way of loyalty from their infants. They do expect, however, that the infant will prefer them to strangers! Infants oblige quite nicely. Likewise, the infant demands only that the parents be committed to their caretaking function. As the child matures and his social world widens, the loyalty-commitment contract expands. During the preschool period, parents demand that the child maintain her loyalty and affection for them despite attendance at a full-day child-care facility and the ministrations of non-parental caregivers. The child, in turn, demands that the parents maintain their commitment to her as new children are born into the family, despite the new demands upon parental time and energies.

Once the child enters school, parents generally expect that the child's loyalty to his family will supersede that to his teacher or to his peer group. On his side, the child demands that parents show evidence of their commitment to him by the time and energy they give to him as a person. This is sometimes difficult when there has been separation and divorce. In such circumstances, the most serious problems revolve around loyalty and commitment. Should the child be most loyal to his biological father or his stepfather? The separated parent may also experience questions about how best to show commitment. At the very least, communication, in whatever form, must be maintained. Calling and writing a child on a regular basis, and particularly on special occasions, is an important way for a parent to demonstrate commitment.

In adolescence, the loyalty commitment clause takes on a somewhat different coloration. Parents must give up the demand that loyalty be demonstrated by preferring family to peer activities. Rather, parents now expect that their adolescent will be loyal to the family's values and beliefs. Adolescents, in turn, now expect their parents to live up to the values and to the beliefs they espouse. Although there often seems to be a serious breach in the loyalty commitment clause in early adolescence, when young people seem to defy what their parents stand for, this is only temporary. Most young people eventually subscribe to most of their parents' value and belief systems.

This model of parent-child contracts is just that: a model. It was derived from observation of middle-class families in America. Nonetheless, I believe contracts like these are written by parents and children of all cultural, ethnic, religious, and racial groups. Frames and contracts, or metaframes, are the basic tools of socialization for all families. Contracts are important not only for understanding normal socialization, but also for comprehending disruptive behavior. When parents break contracts over extended periods of time, children and adolescents will show the effects of the resultant stress.

Child rearing is not easy. There are no simple, quick-fix solutions to human problems. However, knowing about how children grow and develop and about the power of frames and contracts can help us better understand our children and can help them to grow up to be the caring, responsible, productive individuals we want them to be.

Selected Readings

Elkind, D. (1988). *The Hurried Child.* Reading, MA: Addison-Wesley. Describes some of the pressures on children to grow up too fast, the stress it engenders, and the effects of this stress on young people.

Gordon, T. (1989). *Teaching Children Discipline.* New York: Random House. Useful suggestions for building self-control, self-esteem, and self-reliance in children, by the author of *Parent Effectiveness Training.*

Ginott, H. (1956). *Between Parent and Child.* New York: Avon. A ground-breaking book that describes how the words we use with children often say something different and have different effects than those we intended. Provides important guidelines for communicating effectively with children.

Winn, M. (1984). *Children without Childhood.* New York: Penguin. Talks about the dramatic changes, since the 1960's, in the way in which we treat children. Calls for adults to take a more protective, nurturing approach to children.

7

Mental
Development

As in the case of physical and social growth, mental development shows both continuity and change. For example, the preschool child has already acquired elementary concepts of number, space, time, and causality as well as a multitude of other ideas regarding the natural and social worlds in which he lives. These conceptions, however, are different than those held by older children and adults. Put differently, the continuity of mental development resides in the fact that the child must struggle with the same intellectual problems during each growth period, but with progressively better mental equipment and with correspondingly better results. Mental growth, then, can be envisioned as an expanding spiral wherein the same issues are repeatedly returned to but at higher levels of abstraction and elaboration.

There is a parallel between the progressive construction and reconstruction of an idea in the child's mind and the progressive construction and reconstruction of concepts in the history of science. Among the ancient Greeks, the atom was regarded as the smallest building block of matter. Later, it was discovered that atoms, far from being single particles, are in fact miniature universes with a central core about which circulate a variety of still smaller particles, such as quarks and masers. Both the ancient Greeks and modern science have proposed a concept of the atom in connection with finding the irreducible elements of matter, but the atomic concepts of today are far more elaborate and abstract than those held by the ancient Greeks. In the same way, the preschool child has concepts of space, time, and number, but these are more limited and concrete than the space, time, and number concepts of older children and adults.

I am emphasizing this parallelism because it is often obscured by the child's use of language. During the elementary school years, children will use terms correctly in a grammatical sense without really understanding their full meaning in the conceptual sense. Although six- and seven-year-old children may use the terms *life* and *death*, they do not understand these terms as having to do with biological processes. The understanding of life and death in biological terms must wait until the child attains the age of nine or ten. For younger children, death is a kind of going away from which it might be possible to return.

In talking about mental development, therefore, we need to distinguish not only between words and concepts, but also between the growth of mental abilities (learning and reasoning processes) and the kinds of knowledge acquired through the utilization of these abilities. To illustrate, consider two boys of equal intelligence who grow up in quite different environments. One boy puts his intelligence to work acquiring the skills and knowledge he will need to pursue a career in the professions. The other boy puts his intelligence to work learning the skills and knowledge he will need to acquire and sell drugs without being caught. Obviously, many different factors operate to determine how mental ability will be used and what kinds of knowledge and skills children will acquire. The point of the illustration is to highlight the fact that we have to separate mental processes from their content and the use to which they may be put.

In the following sections, we will first review the development of the various mental abilities and then look at how children use these abilities to construct their knowledge about the natural and social world. Put differently, we will first look at *how* children think before we turn to the matter of *what* they think.

The Development of Mental Abilities

There is some disagreement among psychologists as to how best to describe our mental abilities. Traditionally, mental development has been regarded as the development of *intelligence,* or adaptive thinking and action. Intelligence as adaptation can be viewed quantitatively, as a more or less fixed level of adaptive capacity, or brightness, which can be measured by intelligence tests. From this quantitative perspective, although mental ability and knowledge increase with age, a child's relative brightness, his intellectual standing in relation to his peers, remains the same.

Intelligence can also be viewed qualitatively, from the perspective of the stages in the evolution of mental ability. Piaget's stages—sensorimotor, preoperations, concrete operations, and formal operations—reflect this qualitative approach to intelligence. Whereas the mental testing approach is focused upon *individual* differences in adaptive ability, the Piagetian approach focuses upon *age* differences in children's thought and action. The two approaches are not opposed; they just focus upon different dimensions. To assess individual differences, we have to keep age constant. To assess age differences we have to keep individual differences constant.

Recently, Harvard psychologist Howard Gardner has argued that there are multiple intelligences, and Yale psychologist Robert Sternberg has described intelligence as having three main components. In addition, other writers describe mental development in information-processing terms. Although these new approaches have merit, most of our knowledge about the development of children's mental abilities is organized around the more traditional categories of perception, language, learning, memory, reasoning, and problem solving. These are the categories that are used here. Where appropriate, however, I refer to these more recent innovations.

Perception

In the broadest sense, perception has to do with the ways in which we read the information that comes to us from our senses. We probably know most about visual perception, but we are beginning to learn more about the development of hearing, touch, and smell perceptions as well. We are also learning more about the interaction of information that comes from different senses at the same time.

A great deal has been accomplished in the perceptual domain by the time the child is of school age. By the end of the first year, infants already give evidence of depth perception and prefer pictures of regular faces to those of irregular faces. As we have already noted, infants also have considerable sensory integration and are able to look at what they touch and orient themselves to sounds coming from different directions. Infants can also distinguish between the basic tastes of sweet, sour, bitter, and salty. By the time they reach school age, most children can discriminate and label the basic colors and geometric shapes.

By the age of five or six, therefore, the child's basic perceptual skills are fairly well advanced. During the childhood years they undergo increasing refinement. Several general principles seem to hold true for visual perceptual development during the school years. First of all, as the child grows older, he is less and less bound by the organization or lack of organization of visual materials he looks at. Increasingly, he is able mentally to reorganize materials into patterns that are more interesting or satisfying. For example, when young children are presented with a card upon which pictures of familiar objects are pasted in a disordered array, they have difficulty in naming all of the pictures. They make errors of *omission* (failure to name all of the pictures) and of *commission* (naming the same picture twice). Children of seven or eight, however, name all of the pictures without errors of either omission or commission. They impose, or construct, an organization of the pictures on their own.

Another characteristic of the older child's perception is that while the young child tends to focus upon a limited aspect of an arrangement or picture, the older child is likely to explore the entire field systematically. When young children are asked to compare complex figures, such as two houses, that are alike except for the number of windows, they say the two are the same if they find only one similarity without any further exploration for possible discrepancies. Children of seven or eight explore both houses systematically before deciding whether the two are alike or different. Language enters in here, of course, because young children understand *same* to mean alike in *one* characteristic. Older children assume that *same* means alike in *all* characteristics. So the child's perceptual performance coincides to a certain extent with his language comprehension.

Not only do children explore their perceptual world with greater exactness than they did earlier, they are also able to construct higher order perceptions with the perceptual material they are provided. To illustrate, when young children are shown a drawing of a figure with an apple for a head, a pear for a body, bananas for legs, and grapes for feet, they name only the fruit and fail to see the figure. Children of seven or eight, in contrast, are able to grasp that the same shape can be that of an apple or a head and so on, and so they construct a superordinate perception, namely, "a man made out of fruit." This ability to construct and reconstruct visual arrays is also shown in their growing ability to read words upside down, to unscramble scrambled words, and to read sentences in which there are no spaces between the words.

During the elementary school years, then, perception becomes increasingly freed from the authority of the immediate physical configuration, and the child is progressively able to find order in disarray, to take in all of the many and varied details of illustrations, to integrate parts and wholes, and to organize existing organizations into new and higher level organizations. The older child literally sees the world differently than the young child.

It is not possible to leave the topic of perceptual growth without mentioning reading. Perception was once regarded as the leading factor in a child's reading difficulties. The consensus of workers in literacy today, however, is that reading is but a part of language and that reading difficulty is first and foremost a language difficulty. If we wish to improve reading, we have to look at all facets of a child's language development. For example, writing is now seen as an important step in learning to read. Many programs now utilize "invented spelling" in the sense that they encourage children to write stories without worrying about whether or not they are spelling words correctly. Children are quite good at reading their own writing, and this gives them the sense that "Yes, I can read."

In addition to writing, the "whole" language approach also emphasizes the importance of listening and auditory discrimination. We have to talk and read continually to children so that they can develop their auditory discrimination skills. Finally, we need to give children frequent opportunities to talk and express themselves, to converse with others, to tell stories, and to ask questions. When we view reading as part of the child's language development, we get away from looking at it as a matter of visual perception alone. It is not.

Language

As I suggested above, language is so closely tied up with the growth of perception and with learning, reasoning, and problem solving that it is highly arbitrary to treat it in iso-

lation. It is nonetheless true that despite their close interdependence, language and thought are distinguishable and
do not always run parallel courses of development.

In general, language tends to mature earlier than both
perception and thought. Most children have a fairly large
vocabulary and have mastered the basic grammatical rules
of tense, pluralization, and word order by the time they enter
first grade. Nonetheless, they have still to master the finer
points of grammar. Until about the age of nine, some children have trouble with constructions such as "John is easy
to see" and may not be sure who is doing the seeing. This
is difficult because in most constructions such as "John is seeing
the doctor," it is John who is doing the seeing. Up until about
the age of nine, children continue to improve their knowledge of *syntax*, the variety of ways words can be organized
into phrases and sentences to give different meanings.

We saw earlier that preschool children can already
use language to guide and direct their own behavior. Learning
to use language to guide and direct someone else's behavior,
however, is a much more difficult task, and children only
acquire this skill at about the age of eight or nine. In one
study, kindergarten and second grade children were required
to tape-record instructions as to how to build a block tower
so that another child could build it from the instructions alone
and without a model. The instructions from the kindergarten children were often incomplete, contradictory, and
ambiguous. Second grade children gave instructions that could
be followed, although they were not always complete.

When they were asked to build the tower from the
taped instructions, again there was an age difference. Kindergarten children sometimes recognized that the instructions were unclear, but they did not appreciate that this might
make it difficult for them to build a tower that would look
like the model. Second grade youngsters, in contrast, often
looked puzzled when the instructions were unclear and
understood that without clear guidance they might not be
able to build a tower that was a copy of the original model.
It should be said, however, that even adults have been known
to give poor directions!

Although school-age children are still learning the finer
points of syntax and how to use language to guide another
person's behavior, they are also beginning to take pleasure
in their mastery of language. This mastery is evident in the

child's playful use of language. Earlier I gave an example of a child who played with language once he had mastered an articulation problem. Now children play with language once they have mastered the meaning dimension of language. At this stage, children enjoy simple puns, such as, "Why did the tomato blush? Because she saw the salad dressing!" Elementary school children take great pleasure in such jokes and in riddles, deliberate wrong pronunciations, and wrong words. In their appreciation of language humor, children give evidence of their new mastery of both thought and language.

One aspect of language growth during the elementary school years was first described by Vygotsky. This is the progressive internalization of language and its use as a tool of thought. Young children think with the aid of images, rather than with words. That is one of the reasons their thinking is transductive. As children grow older, however, speech is "miniaturized"—Vygotsky says that whispering is a stage along the way—until the child can talk to himself without being heard by others. There is a stage, Vygotsky points out, when children have internalized language but still mouth the words. Although this internalized language may not be the same as thought, it does help to organize and direct thinking and does provide tools for use by thought processes.

Although the pattern of language development sketched here probably holds true for most middle-class children whose native language is English, it may not be so for children of other backgrounds and languages. Some children may be handicapped if their native language is not the language of the larger society. One problem arises when a mixed language appears that is not a good model of either language. Children from Spanish-speaking families who learn "Tex-Mex" or "Porcho" learn neither good English nor good Spanish. For example, in Spanish one says, "Hace mucho calor," or literally "It makes very hot." In Tex-Mex, however, this phrase is anglicized into "Es mucho calor," or "It is very hot." As they move into the higher grades, many children whose native language is Spanish have educational problems that are attributable to not speaking either good English or good Spanish.

Another problem occurs when the majority language is looked upon as the language of the oppressor and victimizer. Many African-American children and teenagers will not speak standard English because this means, in effect, that they have sold out to the larger white society. Even doing well in school is sometimes viewed as giving in to the values of white society. In this case, language is viewed as a vehicle of discrimination and oppression. Unfortunately, children who do not learn, or who refuse to use, standard English will fail in our educational system, and this only compounds the problem.

The difficulties school-age children have in some aspects of communication, coupled with the problems of children who are bilingual or for whom standard English is an anathema, pose serious problems for teachers. The sophisticated use of language by children from advantaged homes often leads teachers to assume that their comprehension is on a par with their linguistic skill, and this is often not the case. A very bright girl, for example, had trouble reading fairy tales. She was so puzzled by the phrase "once upon a time" that she could not proceed. What, she wondered, does "upon a time" mean? This is but one of the many expressions used by adults that puzzle and confound children. Teachers have to be careful to use concrete language that instructs, rather than abstract language that obstructs, children's understanding.

With children who come from bilingual homes or from homes where nonstandard English is spoken, the reverse problem can occur. The child's nonstandard English may lead the teacher to underestimate his intellectual powers. One of my students, for example, was tutoring an African-American elementary school child who was regarded by her teacher as mentally retarded, although she had never been tested. After working with her for some months, he so doubted the diagnosis that he tested her himself and found that she had an IQ of 125.

In defense of teachers, it should be said that they often do a miraculous job with very limited resources. I have seen teachers handle a class with children who spoke as many as seven different languages and from as many or more different cultures. Many teachers have to work with classes so large that individualization is almost impossible. Likewise, materials and equipment may be hard to come by, and the available curriculum materials dated and inadequate. Finally, most teachers have not been trained to deal with cultural and linguistic diversity. To their credit, many do extraordinarily well given the constraints and pressures under which they work.

Learning

In general, we speak of learning when there is a change or a modification of behavior as a result of experience. One form of learning is *classical conditioning.* For example, an infant may recognize the sound of his mother's footsteps and start to smile and vocalize when he hears them. His smiling and vocalizing have been conditioned to, or associated with, the sound of the mother's footsteps. Another form of learning was discovered and labeled *operant learning* by famed psychologist B.F. Skinner. In his work, Skinner found that once a particular behavior occurred, it could be made to reoccur if it was *reinforced,* or rewarded in some way. A child who, for whatever reason, shares his toy with a friend will likely do so again if the parent or teacher compliments him on his action.

Another form of learning has been described by Jean Piaget. He terms this mode of learning, *reflective abstraction.* Although Piaget recognizes both classical and operant learning, he also suggests that learning can be the modification of experience as the result of behavior, as well as the reverse. That is to say, children often create their own experiences and learn from these created experiences. That is what Piaget means by reflective abstraction. To illustrate, a child may arrange a set of stones to form a circle, then a square, and then a triangle. As a result of these experiences, which he has created himself, the child learns that no matter how he arranges the stones, their number remains the same.

Although learning from reflective abstraction, from experiences we create by our actions upon things, is present at all age levels, it is particularly prominent at the preschool level. Young children learn best through the active exploration of materials that allows them to learn the properties of things through their own actions upon them. At the elementary school level, children learn from reflective abstraction when they contrast and compare more complex patterns, arrangements, and concepts. At the adolescent level, the use of simile and metaphor illustrate a high-level form of reflective abstraction that allows young people to arrive, by their own mental actions, at the similarities between diverse concepts.

Although the basic modes of learning are the same, children vary widely in the circumstances under which they learn best. Children, and for that matter adolescents and adults, vary in their learning styles. These learning styles have little to do with intelligence and everything to do with personality, sensorimotor orientation, and temperament. A few examples of learning styles may help to illustrate how important style is for effective learning.

Harriet's parents provided her a desk, a comfortable chair, a bookcase, and a study lamp in her room so she could have a quiet place away from the television, telephone, and conversation of the downstairs living areas. However, she still got poor grades. After an evaluation of her learning style, it was found that she learned better in noisier settings with people nearby. After she began studying downstairs on the dining room table, Harriet's grades improved. A similar style is exhibited by those individuals who have to have the radio blaring as background for their studying.

Some young people who know their own learning style may begin to demand that information be presented in a way that is appropriate for them. One young man told his teacher, "I need to see the assignment, not just hear it." He had a predominantly visual learning style. Another example: Some auditory learners may have trouble with a "look-say" approach to reading. They do better with an auditory phonics approach. Indeed, the controversy about whether look-say or phonics is the best reading method may best be answered by asking "for whom?". Look-say may be best for visual learners, whereas phonics may be the best way to teach auditory learners.

Sometimes an educational system imposes a learning style that impedes rather than facilitates a child's learning. A case in point is Ross, an eight-year-old who had received his early schooling in Jamaica. In New York, he attended a school I ran for what I called "curriculum-disabled children"—children of average ability who were operating below the academic norm. Ross was very bright, but in Jamaica he had been taught to learn by rote, and this was now his preferred learning style. Whether it was reading, math, or social studies, Ross tried to memorize everything. He was a good auditory learner, so this imposed learning style fit him quite well, but he needed to learn other styles more appropriate for other materials, and after about a year he was able to do so. Although we should recognize a child's learning style, we need not be bound by it and should help the child to be flexible and to use other styles as well.

Before closing this section, it is important to say that talking is also a learning style. In talking, a child creates his own experience so that it is a form of reflective abstraction, and the child learns from experiences that he has created. We don't fully appreciate this either at home or at school. I recall visiting a first grade classroom on Cape Cod and observing a young man who seemed to be bursting with something to say. The teacher, burdened with too large a class, could not attend to him. I took an opportunity to talk to him during snack time and asked him if he had any news for me. He literally burst forth with "We have a brand new four-wheel drive, and we are going out on the dunes at Sandy Neck." Putting that information into words and listening to his own language constructions is an important mode of learning. We need to take some of the curriculum pressures off of teachers so that they can, as they used to, start the day with a circle where every child gets a chance to talk.

It is important for parents to give children a chance to express themselves at home as well. I was as guilty as most parents in this regard when my children were small. Sometimes when my sons had something of burning importance to tell me, I would cut them off with, "Tell me later, when I am not so busy." But later, the excitement is gone. Children need to talk when the fire is within them, not when it is cold ashes. Now when I am with children, I try to attend when children want to talk, not just when I want to listen. This isn't always possible, of course, neither at home nor at school, but it is possible more often than we would like to admit. Perhaps if we appreciate that talking is an important form of learning, we will be more willing to take the time to attend to what young people have to say.

Memory

Three types of memory are generally recognized and are already apparent in early childhood but become more elaborated in childhood proper. *Sensory memory* has to do with the immediate awareness of images and sensations that disappear quickly but may be transferred to short-term memory.

Short-term memory is our working memory, the full gamut of information with which we are currently working. *Long-term memory* is a storehouse of memories. The information-processing model is useful here. Short-term memory is like the RAM of the computer that has, say, the word processor and the document on which you are currently working. Long-term memory is like the ROM that has all the documents that you have previously composed.

In general, short-term memory increases with age through the elementary school grades. A simple test of short-term memory is the digit span test. We say a series of numbers and have the child repeat them back to us. Children of five or six can remember two or three digits, whereas adolescents can remember five or six. It is generally accepted that even among adults, short-term memory is limited to about 7 "chunks" of information. It should be said, however, that some children manifest eidetic memory, which is like photographic memory. They can, for example, often beat adults in games of concentration where you have to identify turned over pictures or playing cards.

Recent research has focused upon the strategies children use to enhance short-term memory. For example, a child who has learned to use the phone may ask his mother for his grandmother's phone number. Then as he rushes into the next room to use the phone, he repeats the number over and over again so as not to forget it. This is a *rehearsal* strategy that all of us use on occasion. In general, children do not spontaneously use rehearsal until after first grade. When shown pictures that will be taken away and that they will be asked to recall, first grade children did not rehearse until asked for the information, whereas children in the later grades talked to themselves under their breath until asked to recall the pictures. The older children recalled more pictures than did the younger children. Even children as young as three can sometimes be observed to use rehearsal, but it is much more common at the later age levels.

Another memory facilitation strategy is *categorization*. This technique is employed when a number of different elements are to be memorized and when they can be grouped within a larger category. Because we may have some of the members of the category already stored in long-term memory, the category approach builds upon previous learning and memory. Ordinarily, children below the age of ten or eleven do not use categorization spontaneously. They can, however, be taught to do so. Even so, they will not transfer this strategy to other learning situations.

Still a third memory facilitating strategy is the use of *external aids*. Such aids vary from making lists, to asking someone to remind us, to setting an alarm on our computer, to writing appointments in a date book. Apparently, even kindergarten children recognize and make use of such external aids, and they use them more frequently as they get older.

Finally, a useful memory strategy is that of *elaboration*. For example, when I worked as busboy at a resort during the summers, I had trouble remembering the guests' names. One guest, whose name was Bill, always gave me what seemed like a huge tip, namely, five dollars. I remembered his name by calling him "Five Dollar Bill"—to myself, of course. Likewise, a character in the "Peanuts" comic strip remembered the combination to his locker by associating the numbers with already remembered numbers. The combination was 3-24-7, which he remembered by thinking, "Babe Ruth was number 3, Willie Mays was number 24, and Mickey Mantle was number 7."

It should be said that all of these memory strategies— rehearsal, categorization, external aids, and elaboration— employ what Vygotsky called *verbal mediation*. Up until a certain age, children use inborn intellectual skills. After about the age of six or seven, however, their thinking is further elaborated by the use of cultural tools, namely, language. Language is a learned cultural tool that extends our inborn memory capacity. The effectiveness of verbal mediation is determined by language but also by the availability of peers and adults who provide models of verbal mediation for the child to follow. This is what Israeli psychologist Reuven Feurerstein calls *mediated learning*.

Investigators have also recently been interested in what is called *metamemory*, the child's knowledge about and understanding of memory processes. Young elementary school children have a general understanding of terms such as *learn, remember,* and *forget.* They appreciate that study improves learning, that memory can be facilitated with external aids, and that forgetting is a matter of the passage of time. Older children also grasp that there are individual differences in memory ability and that some things are easier to remember than others. By sixth grade, children also regard categorization as a more beneficial learning aid than rehearsal.

Memory, like perception and language, is also affected by the child's level of cognitive development. Piaget, for example, demonstrated that children's memories of certain patterns change spontaneously with age. When children are shown various figures and asked to reproduce them, young children may reproduce them incorrectly. When six months or a year later they are asked to reproduce the same figures again, they often reproduce them correctly! Piaget believed that it is not just the memory that has changed, but rather the mental framework within which the memories are stored that has changed, and that has brought about the specific change in the child's recall of the figure. Piaget's major point is that memory is always a *reconstruction* and not a simple *copy* of what was originally perceived.

Reasoning

Since ancient times, the age of six or seven has been regarded as the age of reason. The reason referred to by the ancients, however, was the reasoning of Aristotle, syllogistic reasoning. This reasoning took the following classic form:

All men are mortal [major premise].
Socrates is a man [minor premise].
Therefore, Socrates is mortal [conclusion].

Indeed, this is the reasoning that school children acquire and that largely replaces transductive reasoning. As we shall see, however, another still higher level of reasoning emerges in adolescence.

Piaget called the Aristotelian mode of reasoning *concrete operations*. He argued that these operations form an interconnected group much like the operations of arithmetic. Addition, for example, can be reversed by the operation of subtraction, and multiplication can be reversed by the operation of division. From this perspective, once the child has concrete operations, we can predict from his performance on one task how he will be able to perform on others.

Concrete operations enable the child to do a number of things that he was unable to do at a younger age. First, he can now follow rules and play games with rules. Moreover, because much of formal education involves the inculcation of rules, he is able to profit from such instruction. Second, he is now able to grasp units, whether these be in reading, math, science, or social studies. The unit concept presupposes the understanding that a single object can possess two properties or relationships at the same time. Third, the child is able to nest classes and relationships.

With respect to rules, consider first children's new ability to play games. In a simple board game such as Candy Mountain, the basic rule is: "Move your token as many spaces as the spinner says" (major premise). The child flicks the spinner with his finger. "The spinner says three" (minor premise). "I move my token three places" (conclusion). Young children who cannot yet engage in such reasoning are not really able to play simple board games. To be sure, they play according to a rule, but it is the rule, "I win, you lose!" Not surprisingly, older children complain that when younger children play the game, they "cheat."

Learning rules is a critical component in children's academic achievement. For example, a common spelling rule (not a very good one!) is "*i* before *e* except after *c.*" Likewise, a common pronunciation rule is "when two vowels go walking, the first one does the talking." Both of these rules require syllogistic reasoning to be applied. In a particular instance, say an encounter with the word *speak*, the child must say to himself:

When two vowels go walking, the first one does the talking
[major premise].
In this word, speak, *the first vowel is* e *[minor premise].*
In this word, the e *does the talking, so I say "speak" [conclusion].*

Children's understanding of rules at this age has far-reaching consequences. For example, it enables children to play with other children in organized games with rules. Moreover, children get obsessed with rules and are unhappy when they are broken or when they are bypassed. The child's sense of morality is very much tied up with his sense of rules. During the early elementary school years, the child believes that breaking the rules is bad absolutely, but later, toward the age of nine or ten, he begins to take intention into account as a mitigating circumstance.

The attainment of the unit concept, the understanding that one and the same thing can be two things at once, enables the child with concrete operations to understand both elementary mathematics and basic English phonics. For example, a true understanding of number requires the child to grasp the fact that one number, say the number 3, is like every other number in the sense that it is a number but is different from every other number in its order of enumeration. It is the only number that comes after 2 and before 4. Once children understand a number in this unit sense, they can perform all of the elementary operations of arithmetic.

Something similar is required to comprehend English phonics. What is difficult about English phonics is that one vowel or consonant sound can be represented in different ways. For example, the *ay* vowel sound can be represented by the long *a* as in *ate*, by the vowel combination *ai* as in *vain*, or by the vowel-consonant combination *ay* as in *say*. In the same way, the consonant sound *k* can be represented by the letter *k*, by the letter *c*, or even by the first sound of the combination of the letters *qu* as in *quote*. To comprehend phonics, then, the child has to be able to understand that one and the same sound can be represented in different ways, depending upon the context. Once the child understands the letter as a unit that is the same and different from other units, he can understand that the letter can represent both the same and different sounds as other letters.

Concrete operations also enable children to nest classes and relationships. Nesting simply means being able to group smaller classes within larger superordinate classes and to subordinate single relationships to multiple relationships. With respect to nesting classes, imagine that you are in a kindergarten with ten boys and eight girls. The children take roll every morning and know how many children there are in the class as well as the number of boys and girls. If you ask a five-year-old child in this class whether there are more boys or girls in the class, he will instantly respond, "More boys than girls, eight girls and ten boys." If you then ask, "Are there more boys or more children in the class?" the child appears perplexed and answers, "There are more boys than girls." At this stage, the child does not have a general concept of children that subsumes the class of boys and the class of girls. By the age of eight or nine, children can nest all sort of concepts. They know that eagles and robins are birds and that tulips and roses are flowers.

Nesting family relations follows a similar pattern. For example, if you ask a five-year-old child whether he has a brother, he may answer, "Yes, his name is Robert." If you now ask the child, "Does your brother Robert have a brother?" he is likely to answer, "No." At this stage, the child cannot nest the brother relation within a pattern of relationships and grasp that if he has a brother, his brother must have a brother as well, namely, himself. Children of seven or eight, however, readily acknowledge that their brothers have brothers. Similarly, if you show a child of five or so three objects and ask whether the one in the middle is on the right or the left of the object on the right, the child will say that it is "in the middle." He is as yet unable to nest relations and see that one and the same object can be both on the right of one object and on the left of another. Older children handle this question with ease.

Problem Solving

Problem solving can be thought of as the bringing together of perception, language, and reasoning to overcome barriers and reach a desired goal. Problem solving occurs at all age levels but becomes more elaborate as children mature. An example of problem solving at the preschool level is the child who observed his mother place some cookies in a high cupboard. After his mother left the room, he looked about, saw the kitchen chair, immediately moved it over to the cubboard, climbed on it, and retrieved the cookies. Although he had climbed stairs many times, he had never before used a chair to climb in this fashion. This is an example of problem solving by *insight*, a sudden "aha" experience.

Although early psychologists thought problem solving involved primarily trial and error and insight, recent advances in information-processing theory have provided a new way of looking at this form of mental activity. From an information-processing point of view, problem solving has four components: the encoding of information, the construction of strategies, the automatization of these strategies and their generalization. As children mature, so too does their level of information processing and thus their problem solving.

When a child is confronted with a problem, such as adding the numbers 7 and 10, he must first encode this information by storing it as mental representations in short-term memory. Then he must call upon a strategy to overcome the barrier, two different numbers, and attain the goal, the sum. One strategy is to simply count all of the numbers. The child will first count from 1 to 7 and then continue to count another 10 to arrive at the sum of 17. Older children will use a somewhat different strategy and start with the larger number, 10, and then count upwards to 17 from there.

As children practice these strategies, they become increasingly automatized: automatic and unconscious. As adults, for example, we no longer count when confronted with the addition problem; the answer is almost immediate. We are not aware of having used any strategy; the solution seems obvious. However, this is only because the strategies have been automatized, and we are no longer aware of them. We see a similar phenomenon with Piaget's conservation problems. After the child has attained conservation and recognizes that a quantity remains the same despite a change in its appearance, it seems to the child that the equality is perceptually obvious rather than a product of mental activity.

Although automatization is very adaptive, it sometimes presents problems in education. As adults who have automated so much of our learning, it is sometimes difficult for us to appreciate the learning difficulties encountered by children. Teaching children to read is a case in point. As adults, reading has become so automatized that it appears to us that the meaning of the word rests upon the page rather than in our heads. This makes it difficult for us to appreciate the problems reading presents to children who have not yet automatized decoding. When beginning teachers try to instruct young children, they often adopt what might be called the "look harder" theory of reading. If children will only look harder, they will "see" the word, be able to read and understand it. We have to be aware of automatization when teaching children.

The final stage of problem solving is generalization. After the child has learned successful problem-solving strategies and these have become automatic, he begins to extend these strategies to new situations. The ability to generalize strategies is in part a function of the child's level of development. When children and adolescents are presented with problems that require rather simple strategies, adolescents are more able to shift strategies than is true for children. Adolescents' readiness to shift strategies is a function of their more elaborate mental abilities.

Children's limited ability to generalize strategies and to shift them is demonstrated in other investigations. In one study, children and adolescents were confronted with a game that involved pushing three levers so as to attain the most rewards, tokens that could be exchanged for toys, candy, or money. The levers were programmed so that one paid off 33 percent of the time, another paid off 66 percent of the time, and the other paid off 10 percent of the time. The winning strategy was to push only the 66 percent lever. Adolescents quickly adopted this strategy after trying out several others. Children, however, stuck to a "win stick, lose shift" strategy and were never able to give this up and adopt the simpler, more lucrative strategy.

The years of childhood, therefore, are witness to a very impressive transformation of children's intellectual powers. In perception, language, reasoning, and problem solving, children make great advances over what they were able to achieve as young children. They still have limitations, but they have come a long way. Children make similar enormous advances in their fund of knowledge and skills.

The Growth of Knowlege

In this section, we will review some of the changes that occur in the elementary school child's understanding of the physical and social worlds. First we will look at changes in his concepts of quantity, space, time, and causality and then at his revised conception of morality and religion.

Among the most difficult concepts children have to learn are those of more, less, same, all, some, few, and many. These terms are difficult because they are used in such a wide variety of ways and contexts and in relation to an enormous array of dimensions. The child hears remarks such as "How much more do you need?" and "There is no more soda left" and "We need some more bread" and must try and make some sense out of these quantitative expressions.

Not surprisingly, the young child interprets quantitative terms as referring to actions. For example, a young child is accustomed to hearing the word *more* in the context of his mother asking whether he wants "more" to eat or to drink. As a result, he regards any collection or amount of substance to which an additional quantity has been added as having more than another quantity to which nothing has been added. Toward the end of the preschool period, the child comes to judge quantity by a particular visual property, such as height or width. To see whether he has more chocolate milk than his sister, a boy will push his glass next to his sister's and compare their levels.

It is only after children have attained concrete operations, however, that they come to understand quantity in terms that are comparable to those understood by adults. This is true because children are now able to understand quantity in unit terms. The growth in understanding of quantity terms is well illustrated by Piaget's conservation tasks. In these tasks, the child is confronted with a conflict between a judgment based upon perception and one based upon reason and logical deduction. Before the child has concrete operations, he tends to make judgments on a perceptual basis. After attaining concrete operations, however, he is most likely to make judgments on the basis of logical deduction.

Piaget's number conservation task is a case in point. If a preschool child is shown two equal sets of pennies that are aligned in identical rows, he will agree that both sets of pennies have the same "number." If, however, the pennies in one of the rows are spread farther apart than the pennies in the other row, the child will say that the longer row has more. The child is unable to "conserve" quantity because the perception of difference cannot be superseded by the deduction (both had the same before; nothing was added or taken away; therefore, both remain the same) of concrete operations. Once children attain concrete operations, however, reason wins out over perception, and the child judges the two rows to have the same number. With concrete operations, the child is able to overcome the press of perception and conserve quantity.

A similar transition can be observed with respect to the conservation of length. If a preschool child is shown two unsharpened pencils that are aligned so that their ends do not overlap, the child will say that they are the same length. If we now push one of the pencils so that it extends beyond the other pencil at one end and repeat our question, we get a different answer. The child now says that the pencil that extends beyond the other one is longer. For the young child, longer means extending beyond and not more units of length as it does for the older child and adult. Older children conserve length because their reasoned judgment supercedes the perception of difference.

A rather interesting development of quantitative concepts occurs with respect to the concepts of substance, weight, and volume. Although the assessment of the concepts involves the same conservation task, children do not attain conservation of these tasks at the same time. Piaget calls this phenomenon *decalage*, or separation. It occurs not only because these concepts are logically more difficult, but also because of the intuitive conceptions of mass, weight, and volume that children bring to the task.

The demonstration is easy to arrange. We need two identical clay or plasticine balls and three children aged seven, nine, and eleven. We examine each child individually and out of earshot of the others. Let us begin with the seven-year-old. We show him the two clay balls and ask him if both balls contain the same amount of clay. After he has agreed that the two balls do indeed contain equal quantities, we roll one of the balls into a "sausage" so that it is now longer and thinner than the other. If our subject is like most children of this age, he will reply that the ball and sausage both contain the same amount of clay for one of three deductive, rather than perceptual, reasons: (1) nothing was added or taken away, so they are the same; (2) what the sausage gained in length, it lost in width, so the amount is the same; or (3) if you make the sausage back into a ball again, they would be the same, so they must be the same now. With regard to mass, therefore, seven-year-old children can use their reason to overcome the perceptual impression of difference and understand the conservation of matter.

Suppose we now roll the sausage back into a ball and ask the seven-year-old, "Are both the balls the same weight?" Suppose, in addition we make available a small balance scale and a bit of extra clay so that he can weigh the two balls and add additional clay, if necessary, to make them equal. After he agrees that the two balls have the same weight, we again roll one of them into a sausage and repeat our question. This time the seven-year-old replies that the sausage weighs more because "it is longer." He discards the scale and uses his hands to weigh the two pieces of clay. Because the clay sausage does not touch as much of the palm as the ball does, the child thinks it weighs less. One boy explained the inequality by saying that you weigh more sitting down (when you are more folded up like a ball) than when you are standing up (when you are more stretched out like a sausage). In this instance, the child's intuitive concept of weight interfered with his difficulty in overcoming perception and grasping the conservation of weight.

If we now repeat the experiment with the nine-year-old child, we discover that he judges the ball and the sausage to have the same amount of clay and the same amount of weight. In justifying his conservation of mass and weight, he uses the same three explanations as the seven-year-old employed in justifying his conservation-of-mass judgement. If we ask whether the two balls have the same amount of volume, or take up the same amount of space, the child will agree that they do. Then we make one of the balls into a sausage again and repeat the question. This time the nine-year-old argues that the ball takes up more space than the sausage. His intuitive sense of space prevents him from using the same explanations for the conservation of volume as he did for mass and weight.

It is only when we test the eleven-year-old that we find a young person who understands that the mass, weight, and volume of matter is conserved despite a change in an object's appearance. At this age, the child's reasoning powers are such as to overcome even his most complex intuitive ideas about quantity. Apparently, the more closely our concepts are tied up with our actions, the more difficult it is to extract these conceptions from perception and to conceptualize them rationally. Weight is more tied to action than is mass, and volume is more tied to our bodies in space than is weight. The delay in the attainment of weight and volume concepts is not due to a lack of mental ability to conceptualize them, but rather to the difficulty of extricating them from our perceptual experience.

These findings are sometimes used to argue against the Piagetian stages. The argument is that, rather than general operations, different tasks present different levels of complexity. Although this is certainly true, it ignores what the child brings to the learning situation. The value of the *decalage* approach to this issue is that it emphasizes not only how much the child must learn, but also how much he must unlearn in his construction of reality. Put differently, it is as much the difficulty of unlearning our intuitive conceptions of mass, weight, and volume that accounts for the age differences as any intrinsic difference in the task itself.

The findings regarding *decalage* are not really surprising. They demonstrate once again that sheer intellectual power is no guarantee of objectivity. We encounter this phenomenon daily. It is simply easier to judge by appearances than it is to collect evidence and arrive at a reasoned judgment. The roots of prejudice lie in the fact that the presence of reason is no guarantee that false ideas will be rooted out. In the case of the child constructing his world, however, the child does overcome his subjective prejudices and does eventually arrive at objective quantity concepts.

In summary, then, the child begins with rather different conceptions of quantity than those held by adults. It has to be emphasized that these conceptions are different, not right or wrong. The young child who judges quantity in perceptual terms is acting in an age-appropriate manner, not giving wrong responses. As the child begins to think in unit terms, he is progressively able to overcome his intuitive impressions of number, length, mass, weight, and volume and to think of these quantities in a manner comparable to that of older children and adults.

Spatial Concepts

Space is a fundamental framework by which all of our behavior and experience is bounded. The growing child must learn to deal with many different spatial concepts and rela-

tions. He must, for example, master *body* space and become
aware of the positions, movements, and coordinations of his arms and legs. He must develop a sense of *action* space, the world of walking, riding, building, running, and playing. He must also acquire a sense of *living* space, the world of his room, his house, the backyard, the neighborhood, and the school. Early on, the child must deal with *representational* space, the space depicted in drawings and pictures. He must learn *topographical* space, the world of lakes, forests, oceans, and mountains. He must also learn to comprehend *map* space, the two-dimensional representations of three-dimensional space. Eventually, he must begin to appreciate *geopolitical* space, the space occupied by different countries around the world. Finally, he must learn about celestial space, the world of sky, sun, moon, planets, and stars.

As we might expect, the child masters body and action spaces first and only later gradually conquers the many other spaces in which he must live. It is during the elementary years that the child begins to grasp the broader spatial worlds that surround him. In each case, the child starts out with his own ideas, which he has to give up or elaborate as he comes to understand the spaces as they are understood in the larger society.

When we turn to representational space, we again encounter characteristic misunderstandings in young children. To illustrate, six- to seven-year-old children still draw pictures with *transparencies,* that is, with features showing that would not be seen in fact. A man on horseback, for example, is drawn so that the line of the horse's body is showing through the man's body. A woman in a boat is drawn so that you can see all of her body in the boat. At this stage, too, children use no perspective in their drawing. Only toward the end of childhood do children learn and employ representational conventions such as profiles with one eye and drawings with perspective.

With respect to geographical space, the child begins by assuming that his world is the only world. A young child growing up in the Midwest may have trouble understanding what the concepts of mountain or ocean really represent. Likewise, a child growing up in the Southwest may not be able to envision the lush greenery of the Northeast. Television can help in this regard, but it is only as children gain a better sense of geographical distance and travel that they come really to appreciate geographic diversity.

A similar pattern occurs with respect to the child's sense of geopolitical and map space. Young children have great difficulty in imagining distant places, and "far away" is often understood in concrete terms as differences in styles of clothing, language, mode of life, and shelter. Children appreciate that Eskimos live in igloos before they fully appreciate the distance to the Arctic. Only in later childhood, by age nine and ten, do children begin to appreciate the vastness of the distance that separates us from those who live in the far north.

Young elementary school children encounter similar difficulties with map space. I once taught a second grade class in upstate New York. We were in Rochester, New York, and had a map that showed Lake Ontario, Toronto, Canada, as well as neighboring Erie, Pennsylvania, and all of New York State. When I started asking about distances, I found that the children believed it was farther from Rochester to Toronto (about sixty miles across the lake) than from Rochester to New York City. It seemed to them that any two cities within the same state were closer together than any two cities located in different states. They also had trouble understanding how one and the same boundary line could belong to two states at the same time. Only at the later grades do children understand that states can share boundaries.

Finally, with regard to celestial space, children learn the names of the stars and planets much before they can appreciate celestial distance or movements. Piaget observed that children's first ideas about celestial space have an egocentric quality. The young child believes that the moon follows him when he walks at night. He also believes that the clouds are alive because they move. As the child's quantitative thinking matures, he is better able to understand celestial movements. It is not until adolescence, however, that he can comprehend notions such as light years and the fact that the earth revolves around the sun, and not the reverse.

By the end of the elementary school period, children have mastered the basics of their many spatial worlds, but these worlds are far from complete. It is only in adolescence that young people acquire a true sense of geographical, geopolitical, and celestial space. Even so, children make enormous progress over the period from preschool to early adolescence and are able to operate comfortably in the immediate spatial world of home, school, and community.

Time Concepts

During the school years, the child must master a number of different time concepts, including psychological time, clock time, and calendar time. During the preschool years, psychological time is about the only time perspective the child has. A child measures time with regard to his activities. To the young child, there is little difference between "later," "in a few minutes," or "next week," which are all understood as simply meaning "not now."

The development of a child's time concepts moves in two directions: to the smaller divisions of clock time and to the larger divisions of calendar time. Preschool children distinguish first between day and night and then between various activities that occur in the course of their routine day. By school age, the child is on his way toward the mastery of clock time, first by full and then by the half and quarter hours. Progress in calendar time concepts is somewhat less rapid. The child learns the days of the week first, then the months. Only late into middle childhood does he begin to appreciate years and printed dates. The child's understanding of calendar or historical time does not, therefore, come about until the child is eight or nine years of age. In fact, a true comprehension of historical time and realistic planning for the future does not emerge until adolescence.

A measure of the child's progressive comprehension of both time and space can be gathered from children's literature. This literature reflects the child's level of conceptual development and thus his level of spatial/temporal understanding. Fairy tales for preschool children contain little in the way of time and space terminology other than perhaps "once upon a time." Stories for school-age children begin to have elementary spatial and temporal concepts. In *Winnie-the-Pooh*, there is a forest, birthdays are described, and time is described in the sense that Pooh sometimes forgets things he is to do the same or the next day. Finally, at adolescence, stories such as *The Hobbit* contain elaborate and complex space/time depictions. Children's literature, then, can give us good practical guides to young people's expanding understanding of space and time.

One of the major cognitive tasks of the school-age child is the progressive differentiation between psychological and physical causality. That is, he must eventually distinguish between events that are brought about as the result of human actions and intentions and those that are occasioned by physical laws or by chance. Preschool children do not make this distinction and often assume that physical events have psychological causes, and vice versa. Young children believe that physical events, like psychological events, have a purpose: that the sun shines for a reason and that rain has a purpose.

On the other hand, the child attributes psychological events to physical causes and believes that dreams "come in through the window at night." He may even believe that his thoughts and feelings are tangible and visible to others. That is why young children are not good at keeping secrets. They seem to believe that their thoughts are visible to others and that others will know the secrets, so they talk about them.

As the child enters school, he progressively modifies his causal conceptions in keeping with those of older children and adults. This comes about in part as the child continually checks out his causal conceptions against those of his peers as well as his parents and teachers. In addition, the child also needs to be able to put his intuitive understanding of causality into words. That is, the child already knows such causal connections as that turning the light switch makes the light go on and that when a glass drops it is likely to break. He also understands a great deal about psychological causality. Afraid that he will be blamed for spilling his milk, he may defend himself by saying, "It was only an accident!"

These understandings, however, are still at a nonverbal level. He is not yet able to put into words his understanding that "turning the switch makes the light go on" or that "Spilling the milk makes my mommy angry." During the elementary school years, the child both increases his understanding of causal connections and his ability to put those connections into words. One evidence of his new causal understanding is his distrust of magicians and of magic tricks. He is no longer taken in by the seeming noncausal events and wants to know what goes on behind the scenes and how the trick is done. Likewise, he now recognizes that dreams have psychological causes and can relate them to scary movies or TV shows. He also recognizes that physical events have physical causes, and he has a beginning understanding that the motions of sun and moon are entirely physical phenomena.

Nonetheless, at times of strong emotion, the child may revert to more primitive conceptions of causality. This happens because the development of causal concepts is somewhat different than the development of other concepts. In the attainment of number, for example, lower level concepts of sameness and difference are *integrated* within a higher level concept of a unit. Even when he is upset, the child does not revert to lower level concepts of number. Higher level concepts of causality, however, are simply *substituted* for lower level ones. The lower level concepts are not incorporated within the higher level ones. At times of stress, it is easy to slip back to earlier ideas of what leads to what.

A few examples may help to illustrate this point. A child who has a good sense of psychological causality may nonetheless take a good-luck coin or baseball card with him when he goes to the dentist, in hopes that this may make it hurt a little less. He may get angry and hit a battery-operated toy when it fails to work, as if the toy had bad intentions toward him. Children, of course, are not unique in this regard, and adults can also revert back to earlier causal conceptions. Such conceptions remain latent beneath the higher level causal ideas that have been substituted for them. An adult may, for example, use body English on a bowling ball or a golf putt to help the ball gain its desired goal.

The development of the child's causal conceptions, therefore, takes a somewhat different path than his conceptions of classes, relations, and numbers. Unlike those conceptions, which are attained by progessive differentiation and higher order integration, higher order causal conceptions are merely substituted for lower level ones. During the elementary school years the child gains a clearer understanding of both physical and psychological causality and is better able to verbalize these relationships. Nonetheless, because these higher level conceptions are attained by substitution, children and adults frequently fall back upon earlier causal conceptions at times of stress.

Moral Concepts

Morality has to do with our ideas regarding what is right and what is wrong and how right and wrong behavior should be punished and rewarded. The classic work on the moral judgment of children was done by Jean Piaget. His work was later elaborated by the late Harvard psychologist Lawrence Kohlberg.

Piaget argued that there are essentially two forms of morality. One of these is derived from the child's experience with adults. The morality of *unilateral* authority is derived from adults in the sense that the adult sets the rules and enforces them. In general, the morality of unilateral authority appears in early childhood and is objective in the sense that the child believes that badness is associated with the amount of damage done. The young child believes that a child who breaks three cups while helping his mother set the table is more culpable than a child who has broken a single cup while trying to get cookies he was forbidden to eat.

After the child attains concrete operations and begins to interact with his peers and to participate in the culture of childhood, he attains a second form of morality, that of *mutuality*. In the course of playing with his friends, the child learns to make and break his own rules and to set his own rewards and punishments. At the same time, a new factor enters into his assessments of good and bad and how punishment should be meted out. He now begins to take the person's intentions into account. In the dilemma described earlier, the child of eight or nine is likely to say that the child who broke one cup did something bad and should be punished more than the child who broke three cups because the latter was doing something good.

Unilateral authority thus occasions an objective morality while mutual authority occasions a subjective morality. To illustrate, six- and seven-year-old children regard a pupil who lies about the grades he received on his report card as less culpable than a child who claims he has seen a dog the size of a house. At the early elementary school level, children reason that the child might have received the grade he said he did, whereas a dog the size of a house is physically impossible. The lie about the dog is thus more serious because it is more at variance with the objective world.

In contrast, older elementary school children say that lying about the grade is more serious than lying about the dog. They reason that the child who lied about the grade intended to deceive his parents, whereas the child who lied about the dog intended only to amuse them. Deception is a more reprehensible intention than amusement and should be punished more.

The objective character of unilateral morality can also be seen in the young child's judgment regarding punishment. Up until about the age of six or seven, children assess an action's "badness" or "goodness" on the basis of whether it was objectively rewarded or punished. For example, children at this age argue that a child who is unfairly spanked by his mother must, of necessity, have done something bad. Older children, however, recognize that a child can be punished unfairly. For them, objective punishment is not necessarily an index of subjective guilt.

Another dimension of moral development has to do with the relationship between personal injury and property damage. When intention is held constant, children at all age levels, from kindergarten to sixth grade, judge personal injury (say, a bloody nose) as more serious and more punishable than property damage (say, a broken toy). Young children say that a bloody nose "hurts" more. By second grade, children express a kind of "cold cash" morality and say that a "bloody nose costs more" (in doctor's bills) than a toy. Finally, among the oldest children, a genuine humanism emerges, and they say personal injury is more serious than property damage because "it's another person; you shouldn't hurt people."

It should be said that both unilateral (objective) and mutual (subjective) authority and morality are important in everyday life. We all have to respect unilateral authority. For example, we obey traffic rules and pay income taxes even though we did not make the rules and may not always agree with them. Some degree of unilateral authority is essential for a society to function. Yet for a society to function as a democracy, there must be room for mutual authority as well. The electoral process is the one in which we engage in mutual authority. We also operate according to mutual authority in our marriages, our friendships, and many social relationships. One of the dangers of the disappearance of the culture of childhood is that children may not have the opportunity to acquire a solid sense of mutual authority, of their ability to make and break their own rules.

In his work, Piaget distinguished only two levels of authority: unilateral and mutual. Lawrence Kohlberg distinguished still a third level of morality in adolescence, and he argued that the unilateral and mutual authority of Piaget could be further subdivided. His six stages of moral development are described in the accompanying box. Kohlberg's last two stages, which he calls the *post-conventional level,* go beyond Piaget. They suggest a higher order integration of unilateral and mutual authority into a superordinate transcendent morality of abstract principles of goodness and justice.

Kohlberg's Stages of Moral Development

Level 1   *Obedience and Punishment Orientation*
Obey rules so as not to be punished.
Level 2   *Naive Hedonism Orientation*
Obey rules to obtain rewards.
Level 3   *Good Boy Orientation*
Obey rules to win social approval.
Level 4   *Authority and Social Order Orientation*
Obey rules because everyone else does.
Level 5   *Moral Principles Orientation*
Obey rules that have been mutually agreed upon.
Level 6   *Individual Principles Orientation*
Obey transcendent moral beliefs that have been individually arrived at.

Although Kohlberg was able to provide evidence for his stages by following the same subjects over a number of years, his work has been challenged. One of his students, Havard psychologist Carol Gilligan, has used his work to mount a more general feminist critique of developmental psychology. She argues that Kohlberg's stages were arrived at by studying the cognitive development of boys and young men. When girls and young women are examined using

Kohlberg's procedure (using moral dilemmas to assess a subject's level of moral development), young women seldom attained Kohlberg's last two stages, stages he regarded as the most advanced and mature levels of morality.

Gilligan objects that women have a different conception of morality than men. For women, interpersonal relationships are more important than abstract principles of justice. When the stages of moral development derived from the study of young men is used as the standard, women do not attain the same level of moral development as men. Gilligan's point is that young women have a different moral "voice" than men but it is not, in any way, an inferior or lesser voice.

Before closing this section, a word or two needs to be said about moral judgment and action. For both boys and girls, young men and young women, moral action is likely to be situationally determined. That is to say, general moral principles are seldom guides to action in very concrete situations where many different factors operate. For example, a child may take something from a store because he is dared to do so by friends, even though he knows this is wrong. In general, the models of moral behavior the child has observed may be the most important determinants of his own moral behavior.

Religious Concepts

In talking about children's understanding of religious conceptions it is useful to distinguish, as William James, famed Havard psychologist, did, between institutional and personal religion. *Institutional religion* has to do with its formal aspects, with theology, sacraments, and rituals. *Personal religion*, in contrast, has to do with the individual's unique response to the various facets of institutional religion. Psychologists are in general agreement that there are no uniquely religious motives, feelings, or ideas but that these become religious in association with the elements of institutional religion. Put differently, personal religion is the individual's response to and interpretation of institutional religion and does not occur outside of or independently of the church as an institution.

A child's religious development follows two different paths. One of these, the path of spontaneous religion, involves the child's efforts to make sense out of the elements of institutional religion. The other path is acquired and derives from religious instruction and participation in religious observances and practices. Spontaneous religion is most prominent in young children and is gradually replaced by acquired religion as the child receives religious instruction and increases his participation in religious rituals and ceremonies both at home and at the church or synagogue. An exception occurs in early adolescence when, for a few short years, many young people revert to their own spontaneous religion.

The transition from spontaneous to acquired religion can be illustrated by the evolution of the child's understanding of his religious identity and by the evolution of his comprehension of prayer. To explore these conceptions, I interviewed hundreds of children, aged four to thirteen, from Protestant (Congregational), Jewish (Conservative), and Catholic backgrounds. For both identity and prayer conceptions, I found that the child's understanding proceeds through a series of stages that are related to age.

At the first stage in the evolution of his religious identity (usually ages five to seven), the child has only a general notion of the meaning of terms such as *Catholic, Protestant,* and *Jew.* In his spontaneous attempt to understand these terms, the child confuses them with national and racial designations. A child at this stage will, for example, reply to the question, "Are all boys and girls in the world Protestant?" with an answer such as, "No, some are Russian and some are Japanese." Similarly, when children at this stage are asked how a Protestant is different from a Jew, they might reply, "Because some people have black hair and some people have blonde hair." Furthermore, children at this stage believe that having a religious identity is incompatible with other identities and say that they cannot be Americans and Protestants at the same time (a reflection of young children's inability to nest classes.)

At the second stage in the understanding of religious identity (usually ages seven to nine), children show some transitional ideal halfway between their spontaneously elaborated meaning of religious terms and the meanings generally accepted by adults. When asked if all boys and girls in the world are Protestant, they reply, "No, because I know a boy who is Catholic." By this stage, children relate their own religious denominations to other denominations and no longer confuse them with national and racial concepts. In addition, they now think of their religious denominations in terms of particular and religion-appropriate actions. (A Protestant goes to a Protestant church. A Jew goes to a synagogue.) They can also nest classes and appreciate that one can be a Jew, Protestant, or Catholic and an American at the same time.

By the time they reach the third stage (usually ages nine to twelve), children's conception of their religious denomination appears entirely acquired and in keeping with those of institutional religion. It is a more abstract conception in the sense that the child now thinks in terms of general categories rather than in terms of specific experiences or actions. At this stage, the child says that not all boys and girls in the world are Protestant because "there are different religions in the world," and a Protestant is one "who believes in Christ, but not in the Pope." The question of whether one can be both a Protestant and an American is dismissed with the reply "They are different things. One is your country; the other is your religion."

The evolution from spontaneous to acquired conceptions of religious identity holds equally true for Protestant, Catholic, and Jewish children, although there are some differences. Protestant children at the first stage are frequently confused by the terms *Congregationalist, Presbyterian, Lutheran,* and *Baptist.* Catholic and Jewish children, who do not have this wealth of sects and terms to confuse them, are aware of their denominations earlier and are somewhat clearer about them. This difference is, however, erased by the second stage, when children have learned their particular Protestant denomination.

Children's spontaneous religious conceptions can sometimes be amusing. One boy told me, "Yes, you can be a Protestant and American at the same time, but only if you move!" A boy of eight was rather ambivalent about whether a dog or a cat could be Protestant: "If he belongs to the family, he would be Protestant, but I don't think the minister would let him into church—he might bark! So maybe he couldn't be." Some of the children's remarks were actually quite profound, like the five-year-old girl who remarked, "God doesn't have birthdays and Jesus does."

The child's understanding of prayer goes through roughly the same developmental stages. At the first stage (usually ages five to seven), children regard prayer as asking God for things. Many young children picture God as an old man with a beard who gives gifts. Children at this stage usually ask for things such as candy or toys for themselves. If prayers are not answered, they "get mad" or "yell and scream" or "get angry at God."

At the second stage (usually ages seven to nine), prayer is understood as a kind of talking to God as well as asking him for things. He is thought of more in terms of his personality traits, such as goodness and kindness, rather than in regard to his appearance. Seven- to nine-year-old children pray not only for things for themselves but also for their families and for their pets. If their prayers are not answered, they are disappointed but take responsibility for why this was not the case—the prayers were not good enough, not phrased properly, and so on.

At the third stage (usually ages nine to twelve), children begin to understand prayer as a kind of private conversation. Correspondingly, at this stage they think of God in relationship terms, such as Master or Father. By this age, the young person's prayers have become altruistic and general. He prays for peace on earth and for food for needy children. If his prayers are not answered, the older child argues that God can only help him realize his prayers but that he himself shares some responsibility for their fulfillment.

In general, then, for both religious denomination and prayer, the child's religious understanding moves from spontaneous, concrete, and confused conceptions to those that are acquired, abstract, and in conformity with institutional religion.

The concepts of quantity, space, time, causality, morality, and religion are some aspects of the development of mental abilities and ideas during the elementary school years. Although this is only a limited sampling of the child's broadening understanding of the physical and social worlds, it may suggest how much children have to learn and how much they must unlearn and relearn. The growth of understanding is always a reconstruction and representation of previously held conceptions. It is never a simple addition of new information.

Moreover, a review of the child's ideas about the world indicates how great a gap there is, at least initially, between the adult's view and the child's view of the world about them. It must remind us once again of the extraordinary effort and time children have to expend in coming to understand the world from the adult's point of view. It seems only fair that, as parents, we make an effort to see the world from the child's perspective.

Selected Readings

Coles, R. (1985). *The Moral Life of Children.* Boston: Atlantic Monthly. Challenges Kohlberg's position and argues that even elementary school children can live profoundly moral lives. Buttresses this position with remarkable quotations from children discussing their experience.

Donaldson, M. (1979). *Children's Minds.* New York: Norton. Makes the important point of how much children's learning depends upon the social and physical context in which that learning takes place. Suggests strategies that will help us to use contexts more effectively.

Ginsburg, H.P., & Opper, S. (1990). *Piaget's Theory of Intellectual Development,* 3rd ed. Englewood Cliffs, NJ: Prentice Hall. A well-written, accessible introduction to some of Piaget's major experiments, findings, and conceptions.

Siegler, R.S. (1991). *Children's Thinking.* New York: Prentice Hall. A comprehensive, readable overview of the literature on the development of children's perception, language, and thought.

Vygotsky, L.S. (1978). *Mind in Society: The Development of Higher Psychological Processes.* Cambridge, MA: MIT Press. Provides an introduction to some of Vygotsky's major concepts about language, memory, play, and the interaction of learning and development.

8

Age Profiles

Year-by-year profiles, as I noted earlier, reveal patterns in the development of temperament, self-concept, social relations, and school orientation that are sometimes obscured by looking at development over a larger time frame. Some of this yearly ebb and flow of development is described below.

The Six-Year-Old

One of the most notable traits of the six-year-old is high activity. Looking in on a first grade class—with the constant motion, jiggling, shoving, pushing, and talking—can give you a distinct experience of seasickness. Whether sitting or standing, six wiggles and squirms. Six makes faces, imitates the latest dances he has seen on TV, and is constantly bouncing out of his chair, even during the evening meal. He also engages in a lot of boisterous play and verbal attacks. Phrases such as "You are funny looking" and "You stink" are frequent. At this age, however, the child is much more ready to dispense verbal abuse than to receive it. Six is very sensitive about being called the names he is so ready to apply to others. Although he likes to roughhouse, he may not know when or how to stop and he may get hurt.

By age six, children are interested in games with rules that can be played by several children or by children and adults. Games in which each child takes a turn throwing dice or spinning an arrow are popular. Simple motor games, such as Tee Ball, are also popular. Most six-year-olds are able to ride a two-wheeler and handle it well. Although they attain mastery in these areas, six-year-olds have difficulty with more complex board games, such as checkers and chess. Even tick tack toe may not be easy for them. In comparison to spinner games, these more elaborate board games involve multiple rules, rather than a single rule (move your token as many places as the number pointed to by the arrow or that shows up on the die), and thus require more intellectual power than most six-year-olds can muster.

On the other hand, six-year-olds enjoy and are quite ingenious at making things. They engineer toy boats out of pieces of wood and create paperweights out of painted stones. Fabricating new things is high on the six-year-old's list of favorite activities.

Six tends to be a bit clumsy and a dawdler. Parents often have to fight to get him dressed and off to school or to other activities. On his side, however, the six-year-old wants things done at once, and he gets upset if his parents do not drop everything to do his bidding. In fabricating activities, as in his play, he may not know when or how to stop and may exhaust himself and get angry that he has run out of steam. Six also has trouble controlling his insatiable appetite for sweets. It is not unknown for six to waken before his parents and scour the house in search of candy. If he finds it, he may devour it in large quantities. Six, in fact, is almost always eating, particularly after school.

The six-year-old needs to be at the center of things, to be first, and to win. He is seldom modest about his accomplishments and may exclaim, "I'm pretty good, aren't I!" At this age, the child is assertive, bossy, and extremely sensitive to real and imagined slights. He feels he is being treated unfairly if a sibling gets a birthday present and he doesn't receive one at the same time. He gets upset if someone gets a larger portion of anything than he does, and when he gets the lion's share, he takes it as his due. Six is also very free with unasked-for opinions and advice. He demands attention from parents and is oblivious when they are involved with activities that preclude them from interacting with him. It is also not unusual for a six-year-old to ask a parent to play a game as soon as the parent has come home from work, without giving the parent a moment or two to unwind.

During this age period, the child begins to define his self-concept by putting himself in opposition to his mother. (This is true for girls as well as boys.) Sometimes the child resorts to calling her names ("Stupid idiot," "I hate you, you're so mean"). At other times the child may say "I love you" and write her notes and make her presents. The strain of growing up and of going to school sometimes takes the form of regression. At such times, the six-year-old may engage in baby talk in imitation of his younger siblings and may behave with babyish mule-headedness. Because six is now in school and exposed to new values and standards, he is in somewhat of a turmoil of adaptation. This is a prelude to the similar but more intense turmoil the child will manifest in early adolescence.

The six-year-old can give his parents a hard time. Fortunately, his onslaughts are not as incessant as those of, say, the two-year-old. At this stage, he tends to be a know-it-all, an attitude that quickly gets on his parent's nerves. Equally irritating, given his readiness to attack others, is his adverse reaction to any criticism of himself. When he is not being overly assertive, however, six can also be affectionate and loving. The father is, if not the preferred parent, the parent toward whom the child is most consistently positive. Six-year-olds like to go places and do things with their fathers.

Relations with siblings are often competitive but will vary with the child's position in the family. If he is the oldest, he may get angry about his younger brothers and sisters getting into his things. Nor is he above punching or shoving them to show his displeasure. Occasionally the six-year-old may play with younger siblings, but he prefers children of his own age. Although he wants to play games with older brothers and sisters, he does not like to lose. If he does lose, he will not play the game again.

With respect to peers, six-year-olds often pair up and have best friends with whom they spend a good deal of time. Such pairs often seem to take brutal satisfaction in ostracizing a third child who wants to join their play. Friendships are rather erratic, and the combinations of pairs may change many times in the course of the school year. Six-year-olds also engage in a lot of indelicate "tattling" and putting down of other children ("He didn't even know that!"). They often say that they have boy or girl friends, and these are usually children in their school class whom they admire. Although boys and girls occasionally play together at this age, the movement toward friends of the same sex has already begun.

The six-year-old has a positive attitude toward school and wants to attend. He sometimes changes his mind in midyear, however, and at times proclaims that school is not for him. At such times, he decides that he simply does not want to go to school that day. This may have to do with events going on in school that he doesn't enjoy, or it may reflect a desire to stay home with mother or an urge to sit in front of the TV all morning. Such reactions may also reflect that a full day of school is sometimes tiring for a restless six-year-old. Resisting school may simply mean that he needs a respite from a confining schedule. Because going to school has not yet become a habit or a virtue, the six-year-old does not feel guilty about staying home. Only as he gets older will going to school become the "right" thing to do.

In general, a class of six-year-olds varies markedly from day to day in its level of activity and can be hectic one day and almost somnambulant the next. Children at this age like to work, but they work best in spurts and do not show the persistence they will later. Nonetheless, six-year-olds learn a good deal, particularly in the areas of reading and math. Most children enter first grade able to read a few words. Many leave first grade able to read several primers. First grade children also master the basic arithmetic operations of addition and subtraction. At this stage, fluency is much more important than accuracy. If children are encouraged to read, write, and do math without much attention to accuracy, they will get the "feel" of the skill. Later they can "clean up their act."

Six-year-olds like to bring home their school work, such as math papers and primers. They take pride in the gold stars pasted on their work papers and explain away their occasional errors with such phrases as "I thought she wanted us to plus, but I guess she wanted us to minus!" Six-year-olds really warm up to parental praise and get puffed up with themselves. On the other hand, they can be devastated when a parent or a teacher dismisses their work or is derogatory. Although sixes like to show what they have done at school, they don't like to talk about their school day. They are much more ready to talk about the exploits of their classmates.

In general, then, six is an active, outgoing age at which the child is basically self-centered. His own activities and pleasures take precedence over everything else. His self-centeredness has a certain charm, however, because he is not vain about things he can take no credit for, such as his appearance. On the other hand, he is rather proud of his achievements, both at home and at school. This sort of vanity is easier to accept and appreciate. He is still not fully adapted to school, and his absences may be frequent. Nonetheless, he usually acquires the basics of reading, writing, and arithmetic.

The Seven-Year-Old

Growth is not a regular process that moves by equal increments like the hours of the day. Rather, growth often occurs in spurts, followed by periods of relative quiet. Children sometimes need time to take in and integrate the enormous amount of information with which they are bombarded. I recall visiting a railroad yard with a group of preschool children. At the yard, the children climbed into the engine and sat there while it revolved on a turntable. They also walked through the caboose. On the way home, we stopped for a soft drink and a snack. Back at school, the major topic of conversation was not the train, but rather the soft drink and the snack. It was not until weeks later that the children spontaneously began to talk about the engine, the caboose, and the turntable. It took them weeks to assimilate the stimulation of that experience. Something similar happens when you take young children to a circus or a parade.

Toward the end of the seventh year and the beginning of the eighth, children begin to assimilate the wealth of new experiences to which they were exposed as they entered first grade. This attempt at digesting experiences is seen in the relative quietness of seven-year-old children in contrast with their bustling behavior at six. It is as if their experiences in first grade were comparable to those of the children at the railroad yard. They need time to mull over the experience and to make it their own. Seven appears to be the age when a lot of this assimilative and digestive work gets done.

In part, the reflectiveness and seriousness of the seven-year-old is attributable to the consolidation of the reasoning abilities that the child used at age six to acquire information. At age seven, he uses these same abilities to sift and sort information into categories and to connect the bits and pieces of information that he has acquired. The course of this assimilation process is not always smooth. Sometimes the seven-year-old is brooding, pensive, sad, and negativistic. One might even say that whereas the six-year-old child deals with the world largely with his body, at age seven he begins to cope with his world with the use of his mind. It is not that the seven-year-old is less active than he was at age six. Rather, the setting of activity has shifted, and now the activity takes place within his mental, rather than his physical, action space.

The increased inwardness of the seven-year-old carries with it an increased sense of self and a heightened sensitivity to the reactions of others. Shame is a common emotion at this age and the child is often embarrassed by his body and does not like to expose it or to be touched. Because the child's body self and psychic self are not well separated at age seven, we see a parallel reluctance to expose himself to failure or to criticism. The seven-year-old will often leave the scene rather than make himself vulnerable to possible criticism or disapproval.

It is important to emphasize, however, that the sensitivity of the seven-year-old is geared to what other children, his parents, and his teachers *say* and *do* as it relates to him. It is not a sensitivity to what they *think* about him. Only in adolescence will the child begin to dwell on other people's thinking and worry about what people think about him, regardless of what they say and do. For age seven, however, saying, doing, and thinking are not yet separated.

Perhaps because of his sensitiveness, the seven-year-old often complains about having been treated unfairly and worries about people liking him. This concern is aided and abetted by his first grade experience. In first grade, the child was rated against his peers on such things as his reading, math, and writing abilities. Not surprisingly, the seven-year-old shows concern in just those areas on which his peers, his teachers, and his parents choose to publicly evaluate him. It takes time for the seven-year-old to process these evaluations. Such evaluations are different in content, but comparable in impact, to the comparisons between the child and his siblings made by parents and family friends.

The relatively subdued personality of the seven-year-old has very positive consequences for his interpersonal relations. He is no longer the scourge of the dinner table that he was at age six. The days of bouncing up and down, filling his mouth overfull, and eating with his fingers are thankfully over. In addition to eating in a more civilized manner, the seven-year-old can listen instead of trying to dominate the conversation. He is, moreover, desirous of being helpful around the house and asks to be given chores to do and errands to run. Seven will enthusiastically fetch things, help to prepare dinner, and assist his parents in doing some work around the house. Finally, the child of seven displays a politeness and consideration toward adults that was seldom observed in the stormy petrel of a year earlier.

Although the seven-year-old relates better to his siblings than he did at age six, his behavior will again depend upon the ages, number, and age separation of his brothers and sisters. As a general rule, the closer siblings are in age, the greater the likelihood of quarreling, arguing, and fighting. In families where the age spread between the siblings is much wider, the children usually get along better with one another. They are in less competition for parental attention and favor. At age seven, the child still has a good time with his friends but may also enjoy solitary activities, such as watching television, reading, and writing. When he is with other children who are active and boisterous, seven seems to be in control of himself. He is less likely to get carried away and to allow things to go too far than he was at age six.

At school, the seven-year-old often shows an increased concern with how the teacher responds to him. This may, in part at least, result from the initiation into evaluation that occurred in first grade. Seven is no longer interested in bringing home his work for parental acclaim and approval. He has lost his confident optimism that he can do everything well. In some ways, the seven-year-old is more demanding of the teacher. He is always asking questions such as, "What do we do now?" or "How do we do this?" He is less sure than he was a year earlier that he knows how to do everything before he is told. Now he begins to have a better understanding of the teacher's role as a guide and model for learning, not simply a stimulus to action or reaction.

The seven-year-old is more careful and persistent in his work habits than he was at age six. He likes to know where things begin and where they end. He wants to know how many paragraphs or pages he has to read, how many problems he has to do in his workbook. Seven's literacy and math skills are improving apace, and he may begin reading a variety of materials including comic books. (Many comic books are relatively innocuous in content, yet they provide a powerful stimulus for reading and enhance reading skills.) In contrast to age six, seven reads fluently and with few hesitations. He maintains his speed by skipping words or by guessing at the ones he doesn't know so that he can maintain a steady pace. The seven-year-old is also concerned about how well he did and wants an immediate postmortem of his academic performance.

The seven-year-old, then, is more serious, less active, less talkative, and less impulsive than he was a year earlier. He is also more sensitive to other people's reactions to him. At home, he is tractable, polite, and eager to take on responsibility. He can also be pensive and complaining. Although he enjoys playing with friends, the seven-year-old can also amuse himself with solitary activities. He knows he is being evaluated by his peers, by his teachers, and by his parents. As a result, he is particularly sensitive about those of his achievements that he believes are under scrutiny.

The Eight-Year-Old

The inward pensiveness of the seven-year-old, as he takes time to consolidate his gains and assimilate his varied experiences, paves the way for a new outwardness at age eight. The eight-year-old begins to seek new experiences, and his mood and style are active and expansive. His moving toward people and toward new experience is, however, more mature than it was in earlier expansive periods, such as age four. His interactions with adults are more productive inasmuch as he is now more attentive and responsive to adult communications than he was at age seven.

A new characteristic of the eight-year-old is his judgmental attitude. Perhaps in response to the open evaluations that are made of him by schoolteachers and parents, he adopts an appraising attitude in defense. Clinicians often describe such behavior as identification with the aggressor. For example, a child who has been bullied by a larger child at school may come home and attempt to intimidate a younger sibling. By taking the role of the aggressor rather than that of the victim, the child is able to cope with the anxiety of being a victim. The child of eight years begins to judge and appraise what happens to him and to be concerned with the "why" of events.

At age eight, there is a noticeable separation between the sexes. Boys are beginning to engage in team sports that exclude girls. In addition, groups of boys may shout at groups of girls and tease them by chasing them on the playground and on the sidewalks around the school. Girls begin to form close friendships, to share secrets, and to "gossip" about other children. The boy-girl separation at age eight is far from complete, but the number of such separations and confrontations is greater than it was at earlier ages. We see in the eight-year-old's attitude toward members of the opposite sex a combination of attraction and hostility, a pattern that will be seen again in early adolescence.

Another characteristic of the eight-year-old is his enormous curiosity. He has discovered how much there is to know about the world and has tasted the pleasure of discovery. He collects any number of different things, as any routine examination of the contents of his pockets and his bureau drawers will readily reveal. Mail-order catalogs are of particular interest because of the variety of items shown in their pages. At age eight, the child wants money to buy things, but he also likes to bargain, barter, and trade with his friends. Children vary in their skill at trading. Some shrewd youngsters may, from clever dealing, amass quite a warehouse of toys and books.

The eight-year-old's curiosity does not end with nature and with artificial things; it extends to people as well. An eight-year-old will show this interest in other people by his attentiveness to adult discussions and his eagerness to observe at adult gatherings, such as parties given by his parents. At this age, children are also interested in children from foreign countries and how they live. It is an age when children can begin to appreciate cultural diversity. It is very important, however, for children to learn about human similarities as well as human differences. When we teach children about other cultures, we also need to emphasize our underlying common humanity.

In addition to his new interest in children from foreign countries, the eight-year-old is also interested in how people lived in earlier times. At this age, children have an avid interest in Cowboys and Indians, Knights of the Round Table, and Pilgrims and explorers. Nonetheless, the eight-year-old's sense of historical time is still qualitative rather than quantitative. That is to say, he must use qualitative cues—such as housing, clothing, and implements—to distinguish between the different historical epochs. It is significant, however, that he has gone beyond the primarily here-and-now orientation of the earlier age periods and now thinks beyond the boundaries of his immediate personal experience of time and space.

There are also noticeable advances in the child's self-concept. At eight, the child has more self-confidence than he did at age six or seven. This may be true because the peer group has now become a significant component of his self-evaluation. He now spends more time with age-mates than with parents. Perhaps this new peer group involvement also accounts for his enhanced curiosity about himself as well as about other people and the natural world. At this age, he tries to learn about himself from others and so is constantly "trying himself out" on his parents and peers. He may imitate a parent or a teacher or may try telling jokes or playing the innocent. From the reactions of parents and peers the child gains new information about himself.

This enhanced awareness of his social self is also evidenced in the eight-year-old's language. He now talks about his "self" and judges and appraises himself as well as others. Parents also recognize and remark on the eight-year-old's increased maturity and more distinctive self. They are likely to make remarks such as, "That's Tommy" or "That's Nancy," in response to the child's way of doing things, verbal expression, or style of dress.

Another way in which the eight-year-old seeks to discover himself is through dramatic play in which he takes the role of characters about whom he has read or whom he has seen or heard. Whereas the six-year-old's imitations are simply miming, the eight year-old's imitations are truly dramatic in that he really tries to play the part—often for comic effect. At the same time that the eight-year-old is attempting to discover himself by playing different roles, he is also becoming increasingly aware of and sensitive to his differences from other children. At about third grade, the eight-year-old begins to incorporate social status, clothing, and physical attractiveness into his evaluations of himself and his peers. The significance of these components for the child's self-evaluation will vary with the circumstances of the child and those of his classmates.

In his social relations, the eight-year-old is usually friendly and cooperative. He is less persistent in his activities at home and is not as helpful around the house as he was at the age of seven. This may reflect the fact that the peer group, rather than the family, is now the sun around which his world increasingly revolves. Accordingly, his helpfulness is now more associated with his momentary mood than with an abiding desire to help. Also, because of his new sense of maturity and selfness, the eight-year-old wants mature jobs around the house, such as fixing things or cooking and baking, which are adultlike activities. When the eight-year-old is asked to do what he regards as "baby jobs," such as picking up things or setting the table, he may grumble because he regards such chores as beneath him.

Because of his new concern with himself, the eight-year-old is particularly concerned with what his mother and father have to say about him. He may often dog their footsteps and hang upon every word and facial expression, avidly seeking clues of their reaction to him. The eight-year-old is also discovering that his parents are not perfect and that they can make mistakes. Sometimes, when this happens, he tends to think that if they don't know one simple thing then they don't know anything. On the other hand, because he knows the simple thing that they do not know, he knows more than they do. This results in a kind of *cognitive conceit*, according to which the child secretly believes he is smarter than adults.

As a result of his need for parent input regarding himself in combination with his cognitive conceit, the child's attitude toward his parents is both complex and ambivalent. It is a combination of love, demandingness, anger, and criticalness. Just as he tries himself out on others as a means of self-discovery, he also tests out his parents to learn more about them. This accounts for what seems to be an endless series of demands upon his parents to "do this" or "make that" and so on.

With regard to nonparental adults, the eight-year-old is often more polite with strangers than he is at home. He has learned the basic social frames of greetings and uses *please* and *thank you* appropriately and without prompting. The quality of his interactions with adults is now more mature, and he talks "with" them rather than "to" them. On the phone, for example, the eight-year-old will take a message and even ask questions if something is not clear. He likes to meet new people and to go to new places, and he looks forward to family vacations away from home.

The eight-year-old's relations with his siblings will once again vary with the number and age separation of the children. If he has an older brother, he is likely to try and tag along with his brother and his friends, but not if the older sibling is a sister. The older brother is likely to complain to his parents that his brother is always "bugging" him. If he is the older sibling, therefore, he is likely to be less paternal in his attitude than he was at age seven. In contrast to this kind of backsliding in his relation to older or younger sibs, the eight-year-old's relationships with his peers really begin to blossom. Seeing and being with friends is now one of his dominant motives for going to school.

Friendships between children at this age tend to be closer and more exacting than heretofore. The basis of the relationship is beginning to shift from engaging in common activities to the personality characteristics of some of the children involved. "Sarah is bossy" or "Harold always wants to fight" reflects the eight-year-old's emergent sensitivity to the personality traits of other children. These traits become progressively more important than shared activities in choosing and keeping friends.

At age eight, children generally enjoy and look forward to school. The reasons for this, as already noted, are as much social as they are academic. The presence of bosom friends makes school attractive to this age group. Their attendance is quite good, and when they are absent, they want to catch up on what happened and to make up what they have missed. Like the six-year-old, the eight-year-old is once again interested in taking things home. School products are another way he can get parents to give him more information about himself. For the same reason, perhaps, he spontaneously tells his parents about what he did in school.

His relationship with his teacher is different from what it was at age seven. He is less concerned with the teacher's approval and acceptance and more concerned with acceptance and approval by his peers. Although he can work independently, he still needs directions read, and reread, to him. The eight-year-old child may begin to gossip and even start sending notes to his friends. Sometimes these social activities get out of hand, and the child has to pay the consequences. A teacher may separate him from his peers and seat him close to the front of the class. In dealing with the eight-year-old's breaking of classroom frame rules, teachers need to appreciate that it derives from his newfound sociability, not from a stubborn perversity. They should not mistake a growth phenomenon for bad motives or poor upbringing.

I noted earlier that the eight-year-old is judgmental, and this attitude extends to his own school work. He is always assessing his academic performance. He knows the exact number of mistakes he made ("I got four wrong") and criticizes everything from his handwriting to his artwork. Drawing provides a particularly pertinent example of this self-critical attitude. Although he may have been an avid artist at the age of six or seven, he is ready to give up drawing by the age of eight. He now appreciates the difference between what he would like to draw and what he can actually achieve on paper. For example, trying to draw a face so that it appears three-dimensional is very frustrating, and some children just give it up and never attempt it again. Perhaps these frustrating experiences in childhood help explain why most adults say that they cannot draw.

The eight-year-old is critical of his abilities in all of the academic domains. He is sensitive about being a slow reader or about being a poor speller or about not doing well in math. Because the child's academic performance is no secret to the other children, it often determines their attitude toward him. A child who is teased about his poor academic achievement may incorporate this negative evaluation into his self-image. It can then serve as a self-fulfilling prophecy. Whenever he fails, it is his "due," and when he succeeds, it is only an "accident." He may acquire what has been called a sense of *learned helplessness*. On the other hand, the child who is successful academically builds this evaluation into his self-image and assumes that success is his due and that any failures are unfortunate accidents. With respect to our self-conceptions, therefore, the old saw holds true: The rich get richer, and the poor get poorer.

This, in brief, is the eight-year-old. He is outgoing, curious, and extremely social. He is judgmental and critical, both of himself and of others, and is demanding of information about himself. He is more mature in his social relations, and he talks with, rather than to, adults. Friends are extremely important at this age and become the prime reason for his interest in school and for his good attendance. He is ambivalent about growing up. On the one hand, he is critical of adults and believes that he is smarter than they are. At the same time, he wants to know more about the adult world and to assume more adult household tasks and responsibilities.

The Nine-Year-Old

There is no sharp separation between the overall characteristics of the eight- and the nine-year-old, but rather an increase in the maturity and refinement of behaviors exhibited earlier. The eight-year-old's judgmental tendencies are carried forward by the nine-year-old, but with greater objectivity and discernment. He can say, "That's not so hot, is it?" of something he has done and not feel anxious or guilty about it. In a like manner, he will appraise parents and other adults calmly and dispassionately. The initial shock of discovering that parents are not perfect is long since past, and the nine-year-old can accept parental mistakes and ignorance as a matter of course.

This does not mean, in any sense, that the nine-year-old is an automaton with no feelings. He still shows the bursts of emotion and impatience characteristic of younger children, but the outbursts are less frequent and are under greater self-control. In addition, whereas the eight-year-old was pushed and pulled by other events, the nine-year-old seems to have found his own inner gyroscope. He now chooses activities that intrigue him and keep him involved for hours at a time. While working on a stamp collection or building a model or playing Nintendo, he forgets time and meals. If he is forced to interrupt an activity, he is impatient to return to it.

Perhaps because of this inner-directed quality of his behavior, the nine-year-old appears to be a more "solid citizen" than he was at eight. He gives the impression of calm steadfastness and responsibility that will be the benchmark of his later maturity. We can also observe this new maturity in his dealings with nonparental adults and peers. He now demonstrates a depth of consideration and a sense of fairness beyond what he was capable of just a year earlier. In addition, he is also able to accept blame and take responsibility for his actions. He is at the point where he can distinguish clearly between the act and the intentions that led to it. In making moral judgments, he now weighs intentions more heavily than the amount of damage done.

At age nine, the child also gives evidence of stereo-typical sex-appropriate behaviors. For example, boys are often disdainful of their clothes and of cleanliness. They some-times behave as if a particular shirt or cap is part of their body and are reluctant to remove it at any time. Parents may have to badger them to wash and to change underwear and socks. Girls at this age, in contrast, may become upset and angry about their clothing and appearance. Some girls may even throw tantrums and say, "I hate the way I look" or "I hate this dress." Nine-year-old girls may begin to give their parents a hard time about clothes if they believe that what parents want or can afford to have them wear is not fash-ionable. Although these sex-stereotyped behaviors are, in part at least, learned, they soon become ingrained and habitual.

If we look now at the nine-year-olds self-concept, we see a new self-confidence that derives from his having himself under better control and from his being less perturbed by momentary setbacks. Perhaps this enhanced self-confidence is also rooted in his new tendency to organize and budget his time (often with the help of external memory aids, such as lists and schedules) that give him a new sense of self-importance. Nine-year-olds do have to budget their time. Middle-class children are now taking music and other les-sons, are participating in individual and team sports, and are members of boys' or girls' scouting programs. Parents of nine-year-olds often feel more like chauffeurs than parents.

The increased self-confidence of nine-year-olds makes their self-derogatory remarks less ominous. In a psychologically sound individual, a certain amount of self-derogation is a sign of emotional security and self-assurance. It takes a certain robustness of self-concept to say, "I was wrong," or to poke fun at oneself. Most nine-year-olds have this solidity of self. They can admit their own negative traits and express the wish that they were different without feeling anxious or depressed at these admissions.

The child's new maturity and self-confidence are easily observed in his interactions with his parents. He is less quarrelsome and less demanding than he was a year ear-lier when self-definition was an issue. The intense period of testing out adult reactions is over and gives way to self-directed absorption in a variety of activities. We can ob-serve nine's new maturity in still another way. He does not need to be bribed or bargained with to do simple chores.

Rather, he will accept them as his responsibility and his contribution to the family. He may, however, have to be reminded to do his chores. When it comes to chores, the nine-year-old frequently "forgets" to use his newly acquired strategies for remembering!

In general, the nine-year-old's relations with his mother and father are friendly and accommodating. Although he still enjoys outings and family activities, his own friends absorb much of his social energy. As a consequence, he no longer makes demands upon his parents, as he once did, to alleviate his boredom. In the same way, the nine-year-old gets along well with his younger siblings but may still be a tagalong nuisance to older brothers and sisters.

The close friendships with peers that emerged at age eight are continued and strengthened at age nine. These friendships are almost exclusively between youngsters of the same sex, and there is even overt hostility between boys and girls. Girls say that boys are "always fighting and yelling." In their turn, boys complain that girls are always "talking, laughing, and giggling." At this age, organized games with rules—such as soccer, baseball, football, basketball, and hockey—are becoming widespread among boys. Many boys may begin engaging in these sports at the age of six or seven, however. Girls are also beginning to participate more in team sports and to compete intramurally. Many young people also compete in individual sports, such as swimming, tennis, ice skating, and gymnastics.

School in general is easier for the nine-year-old than it was a year ago. He no longer has trouble getting started in the morning. He may still forget to take his books or neglect to do his homework, however. In some respects, the nine-year-old is hard on teachers. He knows what he wants to do and what he does not want to do, and he shows no hesitation in saying so. He is less emotionally dependent upon the teacher than he was a year earlier because of his new attachment to peers. Now when he dislikes a subject, the dislike may generalize the teacher. In addition, his new sense of independence and his desire to pursue a subject on his own may lead him to resist asking for help when he really needs it.

Academic achievement is important to the nine-year-old. The importance he now attaches to grades probably arises because grades are now the measure he and his peers use in ranking one another. The new importance attached to academic achievement is often hardest on those children who are at the extremes. In large classes, teachers are often forced to engage in "ability grouping" to make instruction manageable. Unfortunately, children in the low group tend to be looked down upon. At the other extreme, gifted children may sometimes be taken out of class to be given special "enrichment." Such pull-out programs highlight that these children are different and may make them the targets of ridicule. With smaller classes, teachers could individualize and not have to employ ability grouping. To avoid such problems, many schools now have teachers for children with special needs, or those who are gifted, come in and work with the whole class so that all of the children benefit from this enriched instruction.

Nine-year-olds have generally mastered the mechanics of reading and arithmetic. Now these skills can be used for gaining information, for solving problems, and for playing board and computer games. Nine-year-olds may still be pretty sloppy writers, and they may complain about having a poor memory, despite their gains in memory strategies. At this age, children increasingly use their tool skills outside of the school setting. They may read books for fun or information and use their math skills in planning a budget or figuring out how to buy a desired item. Many children are also becoming adept at the computer and use it not only to play games but for a variety of school and nonschool writing activities.

The nine-year-old, then, shows a new maturity, self-confidence, and independence from adults. He is inner-directed and self-motivated. His friendships are more solid, but his emotional distance from the opposite sex is greater than it was at age eight. Now the nine-year-old is putting to use his academic skills in his everyday life. For the first time, he begins to appreciate the practical values of schooling. In many ways, the nine-year-old's independence, while trying, is easier on adults than the eight-year-old's demandingness.

The Ten-Year-Old

At the end of his first decade of life, the young person reaches a high point of balance and adaptation to his world that he may not achieve again until age sixteen. By the age of ten, he has crossed and recrossed the stormy social seas of home, school, and immediate community. He is now a seasoned social traveler and takes pleasure in his ability to fit in and to speak the language of parents, peers, and teachers. Because he now copes easily with the trials and tribulations of social travel, he is at peace with himself and with his world. It is, relatively speaking, a halcyon period in human development.

To be sure, there are some exceptions to the general picture of solid adaptation presented by the ten-year-old. He does, on occasion, get extremely angry, depressed, or sad. Such moments are, however, usually short-lived and quickly forgotten. Other negative aspects of "ten-year-oldness" are equally minor in nature. The ten-year-old boy still cares very little about his clothes and usually is hard on them and leaves them scattered about. Ten-year-old girls may be a bit more circumspect in this regard. At the same time, the ten-year-old is pretty good about not losing his belongings.

At ten, girls are slightly more advanced physically than boys and already give hints of the rapid growth sprint that will soon make them taller and heavier than boys of the same age. Ten-year-old girls are already giving evidence of the rounding and softening of body contours that will continue into adolescence. Some ten-year-old girls may even experience an enlargement in the breast area together with a tightening and protrusion of the nipples. Girls of this age are beginning to be concerned about their figures, about menstruation, and about sexual activity. Ten-year-old boys, whose bodies show fewer signs of approaching puberty, are much less concerned about their approaching physical maturity than are ten-year-old girls.

Aside from this sex difference in concern over physical maturation, both ten-year-old boys and girls are remarkably stable youngsters. Fears and anxieties are at an all-time low, and relations with parents, teachers, peers, and siblings are at an all-time high. The exception is with siblings who are between the ages of six and nine. Perhaps because younger children remind them of their own earlier immaturities, ten-year-olds do not treat six- to nine-year-olds very well at all.

If we look more closely at the self-concept of ten, the changes from age nine are worthy of note. At nine, the child was self-conscious and somewhat self-critical and accepting of criticism from others. By ten, however, the young person shows much less interest in evaluating himself and seems to accept himself as he is without worrying too much about his strengths and his weaknesses. He experiences a general feeling of well-being—a feeling that ten is just the right age, not too little and not too big. He has enough, but not too much, responsibility and freedom. To be sure, he is beginning to think about growing up, marrying, and having a career. His ideals are either those of his parents or celebrities, such as motion picture stars or popular athletes. Growing up is a romantic idea, and ten years old is a romantic age.

The ten-year-old likes his family and thinks that it is the greatest. He enjoys going to restaurants and on trips with his family. He does not resent taking time from being with his friends to do things with the family. He develops a new liking and respect for his parents. He now appreciates that their concern about his eating patterns and his dress are genuine expressions of their concern for him. At the same time, he may still ignore their admonitions about eating fruits and vegetables or about wearing warmer clothing. Both ten-year-old boys and ten-year-old girls are spontaneous in their show of affection and concern for both their mother and their father. Children also discover new qualities to value in their parents. This is particularly true with respect to their parents' skills in sports and games. The ten-year-old is, to a much greater extent than at any earlier age, a family person.

Outside the home, ten's interpersonal relations are equally commendable. Ten likes and enjoys his friends. More marked than at earlier ages are sex differences in friendship patterns. Boys are starting to move in loosely organized groups and may play board games, ball games, or computer games together. Within the group, boys may have particular friends, but there is a lot of switching around. Girls usually move in smaller groups and are likely to form more intense attachments. As a result, they also have more serious fallings-out. Falling out may take the form of being "mad" or "not playing" or "not speaking" to one another. This sex difference reflects the fact that, at age ten, girls place more emphasis on relationships, whereas boys place more emphasis on activities.

The solid adaptation of the ten-year-old can also be seen in his school behavior. By and large, he likes school and is a responsible student. He accepts his assignments and gets them done without getting sidetracked and without having to rush to get them done in time. The ten-year-old likes his

teacher and accepts the teacher's authority and knowledge.
He may even describe his teacher's physical appearance and
quote his or her remarks to his parents. The ten-year-old likes
his teacher if he or she is fair and not partial to particular
students. He also appreciates authoritative teachers who are
firm but show warmth. At this age, the young person likes
the teacher to schedule activities and to keep to the schedule.

Ten-year-olds still enjoy being read to by their teachers
and can become intrigued by classics, such as *Robinson Crusoe*
and *Treasure Island*. Both boys and girls of this age are attracted to stories of adventure and mystery. Not surprisingly,
girls prefer heroines and are likely to read books such as
the Nancy Drew mysteries. At this age, girls are also beginning to show an interest in stories about animals, particularly horses. This interest in horses is very common among
girls, and it is an interest that often continues into maturity.
Boys, on the other hand, do not as yet show the interest in
automobiles that will be their guiding concern as they move
into adolescence. TV watching and video games are still an
important pastime, but ten-year-olds are more selective than
they were at earlier ages.

In his studying and other academic pursuits, the ten-
year-old lacks some of the stick-to-itiveness of the nine-
year-old. Prolonged periods of activity have to be interrupted
by getting up and moving about. At ten, the young person is also somewhat more superficial and is more interested in learning facts and memorizing names than he is
in finding causes and explanations. Even his interest in
mystery and adventure is more closely tied to the excitement—the what-comes-next aspect—than to the fun of
unraveling the crime or the mystery. Within the school setting,
then, the ten-year-old prefers to soak up information rather
than to integrate or to digest it. Perhaps this is a necessary preparation for the attempts at knowledge integration
that will come later.

In summary, the ten-year-old is at the high point of
childhood. He is well adapted to his body, to his family,
to his friends, and to his teachers. These relationships and
interactions no longer hold any mystery or fears for him.
He likes other people, and he likes himself. Although there
are occasional emotional outbursts and continued rough
treatment of clothes and occasionally younger siblings, the
ten-year-old is generally a joy to have around the house and

the classroom. He is cooperative, considerate, and responsible to authority. Looking ahead, we know that the halcyon days of the ten-year-old are the calm before the storm. Nature, perhaps in her wisdom or perhaps in her perversity, lulls us into the comforting belief that the ten-year-old is a portent of the young person to be. Unfortunately, we will soon be disillusioned.

The Eleven-Year-Old

In some respects, the age of ten is a kind of platform between the steps toward middle childhood and those that will take the young person toward adulthood. At age ten, the child can look back at where he has been without regressing and can look ahead to where he is going without yet beginning the climb. As he moves toward the age of eleven, however, the growth pressures reassert themselves, and the accelerated pace of growth that marks early adolescence can be seen and felt. The halcyon period is over for parents and siblings as it is for teachers and other adults who have to deal with preadolescents. There is no growth without conflict, and the eleven-year-old is entering a new phase of growth and hence of renewed conflict.

The new growth thrust of the eleven-year-old is evidenced in many different ways. For one thing, his activity levels show a marked increase, and he has trouble keeping still. In this regard, he is reminiscent of the six-year-old. His appetite, too, seems to have increased severalfold, and his stomach, to parents at least, seems like a human black hole. It is not only his appetite for food that is voracious. He also devours new experiences, knowledge about the world, and insights about human psychology.

Perhaps because of his tremendous energy and activity, he often forgets his manners and is loud, boorish, and rude. In stores or on the bus, the eleven-year-old will shout out loudly at his friends and push toward them without sufficient consideration for people in his way. On his bike or skateboard or roller blades, he may take chances that will cause drivers to slam on their brakes and shake their heads. Perhaps the eleven-year-old senses that he is closer to adulthood than childhood and wants to defy the adult world one last time under the aegis of childhood.

His defiance of adult authority comes out in other ways as well. Quarreling is a common feature of eleven-year-old behavior. It is the young person, however, who likes to do the arguing, and doesn't like it when others argue with him. Not only is he argumentative, he is also rather emotional and subject to outbursts of rage, peevishness, and moodiness. The emotional control of the ten-year-old seems to have vanished by age eleven. At this age, he is often touchy and unpredictable. In part, this new emotionality is due to the increased pace of growth and to hormonal changes. It is also due to the concomitant recognition that he is growing up. This awareness of impending change in status brings both hope and new anxieties and fears, all of which contribute to the eleven-year-old's heightened sensitivity.

The young person may demonstrate his sensitivity, emotionality, and argumentativeness more at home than outside it. Particularly with strangers, the eleven-year-old can be cooperative, friendly, lively, and pleasant. On a short-term basis, he can be quite easy to take. It is only under prolonged interactions, at home and at school, that his negative features begin to surface. The eleven-year-old needs to be handled with understanding but with firmness. Although he should not be allowed to run roughshod over people, he should also not be put down too harshly.

When we look at the eleven-year-old's self-concept and at how he is viewed by others, he hardly seems to be the same person he was a year earlier. Because of his new press toward activity and his consequent carelessness, he is often yelled at and disciplined. This, in turn, results in a belligerent attitude: "Everything I do is wrong" and "You are always picking on me." The calm self-confidence of the ten-year-old has given way to renewed self-doubt and sensitivity about himself. This turnabout demonstrates how much the young person's self-confidence is like a social barometer, dependent upon the reactions of other people to him.

As he feels himself moving toward a new level of maturity, the eleven-year-old undertakes new efforts at self-definition. As at age six, he attempts to define himself by open challenges to those in authority. He now confronts his parents with criticisms and accusations as if to get a response—

any kind of response. Eleven needs to be noticed, and he cannot tolerate indifference. Even negative reactions from his parents are better than nothing. Often he lashes out without fully appreciating why he is attacking nor the hurt he may be inflicting. Coupled with this new aggressivity and desire to be noticed is a new defensiveness. Although he will sometimes admit faults, eleven will do so only in a general way, and he will not be pinned down to specifics.

In the eleven-year-old, we see the first signs of independence from parental influence that will become increasingly prominent over the next few years. Both preadolescent boys and preadolescent girls are beginning to differ with their parents as to what profession or career to pursue, and they are beginning to make their own choices. Perhaps because of the new attacks upon their self-confidence, many eleven-year-olds compensate with fantasy. Visions of being a famous singer, actor, athlete, or author and bowing before an admiring audience are common at this age.

Both boys and girls engage in fantasies about the future. In part, this reflects the emergence of new mental abilities that allow them a better sense of time than was true at an earlier age. They often think about their careers and may be quite specific about the particular career path they want to follow. Eleven-year-olds may also think about marriage and some of the qualities they would like to have in their future mates. They say—although their actual behavior often belies this—that they are more interested in personality characteristics, such as kindness, understanding, and honesty, than they are in good looks. They want their prospective partner to be a reasonably intelligent, nice looking person with whom they can communicate.

The changed self-concept of the eleven-year-old parallels a radical change in the quality of his interpersonal interactions. Whereas at age ten, the young person accepted parental authority, he now challenges it. He is critical of his mother's judgment and of his father's temper. Eleven also challenges his parents' child-rearing practices and often accuses them of playing favorites and of being "unfair." In his view, his siblings always get treated better than he does. Although there may be periods of respite when the eleven-year-old will get along with his parents, it is hard to predict when the next negative mood will strike.

Friendships with peers, fortunately, do not suffer the same revolution that we can witness in the eleven-year-old's interactions with his parents. Eleven-year-olds now choose friends on the basis of mutuality of interest and temperament, rather than on the basis of proximity and common activity. At this age, boys usually have one or more best friends and a group of other friends with whom he plays on a more or less regular basis. Girls, in contrast, tend to be part of a small group, all of whom are good friends and among whom pairing is less frequent.

The interactions between boys and girls also change at this age level. Both boys and girls will admit that they are interested in the opposite sex or will acknowledge that they soon will be. Eleven-year-old girls are generally more interested in and more vocal about their interest in boys than the reverse. At this age, girls often spend a lot of time talking about boys and describe them to one another in vigorous detail. Sometimes these descriptions are quietly positive, but sometimes they are laughingly negative.

Boys at this age often show their interest in girls by joking, teasing, or most often by showing off in front of them. Doing handstands, riding a bike no-handed, and skateboarding over curbs are some of the exploits boys engage in to capture a girl's attention. Girls, in turn, enjoy this behavior because they recognize it as an expression of positive interest and a primitive masculine effort to gain attention and to be admired.

The changes that mark age eleven are also obvious in the school setting. Although many eleven-year-old youngsters continue to like school, many others find that school has now become a problem for them—and, it must be added, they are often a problem for the school. The eleven-year-old's high energy level and criticalness make it difficult for him to sit still and to finish his work at a single sitting and without disturbing others. He enjoys school mainly because it is where his friends are. At this age, he would prefer to spend most of his time playing or gossiping with his friends rather than in doing school work.

Eleven-year-olds do not dislike school. They are, however, quite specific in what they do and do not want to learn. Perhaps because of their abundant energy and restlessness, eleven-year-olds like material they can learn quickly and use competitively. At this age, young people delight in exhibiting their skill in rote learning, and it is an age where spelling bees and poem recitals are common. Eleven-year-olds don't want to get involved with more complex subjects such as history and science, however. It is not that eleven-year-olds have lost their intellectual curiosity, but only that they are pulled in so many directions they cannot concentrate a lot of energy toward school work. Schooling is often fatiguing for eleven-year-olds who are exhausting so much energy elsewhere.

In the eleven-year-old, therefore, we begin to see the changes that will become the norm in subsequent years. The pace of growth is beginning to accelerate, and there is an increase in energy and activity level. Self-doubts and insecurity are once again present. This new insecurity is evidenced by the eleven-year-old's reluctance to admit his weaknesses. Interactions with parents and siblings are once again conflictual. The eleven-year-old finds much to criticize in his parents. He complains that he is unduly put upon and flagrantly discriminated against. Only his interactions with his peers remain unruffled. He demonstrates a new dislike for school and many school subjects. He is more interested in rote memorization than in material that requires reasoning and problem solving. School is but one of many activities and interests that absorb the eleven-year-old's energy.

In closing this chapter on the unique characteristics of each age level, it is perhaps well to reemphasize that these are normative descriptions that will fit all children of these ages to some extent but no particular child in every regard. What these profiles do reveal are the patterns of inwardness and outwardness, of integration and disintegration, of self-confidence and self-doubt, and of conformity and rebellion that are missed when we describe development across larger time periods, such as childhood. When we look at childhood, as the unit of growth, the path seems uniformly upward. However, when we look at growth on a yearly basis, we see that the child's progress is anything but uniform. It is helpful to know that even within childhood, one can find periods of calm and periods of storm and rebellion.

III

The Adolescent

9

Personal and
Social Development

Early to middle adolescence, roughly the years from twelve to sixteen, is a dynamic period of rapid growth that propels the child toward adulthood. It is the period during which the young person comes close to her adult stature and appearance. By the time the adolescent is sixteen, she has also reached sexual maturity, in the physical sense, and is capable of procreation. During the years from twelve to sixteen, the adolescent also acquires formal, or abstract, powers of thought. She is now able to reflect upon her own and other people's thinking, to entertain ideals and possibilities, to operate with many different dimensions at the same time, to understand the historical past, and to plan realistically for her future.

These changes, and many others that occur during this phase of adolescence, do not transform the young person into an entirely different individual. The social leader of the elementary school often becomes the social leader of the junior high, or middle, school. The athletic child is likely to make the soccer, baseball, or football team at junior high and high school. Likewise, the scholarly child often maintains her pattern of high academic achievement as she progresses through the grades. Marked changes in personality can and do occur, but continuity, rather than discontinuity, is the general rule of development.

The continuity between childhood and adolescence is evidenced in other areas of growth as well. Many of the interpersonal problems and issues that the child confronts in becoming a social being are reencountered by the adolescent, albeit in a somewhat different form. The parent-child contracts take on a very different quality in adolescence when, say, late hours, use of the family car, and sexual activity are at issue. In the same way, friendships with peers have to be reestablished, but now on a different basis than that upon which they were founded in childhood.

Early to middle adolescence, then, is a time of rapid transformation but also a period of continuity. The processes of growth we observed in the year-by-year development of children continues into adolescence. The ebb and flow of progress toward maturity and regression toward childhood is equally evident in the adolescent years. Without discounting the very real metamorphosis that adolescence brings about, we should not overlook the powerful continuities between childhood and this new growth period.

Facets of Growth and Development

Physical growth from birth to adolescence, although continuous, frequently changes its pace. You will recall that growth during the first year of life is very rapid and that the infant gains about 8 inches of height and triples her weight within the first year. The rate of growth then gradually slows until adolescence, when there is again a sudden spurt of growth in height and weight. On the average, the greatest increase in standing height for girls occurs at around the age of eleven, with an average increase of about 2.5 inches. For boys, the period of most rapid growth usually occurs during the thirteenth year, when boys may gain as much as 4 to 6 inches in height. Weight, on the other hand, tends to increase rather regularly across adolescence, although in mid-adolescence it frequently drops for girls. Because of the different timing of their growth spurts, there is a period, the twelfth and thirteenth years of life, when the average girl is likely to be taller and heavier than the average boy.

As dramatic as the abrupt increase in height is the adolescent's attainment of puberty, or sexual maturity. A number of physical changes, the *secondary sex characteristics*, signal the coming of menstruation, the true mark of sexual maturity for girls. Breast development begins, on the average, at about 10.7 years with the appearance of breast buds. In most girls, pubic hair shows its initial growth, sparse and slightly pigmented, at about the age of eleven. Between the ages of twelve and thirteen, underarm hair becomes noticeable. During this same time period, breast enlargement continues, and the areola and papilla now project beyond the breast. By age fifteen, the average girl's breasts are mature, and pubic hair is of adult color and density but may not cover as much area as it will later.

Embedded in these changes is the appearance of *menarche,* or the first menstruation. Although the age range over which menarche can occur for girls is as much as ten years, more than 75 percent of young women have their first menstrual period between the ages of twelve and fourteen. The fact that a girl begins to menstruate does not necessarily mean that she is fertile and can conceive a child. Fertility depends upon a number of different factors; ovulation is a necessary but not a sufficient condition. The menarche is a very special event for a young girl and brings both fear and anxiety (about the pain and possible embarrassing accidents) and joy and exultation (about having attained the adult estate).

It is much more difficult to determine the exact date of puberty in males because there is no single, dramatic event, such as menarche, to herald its appearance. At about the age of eleven most boys evidence a growth in the size of the testes and scrotum. By age twelve, most boys show some lightly pigmented pubic hair. On the average, most boys have their first spontaneous ejaculation (usually in the form of a wet dream) at about the age of thirteen. At fourteen, most young men have some underarm and facial hair, and their voices have deepened. By fifteen, the penis, testes, and pubic hair are fully developed. As with girls, there are wide individual differences among boys in the ages at which these sexual characteristics appear. Some boys may show some evidence of sexual maturity at age ten, while others may show few secondary sex characteristics until age sixteen.

Studies suggest that in many developed countries, the age of menarche for girls has decreased substantially during the last hundred years—a phenomenon that has been called the *secular trend.* In contrast to the age of thirteen, the average age of menarche for girls in America today, the usual age for menstruation was seventeen a hundred years ago. Improvements in nutrition, health practices, and medical care are probably the main reasons for the secular trend. In underdeveloped countries, the age of puberty may still be much higher than it is in the developed countries. The most recent data on physical growth suggest that American adolescents are no longer attaining menarche at an earlier age than previous generations. Apparently, we have reached our biological limits in this regard.

The changes that occur in the adolescent's facial bones and features are an often overlooked facet of physical development. Yet, because these changes determine the young person's appearance, they have important consequences for her self-concept. In general, the adolescent's bones, including the facial bones, increase in density, hardness, and size during development. This process can sometimes lead to radical changes in facial configuration from childhood to adolescence. During the years when the young person is attaining puberty, her nose and mouth widen, the nose becomes longer and more prominent, and the jaw juts out further. Generally, the top part of the face grows more rapidly than the lower part, and the chin is the last feature to attain its adult size. This may come as some consolation to fourteen-year-olds whose faces seem a little nose-heavy because the lower part of the face has not yet caught up with the growth of the nose and forehead.

Adolescence is marked by other physical changes as well. Body hair darkens and lengthens for both boys and girls. Shaving now becomes a necessary part of grooming for both young men and young women. In addition, certain types of sweat glands, inoperative in childhood, begin to secrete a fatty substance. This gives rise to body odor. The activation of sweat glands necessitates still other additions to the young person's grooming routine. Adolescents also experience marked improvements in their physical capacities. A teenager's strength and endurance increase in combination with sexual development. These changes result, in part, from increases in the size and capacity of the young person's respiratory system. The teenager's ability to eat what seems like impossible amounts of food is witness to her new powers of digestion.

Because the physical changes associated with puberty are so revolutionary, adolescents who attain puberty either earlier or later than their peers are likely to stand out. The effects of maturing earlier or later than average have received a lot of scientific attention. In general, it appears that early maturation is more advantageous for boys than it is for girls, whereas late maturation is more advantageous for girls than it is for boys.

Early maturing boys are likely to be taller and stronger than their peers, and this offers obvious advantages. Late maturing boys, however, are less fortunate. In one study, late maturing boys were rated as lower in physical attractiveness, masculinity, and grooming than their earlier maturing peers. Their peers also rated them as "talkative," "bossy," and "looking for attention." Perhaps because both parents and teachers have lower expectations for late maturing boys, many of these young people have lower academic aspirations than do their earlier maturing peers. In part, at least, these lower aspirations may reflect the lower expectations that both teachers and parents have for late maturing boys.

Late maturation is less of a handicap for girls. They have time to assimilate changes in their bodies and do not have to cope with amorous advances from boys. They also miss the awkward period of being taller and heavier than boys of the same age. Early maturing girls, in contrast, do experience difficulties. They may be less prepared, either by parents or by the school, for the changes they are experiencing. Early maturing girls also tend to have a poorer body image, perhaps because they are experiencing hair growth and body odor before their peers. Because they are often treated as older than they really are, they are more likely than late maturers to engage in "adult" behaviors, such as smoking and drinking. Early maturing girls are also likely to become sexually active at an earlier age than is true for later maturers. As in the case of late maturing boys, social expectations, rather than maturity per se, lead early maturing girls to engage in psychologically risky behaviors. Early or late maturation can therefore present very real problems of adaptation for some young people.

Adolescent Sexuality: Girls

The advent of puberty brings about new feelings, new interests, new attitudes, and many new problems for adolescents. These problems, however, are somewhat different for young men than they are for young women. Although boy-girl differences are present from the start of life, it is only at adolescence that sexual status takes precedence over age status. A child is generally a child first, and a boy or a girl second. In adolescence, however, the young person is a male or female first and an adolescent second. Put differently, although it is reasonable to talk about children without making major distinctions between the sexes, this is not the case when it comes to adolescents.

The physiological maturity of girls, clearly evidenced by the menarche, is not associated with any immediate increase in sexual desire. In general, the girl's sexual desire is much more general and much less focused than is the boy's. She is not as easily aroused as the boy, and she is aroused by different sorts of stimuli. This may be heavily culturally conditioned, however, and there is mounting evidence that as female sexual desire is more liberated and accepted, young women may be stimulated by the same types of stimuli as males. Nonetheless, it is still generally true that girls tend to be "romantic," whereas boys tend to be "erotic."

If we look at the evolution of boy-girl mating interactions, we can see definite patterns. Girls' interest in boys is generally earlier than boys' interest in girls. Girls' "boy consciousness" often initially takes the form of wanting to be noticed and admired by a particular boy. Young women also engage in focused and animated discussions about boys. As in other domains, however, girls show wide individual differences with regard to their interest in boys and in dating. Some girls begin going out with boys at the age of twelve or thirteen, whereas others may wait until they are in high school before they begin to date.

In addition to producing new emotional experiences, interests, and attitudes, sexual maturity can also bring new problems for young women. Girls who suddenly "fill out" must learn to deal with the attention that is now paid to them by boys and by men. They must learn to cope with the whistles and the head-to-toe appraisals they receive as they walk down the street. In addition, they must learn to interact with boys on intimate terms. Whereas girls find kissing and petting pleasurable and do not necessarily feel pressure to go further, this is not true for boys. For them, climactic release is the only reason for the foreplay. When the girl halts his advances, the aroused boy may feel frustrated and angry. The girl, on the other hand, may not understand why the sweet boy she was so tenderly stroking became such a panting, aggressive monster. Learning about one another's emotional and sexual frames is an important task for adolescent boys and girls.

Some of these sexual differences have probably been exaggerated by sex role stereotyping. Less than a half century ago, women were not supposed to enjoy sex but merely put up with it. Little was known about the human sexual response. The work of William H. Masters and Vera E. Johnson, however, has helped us to better understand the differences in the male and the female sexual response. The woman reaches orgasm more slowly than the man, she experiences it as more of a total bodily experience, and her reaction subsides more slowly. Women are more capable of having multiple orgasms than are men. In summary, therefore, women have the capacity to enjoy sexual activity to the same or to a greater extent than is true for men.

As she adjusts to her life as a sexual being, the young woman must also incorporate this experience into her sense of gender identity. Lawrence Kohlberg has suggested that this sense of gender identity goes through a three-phase process of development. First, the child acquires a sense of *basic gender identity* that involves recognition, often verbal, that she is a girl. Next there is a stage of *gender stability,* during which the girl comes to appreciate that she will grow up to be a woman. Finally, there is a stage of *gender constancy,* during which the young person recognizes that gender remains the same despite dress, hairstyle, occupation, and so on. It is a more biological conception of gender.

Other writers, starting from an information-processing approach, suggest that gender identity is a sort of *schema,* or general concept of gender. Once a girl knows that she is a girl, this concept serves to organize her experience in a particular way in keeping with this general orientation. Such schemas tell the child what information to look for in the environment and how to interpret it. Girls, for example, remember "feminine" toys and objects better than they remember "masculine" toys and objects. The opposite is true for boys.

Adolescent Sexuality: Boys

The advent of puberty brings new experiences, attitudes, and problems for boys as well as for girls. Boys find that they are interested in looking at girls, particularly those whom they consider attractive. They experience spontaneous erections and fear that this will be noticed when they go to the black-

board or get on the bus. Most boys engage in solitary masturbation from the age of twelve or thirteen. (Girls also
masturbate, but they start at a later age and do so less frequently than boys.) In the locker rooms and playgrounds there
is a lot of overt joking and denial of this activity, perhaps
because boys are somewhat guilty about masturbation and
half believe the horror stories regarding its consequences.

Boys' interest in girls becomes most evident when
they get to be twelve or thirteen. This interest in girls takes
on a different coloration than does the comparable interest of girls in boys. Girls are seen, talked about, and fan-
tasized about largely as objects of sexual activity, rather than
as persons or as future mates. Studies suggest that boys (and
men) judge women first upon their attractiveness and only
secondarily on personality. For girls and for women, just the
reverse holds true. This may be another sex role stereotype
that is less true today than it was in the past.

The pattern of attaining gender identity for boys parallels that for girls but may be more confining. That is to say,
girls are given more leeway in dress and activities than are boys.
Girls can be tomboys, play baseball and football, wear their
boyfriends' shirts or sweaters, and not be thought of as outland-
ish. At the same time, however, boys who play with dolls or
who play "girl" games such as jump rope or hopscotch would
be immediately subject to ridicule by their peers. And it would
be outrageous for a boy to wear his girlfriend's sweater or shirt.
It is socially acceptable for girls to be a little masculine, but
it is not socially acceptable for boys to be a little feminine.

The Second Sexual Revolution

A major event that has affected adolescent sexuality is the
second sexual revolution, which occurred in the 1960s. The
first sexual revolution took place in the last century, when
young adults began to choose their own mates, rather than
have their marriages prearranged by others for economic,
social, or community reasons. The second sexual revolution made premarital sex a socially acceptable activity for
women as well as for men. Up until the 1950s, even engaged couples often did not have sexual relations until after they were married. After the 1960s, premarital sex became
the norm for both men and women.

Adolescents follow the lead set by adults. When adults did not have premarital sex, neither did adolescents. Now that premarital sex has become socially acceptable for adults, adolescents see it as acceptable for them as well. This is particularly true today when parents who were themselves sexually active before marriage can hardly tell their adolescents, "Do as I say, not as I do!" The statistics on sexual activity are a good index of this changed pattern. In the 1960s, some 10 percent of adolescent girls were sexually active, and the number for boys was 25 percent. Today, close to 50 percent of adolescents are sexually active by age fifteen, and close to 90 percent are no longer virgins by the time they leave the teen years.

As the age for the loss of virginity has lowered, the age for marriage has gone up. Whereas in the fifties and sixties young women married on the average at age twenty and young men at age twenty-two, the figures are quite different today. In the nineties, the average age of marriage for young women is about twenty-five years, and the average age for men is about twenty-seven years. As a consequence, most of the sexual activity engaged in by adolescents is not with their prospective marriage partners, inasmuch as marriage is far in the future. Although young people who engage in sexual activity may be in "love," they do not necessarily look at their partners from the perspective of marriage. Put differently, sexual activity is now separate from commitment to a long-term relationship.

These new patterns of sexual interaction have, among other things, broken down a number of sexual stereotypes. For example, when college students who have been going together break up, it is usually the male who is the most distressed. In many cases, it is the young woman who initiates the breakup. Indeed, at the college level, young women seem to be more pragmatic than young men and may consider the young man's prospects as well as his physical attractiveness. Young men, in contrast, may be more romantic and less practical in their choices. The old adage, noted earlier, that girls are romantic and boys are erotic may still hold true in the early and middle adolescent years, but it may well be modified in young adulthood when boys become romantic and girls become pragmatic!

Despite their earlier, uncommitted sexual activity, young people are generally not promiscuous, and most practice *serial monogamy*; that is, they have a series of monogamous relationships. Unfortunately, this responsible pattern of relationships is not accompanied by an equally responsible use of contraceptives. Less than half of sexually active teenagers use contraceptives and then only irregularly. As a result, there has been an epidemic of venereal disease among adolescents. Although AIDs is not yet a serious menace for sexually active youth, it could well be in the future.

In addition, teenage pregnancies, though not more numerous than they were in earlier generations, are likely to come at an earlier age, and the mother is less likely to be married. It is the number of *unmarried* teenage mothers that increased significantly since the second sexual revolution. Currently, about 1 million adolescents get pregnant each year, and the majority are out-of-wedlock pregnancies. It is estimated that 25 percent of fourteen-year-old females in the United States today, regardless of race or ethnic group, will be pregnant at least once before they leave the teen years.

It is generally conceded that the sex-education programs in the schools have not been successful either in preventing early sexual activity or in getting young people to use contraceptives. Sex education is important, but it is simply not enough. People know the dangers of smoking, and yet they still smoke. Teenagers know the dangers involved in unprotected sexual activity, yet they still engage in it. The issue is not one of knowledge and information, but rather one of risk taking. We need to address the adolescent's readiness to take risks, not her knowledge about the facts of reproduction and sexually transmitted diseases. One way to address this risk taking is to have young people who have gotten pregnant or infected talk about their experience with their peers. This helps young people to appreciate that they are not invulnerable.

Before ending this section, it is necessary to say something about a sexual orientation that causes some adolescents a great deal of difficulty. Homosexuality has been present throughout history and is known in all societies. Facts such as these suggest that, in part at least, homosexuality is a genetically linked normal variation of the human sexual drive. Indeed, homosexuality is no longer regarded by the helping professions as a sexual perversion. Nonetheless, there is still considerable public aversion to gay people. Adolescents, perhaps because of their own insecure sexuality, are often very hostile to their gay or lesbian peers. As a consequence, gay young people, particularly young men, may find it very difficult to make and keep friends, and they may feel socially ostracized and stigmatized. This may explain why male homosexual adolescents make up a disproportionate share of adolescent suicides.

For both young men and young women, the second sexual revolution has permanently changed sexual stereotypes and patterns of sexual and social interactions.

Psychological Development

From the psychological point of view, the major task of adolescence is the establishment of a stable and resilient sense of personal identity. The sense of personal identity is not inborn, the maturation of our biological individuality. It is an active construction that results from an ongoing effort to integrate and make sense of our experience as it pertains to ourselves. Part of growing up is learning about ourselves. In the process, we learn a lot of what we like and a lot of what we don't like about ourselves. We learn that we are attractive or unattractive. We discover that we are generous or stingy, fun or boring, passive or aggressive. We find that we are well coordinated or clumsy, musical or tone-deaf, artistic or lacking in flair and élan. We learn that we are affectionate, obedient children and domineering, nasty siblings. At school we find that we are bright and able or at best average and struggling. These are but some of the bits and pieces we learn about ourselves in the process of growing up.

The task of the adolescent is to bring all of this disparate information together in some cohesive manner that will make sense and that will provide both continuity with the past and guidance for the future. Put differently, the adolescent must construct what might be called a *metarole* that will incorporate and integrate all of the subordinate roles the young person has acquired in the course of growing up. To do this work, the young person requires what famed psychoanalyst and Pulitzer Prize–winning author Erik Erikson called a *psychosocial moratorium*, a period of time during which the adolescent is free from responsibilities and demands to take on the mantle of adulthood. Young people are working on their sense of personal identity when they spend hours listening to records, hanging out with their friends, and attending rock concerts.

Identity formation is more difficult in contemporary society than it was even a couple of decades ago. For one thing, identity formation requires a kind of envelope of adult standards, values, and beliefs that the adolescent can confront and challenge in order to construct and test her own standards, values, and beliefs. This is the familiar process we have seen at earlier stages of development when, say, the six-year-old challenged her parents to get a response and to learn more about herself. Today, however, adults have fewer standards, values, and beliefs and hold on to them less firmly than was true in the past. The adolescent must therefore struggle to find an identity without the benefit of this supportive adult envelope.

As a result of these difficulties and the nature of contemporary society, many young people do not attain a solid sense of identity during adolescence. There are several alternatives to *identity achievement*. One of these is *identity foreclosure*. Some young people decide on an identity early in life and stick with that decision. In some cases, this early choice may result from exceptional talent. Jamie Wyeth chose to paint rather than go to high school, with no untoward consequences. Sometimes, however, identity foreclosure is a matter of convenience or pressure. This often happens when the adolescent is encouraged to follow the family profession or to take over the family business. Identity foreclosure may shut off options for the adolescent that might have been more life satisfying than the one that was imposed upon her.

Another alternative is *identity moratorium*. Young people who leave many identity options open for themselves are said to be in identity moratorium. In our fast-moving society, this may be an adaptive alternative. The job market is changing so rapidly that it may be necessary to keep vocational and other identities open well into college. Sometimes individuals who have attained an identity in one setting, such as the high school, may reenter moratorium after leaving school and the school culture, which provides its own distinctive envelope for identity formation.

A less healthy alternative is what Erikson calls *identity diffusion*. Young people who demonstrate identity diffusion seem to have a kind of patchwork self. That is to say, their identity is not a generally cohesive, consistent whole, but the opposite. Adolescents with a patchwork self seem like chameleons who take on whatever coloration is most suited to the particular circumstances in which they find themselves. They have no genuine identity of their own. Sometimes such young people join cults or very autocratic groups that provide a kind of prefabricated identity that the young person can take on and follow without personal integrative effort.

Identity formation in young women may take a somewhat different course than is true for young men. The pattern outlined above, wherein the young person finds himself by confronting and challenging the environmental envelope of standards and values, may not be the way in which women build their identity. In a recent work, Carol Gilligan and her colleagues followed the attainment of identity in high school girls. They found that young women must first break their ties with others, in some ways suppress their personal beliefs and values, in order to establish new relationships and find a sense of personal identity. For young women, identity formation seems to follow a pattern of breaking relations in order to establish relations. In contrast, for young men it seems to be a matter of breaking rules in order to establish new rules.

Although most adolescents acquire some form of personal identity by the end of this transition period, it is never final or closed. A young person's sense of personal identity continues to grow and change as she progresses through life, pursues a career, becomes a parent, and participates in community affairs. On the other hand, her temperament type—active or passive, outgoing or withdrawn, happy or dour—tends to persist throughout the life cycle.

Social Development

Social interactions in adolescence show both continuity with childhood as well as patterns that are unique to this transition period. As in other domains, there is a divergence between the sexes in the way in which their social interactions evolve during adolescence. This is true for the adolescent's interactions with parents, siblings, and peers.

The friendship patterns of girls over the adolescent period follow a fairly predictable course. Young adolescent girls tend to have one or more best friends (the clique) from whom they are inseparable and about whom they tend to be jealous. To a teenage girl, the loss of a friend of this sort is experienced as a very traumatic event. Toward middle adolescence, the girl is likely to become part of a larger group of boys and girls who date, party, and go to the prom together (the crowd). Her close ties with other girls is now lessened as attachments to boys become stronger. Toward the end of adolescence, cliques and crowds are largely dissipated and are replaced by individual couples as the basic social unit.

Girl-girl friendships in early adolescence can sometimes have an exploitative quality. A plain girl may choose as a friend a pretty girl who will help her meet boys, and the pretty girl may find that her less attractive friend sets her off to advantage. Such friendships are usually not engaged in in a deliberate, premeditated manner, but rather are intuitive and guileless. In addition, there is often an underlying competitiveness among girls with respect to boys, founded on the suspicion that other girls will steal them away. Some girls engage in such "stealing" not because they are interested in the boys, but rather to make the girls whom they were stolen from unhappy and miserable. There is a vicious streak in some adolescents that can assert itself in a number of different ways.

A somewhat similar developmental pattern appears among boys. They, too, develop close friendships with other boys and are jealous about them. At the same time, however, adolescent boys are less likely than girls to form tight cliques and are more likely to be part of a larger group of boys who engage in activities together, such as playing sports, going to the mall, or just hanging out. In middle adolescence, boys usually join a heterosexual crowd in which there is usually no pairing of boys and girls but in which boys and girls may interact as friends. Later in adolescence, young men leave the group and crowd behind as they become involved in dating and the pattern of heterosexual coupling that is the social norm for young adults.

Like the early adolescent friendships of girls, those of boys can also have an exploitative quality. The quiet boy may befriend a boy with an outgoing, engaging personality. A boy whose family has only one car may befriend a boy who owns his own car. As in the case of adolescent girls, such friendships are not entered into because of a deliberate, well-thought-out plan, but are spontaneous gravitations. With respect to boy-girl relations, there is less competition for girls among boys than there is for boys among girls. Boys can show their vicious streak in the merciless teasing and ridicule to which they subject the unathletic or "different" boys at school.

Acceptance and admiration by the opposite sex does not appear to be as crucial for the boy's self-esteem as it is for the girl's. For boys, athletic and academic prowess are rated as more important to a boy's status among his peers than is his attractiveness to girls. For girls, however, at least until recent years, attractiveness to boys was the standard according to which they evaluated themselves and their peers. Today, as vocational and career opportunities for women broaden, achievement is displacing attractiveness as the basis for young women's positive self-evaluation.

According to psychoanalytic writers, adolescence is the period when there is a reawakening of the Oedipus complex, wherein the young person loves the parent of the opposite sex and sees the same-sexed parent as a rival. This conflict is more powerful in adolescence because the adolescent is now sexually mature. For their part, many parents are now experiencing mid-life crises and are anxious about waning physical abilities and attractiveness, about gaining weight and losing hair. This makes the physical powers and attractiveness of their teenagers a constant visible reminder of their own "decline."

Adolescents often resolve this conflict by directing their attachment to a young person of the opposite sex. This new attachment, however, creates its own problems. Teenagers tend to believe that one comes into life with a fixed quantity of love. According to this assumption, if a young woman attaches some of this love to a young man, she must withdraw love from elsewhere. Inasmuch as she bestows only a bare minimum of love on her siblings, she has little in this account to draw upon. The bulk of her emotional investment is in her parents, and she must therefore withdraw love from this source to give to her new love object. Yet her parents have been good to her, and withdrawing love from them necessarily results in guilt. To assuage this guilt, the young woman finds fault with her parents. If they are not so praiseworthy, she need not feel so guilty about withdrawing love from them. Some of the teenager's trumped-up attacks against her parents originate in this way.

The situation is a little different for girls than it is for boys. To appreciate why this is so, we have to recall some observations from infancy and early childhood. As infants, both boys and girls identify most strongly with the mother, who tends to be the primary caregiver during the early years. Around the age of four or five, the period of the Oedipus complex, the child falls in love with the parent of the opposite sex and sees the parent of the same sex as a rival. Because the young child has no chance to win this contest, he or she identifies with the parent of the same sex so as to vicariously attain the parent of the opposite sex. For girls, this is a simple matter because they have identified with their mother since birth. Boys, however, whose early identification was with the mother, must not only identify with the father, but must also sever their identification with their mother. Boys, but not girls, learn about breaking relationships at an early age.

If we return to adolescence and the issue of withdrawing love from parents, boys already have a history of such withdrawal, whereas girls do not. This makes it easier for boys than for girls to withdraw love from parents and to form new emotional attachments. Thanks to this early experience of giving up their identification with their mother, adolescent boys find it easier than young women to break relationships. In young adulthood, however, after women have themselves gone through the experience of breaking relationships, they may find it easier than young men. In any case, adolescent boys still suffer guilt about withdrawing love from their parents, but to a lesser extent than do girls.

This boy-girl difference in the history of their making and breaking attachments may help explain some other phenomena. Because of their greater identification with their mother, adolescent girls often fight more with their mother than adolescent boys fight with their father. This may also help to explain the more abiding attachment of the daughter to her family. This observation may have given rise to the old adage, "A son is a son till he takes a wife; a daughter is a daughter for the rest of her life."

For parents, the situation is different. A father, feeling that his youth and attractiveness are waning, may experience a desire to compete with his son for the young man's girlfriend. Most fathers recognize this thought for what it is, put it where it belongs, and take pleasure in their son's relationship. Mothers may experience the same concerns and feel the impulse to compete with their daughters and to flirt with the young woman's boyfriends. Here, again, most mothers recognize these momentary ideas for what they are and support their daughter's newfound attachment. Some parents may not be able to handle the situation and may embarrass everyone by their antics. Such parents need to seek counseling.

These interpersonal dynamics are more complicated today, when divorce and remarriage are so commonplace. The presence of a stepfather or stepmother in the home complicates the attachment dynamics. We have some data about these dynamics. When daughters who lose their fathers by death are compared with those who lose their fathers by divorce, we can observe clear differences in their behavior in adolescence. Girls who lose their fathers by death tend to be shy with young men and do not date till middle or late adolescence. In contrast, girls who lose their fathers through divorce are likely to be outgoing and seductive with boys. When boys lose their fathers through divorce, they often assume the father's role and may dictate to the mother at what time she should be home from a date!

Despite all of these combinations and permutations of love relationships, most young people eventually discover that love does not come in fixed quantities. They learn the truth that the more love you give, the more you have to give. With that discovery, they reattach themselves to their parents and appreciate that this in no way takes away from their other abiding love relationships.

Sociocultural Change

The transition from childhood to adulthood always takes place in a particular sociocultural and historical context. In many ways, the cultural context determines the ease or difficulty with which young people transit to adulthood. In certain cultures in which puberty is regarded as a sign of adult status, adolescence, as we know it in Western culture, does not exist. Indeed, historian Philippe Aries argues that childhood itself was largely unrecognized in medieval times, when even young children were treated as adults in many respects.

Adolescence as we know it, the long transition between childhood and adult status, is largely a cultural invention. A number of interrelated events gave rise to this invention. One of these was the founding of the republic. The founders recognized that a true democracy required an educated electorate. Universal publicly supported education was the answer. It was instituted in the middle of the nineteenth century. Universal public education introduced a new definition for young people, that of pupils. For the first time, children and adolescents had a unique role and function that clearly distinguished them from adults.

There were socioeconomic reasons for this invention of adolescence as well. With the industrial revolution, many jobs were lost to mechanization. In addition, the machine age required more highly trained and literate workers than did an agricultural economy. The definition of young people as pupils thus served the additional functions of keeping them out of the labor force and providing them with the literacy and technical training required to participate in an industrial economy. There were sociocultural dynamics at work as well. Educating the immigrant children and youth who had arrived in America in large numbers around the turn of the century would help prevent delinquency and crime.

When adolescence was first invented, during the latter part of the last century and the first half of this one, young people were looked upon as immature and in need of adult guidance and direction. Child labor laws were passed to prevent adolescents from being exploited. Compulsory education laws were passed to ensure that all young people went to school. The media, likewise, depicted adolescents as clumsy and naive. High schools offered after-class clubs of many kinds. Adult-organized programs, such as the Explorers and Seascouting, were also available for high school students. In its perception of adolescents as immature, society provided young people with the moratorium Erikson said they needed to attain their sense of personal identity.

Since mid-century, for a variety of different reasons, our perception of teenagers has changed. We no longer view adolescents as immature, but rather as sophisticated, ready and able to deal with the adult world of pornography, drugs, sex, and violence. Many parents no longer have the time or the energy to provide the limits, standards, and values adolescents require to forge their identity. The media portray adolescents as sexually active, used to violence, and avid consumers of alcohol. The schools provide few organized activities for young people outside of team sports. At the same time, society still treats young people as minors and excludes them from congregating at malls and at other places reserved exclusively for adults.

The pressures on young people to be instant adults in some domains while remaining adolescents in others is stressful, confusing, and demoralizing to young people. One result is what has been called the *new morbidity*. Fifty years ago the leading causes of death among young people were diseases such as tuberculosis or polio. Fortunately, medical science has now largely conquered these diseases. Nonetheless, we now lose the same proportion of young people as we did fifty years ago, but to stress-related causes. We lose some ten thousand adolescents a year to substance-abuse-related automobile accidents. The suicide rate has trebled for teenagers since mid-century. Some five to six thousand adolescents take their own lives each year. Alcoholism, venereal disease and violent crime have also become epidemic among adolescents. The new morbidity bears witness to the stresses experienced by young people as a direct consequence of their being perceived as sophisticated.

Certainly, adolescents were never as immature as we liked to believe they were half a century ago. However, they are also not as sophisticated as we might wish them to be today. The belief in adolescent sophistication has been an excuse to abrogate our adult responsibilities toward youth. Adolescents still need the standards, values, and limits that only adults can provide. We need to regard young people as growing in sophistication, but as not quite there yet. They are still very much in need of our adult limit setting, guidance, and concern.

General Characteristics of Adolescents

Adolescent interests show both the continuity with the past and the preparation for the future that we have seen in other areas of adolescent development. Their interest in activities, for example, shifts from solitary to group pursuits. Many of the pastimes that preoccupied young people as children— such as model building, stamp or coin collecting, sewing, or cooking—are usually discarded once children reach adolescence. In their stead, young people participate in team sports or group projects such as working on cars, science projects, putting on plays, or social group activities such as dances and parties. The reading interests of adolescents exemplify this trend. Reading, a solitary activity, tends to reach a peak at about the age of thirteen and to decline thereafter. Here again, however, it is well to recall that there are wide individual differences and that some young people pursue their solitary interests well into adolescence and sometimes into adulthood.

A major concern of many adolescents is clothing. Girls are usually interested in clothing and in being neat and clean in childhood (there are many notable exceptions!), but this orientation usually does not emerge in boys until the age of puberty. After about the age of thirteen or fourteen, however, boys become as clothes-conscious as girls and spend a lot of time in front of the mirror, making sure that their clothing has the proper look. Having the sort of clothing that is "in" or "cool" is particularly important during this transition period. For adolescents, clothing is a sort of badge of membership in the peer group.

Parents have to be a little lenient in this regard. Young children do not require designer clothing, but sometimes an adolescent may need several such items as evidence of being "in." Allowing the young person to buy these items, with the provision that she use some of her own money, is a way to acknowledge the peer group pressure without giving in to it entirely. And the fads change quickly. At one time, it was Bobby socks and loafers, later it was the layered look. A recent clothing fad requires young people to have holes in the knees of their expensive jeans! Hairstyles reflect similar fads. Parents and teachers need to recognize that these are fads that, within reason, can be tolerated.

Young people's vocational interests are also becoming more defined and realistic. Whereas children think about their future vocation in romantic terms—that is, of being something glamorous such as an astronaut—adolescents think about how they want to go about earning their living. What vocation an adolescent eventually chooses depends upon a complex of factors, such as intelligence, talent, training, background, support, and so on. Certain vocations, such as astrophysics, require a high level of intelligence, while other vocations do not. Likewise a person with mathematical talents may work with computers, whereas a person with people talents might work in counseling. Sometimes high schools provide vocational guidance to help adolescents discover the occupation for which they are best suited.

Unfortunately, our school system is geared largely to young people who are going on to college. Most high schools provide very little in the way of preparation for teenagers who are not going on to higher education. This group of adolescents is sometimes called the forgotten half because so little in the way of vocational training is provided for them. Moreover, the vocational education that is available is no longer as highly regarded as it once was before the postindustrial society. Young people who attend vocational schools today may disparagingly be called "vokies." We need to do much more for young people who pursue our much needed, but much undervalued, trades.

It should be said, too, that recent studies of youth work suggest that work during the adolescent years may not have the values for young people that it once did. Youth work was once thought to teach young people responsibility, about the real world, important tool skills, how to manage money, and the effort it takes to earn money. Today most adolescents work in fast food restaurants and spend a large percentage of their time cleaning up or in repetitive tasks. There is little adult mentoring or skill training on these jobs, and many teenagers who earn money on these jobs acquire negative attitudes toward work. Finally, young people who work more than fifteen hours a week may see their grades go down. For a large number of adolescents, work is not the valuable experience it once was.

In addition to maturing vocational interests are the young person's interests in politics, race, and religion. Children, by and large, are free of prejudice other than those they acquire from the significant adults in their world. Left on their own, children will play with other children regardless of race, religion, or ethnic background. In adolescence, however, young people begin to segregate themselves into groups along racial, religious, social class, and ethnic lines. They choose their closest friends from the boys and girls who belong to the same church, ethnic group, or socioeconomic level. This group then becomes the "in" group, and the others become the "out" group. In general, these groupings reflect societal and parental prejudices that were acquired but remained latent during childhood. These prejudices become manifest during adolescence in part because of changes in the adolescent's thinking that enables her to understand general categories. In addition, when adolescents reach sexual maturity, parental fears emerge as a factor in friendship choice. In adolescence, parents become much more adamant about their prejudices.

In addition to these smaller cliquelike groups, the high school is likely to be divided into larger groups, or divisions, that are loosely organized and identified. The names for these divisions vary from locale to locale and from generation to generation. Individuals who are regarded as smart, who do well in school, and who are destined for college are called *brains* in some places, *nerds* in others. The term for the athletic division is more universal: *jocks* seems to be a long-lived favorite. There is also generally a group of young people who are on the fringe of education and acceptable behavior who have been called *hoods* or *baddies* or the like. Generally, once a young person is identified with a particular division, it is difficult to switch and become a member of another. Adolescents, as a group, are not terribly forgiving.

An example of the difficulty young people encounter when they want to change divisions is provided by one of my family court clients. This adolescent girl wanted to move from the hood division to the socially active "mod" group. She began to change her style of dress, speech, and behavior. Although she met some initial resistance, she began to be accepted. Then she contracted the flu and had to be out of school for several weeks. When she returned, the mod division cut her cold. In the interim, her "friends" among the hoods had spread the rumor that she was pregnant and had gone away for an abortion. She then became truant, which was the reason that she was brought to me. In consultation with her parents and me, she decided it would be best if she simply went to another school.

Despite their cliquish behavior and obvious prejudices, many adolescents become concerned about social issues such as racial discrimination, poverty, and political corruption. Although adolescents are often highly critical of adult society in regard to these issues, their own actions often be-lie their words. I once had occasion to go to the airport in Rochester, New York, on a morning when junior high and high school students were on a "Walk for Water." Each student enlisted as many sponsors as possible to pay her a certain sum per mile walked. The funds were to go to help clean up badly polluted Lake Ontario. As I drove, I was impressed by the orderly way in which the young people were walking, often singing songs and being urged on by passersby.

I thought to myself that perhaps I had been too hard on young people and ought to reassess my evaluation of their ability to work toward ideals. When I returned the next morning, however, I was somewhat disheartened. As I drove back along the same route, I saw the city work crews cleaning up the litter that the students had left behind. It seemed to me that the city might have had to spend more money to clean up the debris than the students had collected.

Yet I also recognized that the students were not being hypocritical. They really believed in the cause for which they walked. It was simply that they did not see the connection between messing up the environment and cleaning up the water. It was the symbolism that they were interested in, not the practical reality. It will take a while before they come to appreciate how hard one has to work to attain even partial realization of an ideal.

While adolescents profess liberal ideals and causes, their actual behavior, as in the above example, may be determined by the values of the peer group. It needs to be emphasized, however, that the peer group has no intrinsic power over adolescents. When the peer group unduly influences an adolescent, this is almost always because it fills a parental vacuum. Young people who have been well parented, who have an internalized set of values and beliefs, are not swayed by the peer group. Indeed, such adolescents will seek out and befriend others who share the same values. It is only those adolescents who have no inner-value gyroscope who look to the peer group for guidance and direction.

This is not to say that the peer group is unimportant, even for those young people who move into adolescence with a solid sense of appropriate behavior. Where the peer group manifests its power is in matters of taste, rather than in matters of value. For example, the peer group may determine the adolescent's style of dress and speech, her mannerisms, and her musical and artistic preferences. Al-

though these preferences may sometimes be at variance with
parental tastes, they are reasonably short-lived. We should decide to live with these short-term aberrations (at least from our point of view) in adolescent taste. As parents, we are there for the duration. The peer group influence is a short-lived intrusion into the course of individual development.

The Youth Culture

Since mid-century, with the emergence of the perception of the sophisticated adolescent, we have been witness to the emergence of a unique youth culture. Up until mid-century, young people modeled themselves after adults in their clothing, habits, and musical tastes. Adults had many freedoms that young people did not have. By the sixties, however, all of that had changed. The emergence of rock music as a distinctively youthful musical style set the young apart from adults. The second sexual revolution, which made premarital sex socially acceptable, became part of the adolescent ethos. Drugs and alcohol, through whatever channels, became available to the young. This new youth culture provides contemporary adolescents with many of the prerogatives, once reserved for adults, that made adulthood attractive to youth.

As a result of this development, a new generation gap has emerged. The baby boomers, the first generation of adolescents to experience the youth culture, are now in their forties. Although they retain their appreciation for rock music, they also seem to need to be critical of the upcoming generation, the twenty-something generation, perhaps to deny their nostalgia for their lost youth culture. Likewise, because this generation did not look to adulthood as a liberating step forward, they are less accepting of adulthood than were generations past. Their anger at the younger generation could be generated by resentment and envy of a paradise lost.

However that may be, the upcoming generations have to deal with some harsh realities. Up until this generation, there was a belief in progress, a faith that the world and the people living in it were moving toward a better, more humane, more egalitarian world. Two world wars, the atomic bomb, the Holocaust, the continuation of regional and civil wars, the degradation of the environment, and the deple-tion of natural resources have given the lie to the modern idea of progress. Job opportunities and the prospect of do-ing better financially than one's parents have lessened. All of these considerations tend to blunt the instinctive optimism of young people and contribute to their feeling that adult society has left them a doleful heritage.

There are hopeful signs, however, that we are be-ginning to be concerned about the world that we are leaving to succeeding generations and are working toward amending some of the damage done. This awakening of the adult generation to its obligations to the young is a cause, how-ever slight, for renewed optimism among the young people of today.

The World of Self, Home, and Community

There is both continuity and change in the way in which the young adolescent comes to view herself, her home, her school, and the larger community. She remains herself in tempera-ment and interpersonal style despite the changes in her voice, stature, and appearance. Likewise, although it sometimes seems improbable, her parents are still her parents, and her siblings are still her siblings. The affection she holds for them, although she may demonstrate it less openly, is not seriously altered by the fact of becoming adolescent. In the same way, she carries forward the attitudes toward schooling that she ac-quired as a child as she enters junior high and high school. Although there are sometimes short-lived dips in school performance (the so-called seventh grade slump), young people usually maintain the same level of academic achievement at the high grade levels as they did at the lower levels. Al-though the adolescent's interactions with the larger community are now often more conflictual than when she was a child, it is still the arena for much of her social life.

These continuities notwithstanding, there are changes as well. During adolescence the young person develops a *reflective* sense of self. This new higher order sense of self incorporates those of the early age levels: the *object* self of infancy, the *symbolic* self of early childhood, and the *practical* self of childhood. With the attainment of the reflective self, not only can the adolescent survey all facets of her self as an integrated whole, she can also begin to put herself in other people's positions and look at herself from that new perspective.

In early adolescence, however, young people who have attained a sense of the reflective self make a characteristic error. Because their bodies, feelings, appetites, and intellectual powers are undergoing such rapid and striking changes, they are understandably preoccupied with themselves. As a consequence, when they think about other people's thinking, they assume that other people are thinking about what they are, namely, themselves! They then proceed to construct an imaginary audience that they believe is constantly watching them and appraising their behavior. It is this imaginary audience that accounts for the characteristic self-consciousness of the young adolescent.

To assess this imaginary audience, my students and I constructed a scale with items such as "You were invited to a party and have looked forward to going for over a month. Just as you walk in the door to the party, you discover a large grease spot on your skirt or jeans. What would you do?" Grade school children remarked that they would go in and join the party. Older high school students, ages sixteen, seventeen, and eighteen, said, "They are my friends; they will understand." Young adolescents, however, remarked that they would go home, or spill something on themselves so it would look like it just happened, or hold a hand or a magazine over it. This concern with the audience's appraisal has been associated with susceptibility to peer influence and to identity diffusion and the patchwork sense of self.

Although we never lose the imaginary audience entirely, it is most in evidence in early adolescence, and it can be a powerful motivating force. Many young people work very hard because they envision playing a concerto at Carnegie Hall or catching the winning touchdown pass in the championship game of the season. We all sometimes engage in the imaginary audience fantasy of our own demise—we imagine how people will think about us after we are gone, particularly when those we love have been hard on us. The audience, however, can have a negative impact when young people engage in activities to please the audience that they might never undertake on their own.

If we believe that everyone is thinking about us, concerned with our every thought and deed, we must be something special, something unique upon this earth. Within this frame of mind young people create a personal fable, the belief that they are special and unique. "Other people," the young person thinks, "will grow old and die, but not me. Other people will not attain their ambitions and goals, but not me. Other people will forget their friends when they become successful and famous, but not me." To be sure, we are all unique in some ways, but the fable carries this sense of specialness and uniqueness much further. In early adolescence the sense of specialness and invulnerability is very great.

My students and I have constructed a scale to measure this fable. It contains items such as this: "It seems to me that my teacher likes me better than the other kids even though he or she doesn't say so." These items assess the young person's positive fable of being special and unique in a good way. We also assess the negative fable with items like the following: "When I said something to hurt my best friend, I thought no one in the whole world could have said anything so stupid." We found that young adolescents are more likely than older adolescents to respond in ways that suggest a strong personal fable of specialness and invulnerability.

The personal fable, like the imaginary audience, stays with us throughout life. Many of us, for example, would never get on an airplane or a roller coaster if we did not believe that we are shielded by a cloak of invulnerability and that nothing will happen to us. Once, when one of my sons got seriously ill, I could not believe it was happening to me; things like that happened to others, not to me. In addition to my anguish over my son, who fortunately recovered, I had to deal with this attack upon my personal fable. We have to continually revise our fable as we experience what psychoanalyst and author Judith Viorst calls our "necessary losses."

Although the fable can have positive consequences, it can also have negative effects. This is particularly true for young adolescents today who are often confronted with decision making when their personal fable is at its peak. Some adolescents may engage in sexual activity and not use contraceptives in the belief that "other people get pregnant or catch AIDS, but not me." In the same way, some teenagers may experiment with drugs in the belief that "other kids will get hooked on drugs, not me." Drug and sex education are important and may help young people resist the fabled belief in their own invulnerability, but information may not be enough. Adolescents need to hear from other adolescents who believed in their invulnerability and then became pregnant, diseased, or addicted.

The adolescent's new reflective sense of self also permits her to reconstruct her childhood. Memory is not a fixed entity; we construct and reconstruct our memory as our mental abilities mature. Whereas children often repress and deny what they may have experienced as parental slights and injustices, adolescents reconstruct their memories of their childhood to include all, and usually more, of these injustices and slights. Young adolescents now proceed to pay their parents and their siblings back for all of the injustices, real or imagined, visited upon them when they were children. Whereas children believe that parents can do no wrong, early adolescents often believe they can do no right.

A personal experience may help to illustrate this point. My parents were immigrants, and their English was far from perfect. Yet I never noticed that my parents spoke with an accent until I became an adolescent! At that age I was embarrassed to bring friends home because of the way my parents spoke. Young people will find fault if a parent's profession is too lowly and will complain about their low status and lack of material luxuries. Other adolescents berate their parents for being financially or professionally successful and too materialistic. If parents are orthodox in their religious beliefs, they are too strict, and if they are liberal, they are not orthodox enough. Parents need to have a sense of humor and to appreciate that this adolescent storm, like all storms, will pass.

Younger as well as older siblings do not escape the consequence of the young teenager's reconstruction of her memory of past events. Sometimes older siblings are berated for having excluded them from their excursions and activities. Younger children are often accused, sometimes with reason, of having initiated battles for which the older sib was blamed. The focus of sibling quarrels now shifts as well. In childhood, most of these battles were over toys and prerogatives. For young adolescents, however, many battles with older sibs are over clothes and possessions. Young teenagers often "borrow" without permission an older sib's clothing or possessions, such as a guitar. Some of these conflicts can be avoided if siblings establish freedom/responsibility contracts between themselves: "You might be able to borrow my things, but you have to ask me first."

The young adolescent now treats her younger siblings differently as well. They are now "kids," while she is, if not fully grown up, at least half grown up. This entitles her, or so she believes, to comment upon their cleanliness, eating habits, and manners. In large part, however, these comments are not motivated by her concern for the well-being of her younger siblings. To a much greater degree, these comments about young siblings' appearance and behavior are motivated by her anxieties about the impression these young hellions are going to make on her friends!

The young adolescent's new concern with appearances, stemming in part from the powerful imaginary audience, extends to parents as well. Because she is so concerned with the impression her family is making on others, she becomes hypercritical. What she accepted as natural for her mother and father when she was a child she now cannot abide. Her father should not wear those old paint-stained trousers even when he is working about the house. Her mother should not wear shorts unless she loses some weight. As the adolescent matures and the power of the audience subsides, this criticism diminishes, and she becomes able to accept her parents for their inner qualities rather than for their outward appearance.

The young adolescent's criticism of the family is correlated with her movement into the larger world of the community. Whereas the center of the child's activity is the home, the gathering point for the adolescent can be a pizza parlor, a bowling alley, a movie theater, or a shopping mall. Moreover, now that she is mature, she does not want to be seen in the community with her parents. Going with parents to the mall or to a restaurant is kid stuff, and adolescents are embarrassed to be seen with their parents in such places. Moreover, there are certain stores that are regarded as "dorky" and not fit to shop in. If parents insist upon visiting such stores, the adolescent is convinced that the whole world is watching and laughing at her.

The new level of interaction between the adolescent and the community is often less than harmonious. Young people are not always welcome in the mall, where they can sometimes become boisterous. At the same time, because young people have considerable disposable income, they are welcomed in the record and clothing shops that cater to the youth market. There is thus a lot of ambivalence on the part of the business community toward young people. Although businesspeople want young people to patronize their stores and purchase goods, they do not like the noise, the rowdy behavior, and sometimes the theft that adolescents sometimes engage in.

It is interesting that in places that are exclusively for the young, adolescents tend to be very well behaved. I have attended a number of rock concerts with my sons and have been impressed at how polite and thoughtful the young people were. They were enthusiastic about the entertainment but were generally courteous with one another and orderly at the concession stands. Perhaps it is only in adult settings, where adolescents sense a kind of ambivalence and perhaps latent fear, that they become overly loud and rambunctious.

The young adolescent also has a different perspective on school than she did when she was a child. As a child she viewed the school primarily as a place for academic activities. The organization of the elementary school, largely a set of self-contained classrooms, contributes to this orientation. Children are together for an entire day, and the curriculum is the focus of the class's activities. At the junior and senior high school level, however, the school is organized in a somewhat different way. Instead of being in the same classroom the whole day with the same children, junior and senior high school students rotate from class to class, often with different young people in each class.

As a result of this hourly rotation from class to class, young people spend a lot of time in hallways. This frequent rotation gives the secondary school a powerful social dynamic. Hallways and lounge areas become places to socialize, to be seen, to people-watch, to exchange pleasantries, or to engage in bitter quarrels. It is the social dimension of the school that makes it a natural place for the formation of cliques, crowds, and divisions and for patterns of social ostracism and acceptance. During adolescence, therefore, the school becomes much more than a place for learning; it becomes a stage on which much of the drama of adolescent friendships, rivalries, and hostilities takes place and finds its full expression.

Unfortunately, the social dimension of schools has in recent years taken a more violent turn. It is estimated that more than a hundred thousand young people bring weapons to school each day. Many schools now have weapon detectors. The schools have increasingly become the scene of serious violence and even murder. In talking to a group of middle school students, I was surprised to learn that what they were most concerned about in going to high school was the violence; they were anxious about being attacked and hurt. No community is exempt. In my small private practice I saw a thirteen-year-old from a professional family who attends school in an affluent suburb. He surprised me one day by telling me he was going to take a knife to school to protect himself.

In part, at least, the new violence among youth is a reflection of the abrogation of adult responsibility toward young people. As I wrote earlier, I believe this abrogation derives from our contemporary perception of adolescents as sophisticated and that this perception is held and reinforced by parents, schools, the media, advertising, and the helping professions. We must appreciate that young people are growing in sophistication, but are not there yet. Once we accept this fact, we will reassert our adultness and set limits, standards, and values with love and with care. If we do that, we will begin to see a decline in these evidences of the new morbidity.

The contemporary adolescent, then, comes to view her home, community, and school differently than she did as a child and differently than did her peers of earlier generations. Home, community, and school also view adolescents differently than children and differently than they viewed adolescents in the past. Unfortunately, the new perception of adolescent sophistication often encourages homes, schools, and the larger community to abrogate many of their responsibilities to young people. We need to reinvent adolescents and adulthood if we wish to reduce the stress on adolescence and the serious toll it is taking on their well-being.

Selected Readings

Faber, A., & Mazlish, E.(1984). *Siblings without Rivalry.* New York: Norton. Many useful tips about how to deal with and reduce the battles between siblings.

Gilligan, C. (1987). *In Another Voice.* Cambridge, MA: Harvard University Press. Argues that much of psychology is written by men and ignores the legitimate voice of women. Shows that women's moral development is different from, not inferior to, men's moral growth.

Lerner, R.M., & Foch, T.T. (eds.) (1987). *Biological and Psychosocial Interactions in Early Adolescence.* Hillsdale, NJ: Lawrence Erlbaum. Well-presented summary of some of the ways in which biological development determines how adolescents interact with one another and with adults.

Muuss, R.E. (1988). *Theories of Adolescence*, 4th ed. New York: Random House. Provides a broad historical overview as well as many different theoretical treatments of the adolescent period.

Offer, D., Ostrow, E., & Howard, K. (1981). *The Adolescent: A Psychological Self Portrait.* New York: Basic Books. Describes the results of a large-scale research project. The overall conclusion is that adolescence is a much more psychologically "normal" and healthy period than it is usually described to be.

Rogers, D.E., & Ginzberg, E. (1992). *Adolescents at Risk.* Boulder, CO: Westview Press. Attempts to present some of the factors that place adolescents at risk for substance abuse and other self-destructive behaviors.

10

Mental
Development

Adolescent Mental Development

The extraordinary changes in the adolescent's physical appearance and in her interpersonal relationships often overshadow the equally momentous changes in her intellectual ability. As noted in the discussion of concrete operations, the age of six or seven has, since ancient times, been known as the age of reason. What the ancients had in mind, however, was the syllogistic reasoning of Aristotle.

Our conception of reasoning changed when, in the nineteenth century, a new form of logic was invented, called *symbolic,* or *propositional, logic.* Aristotelian logic dealt with premises about the real world. The truth or falsity of the premises could be checked by a factual standard. Symbolic logic deals with propositions whose truth or falsity is determined by their accordance with a set of general principles, not facts. Propositional logic allows us to deal with probabilities and possibilities. Put more simply, symbolic logic is a logic of what if, rather than one of what is.

One of Jean Piaget's most important contributions was his discovery that adolescents attain a new set of mental abilities, *formal operations*, that enable them to employ symbolic logic. In effect, Piaget contends that in adolescents we can observe what is, in effect, a second age of reason. This new higher order level of reasoning gives a unique quality to both the adolescent's intellectual abilities and to the content of her knowledge.

Qualitative Facets of Adolescent Mental Development

Formal operations give rise to at least four modes of thinking that are unique to adolescence. First of all, adolescents can now think in terms of *possibilities,* even when these are not in accord with the facts of the real world. If we ask an eight- or nine-year-old the color of snow, in a world in which coal is white, the child has difficulty answering. Children find it hard to accept and reason from a contrary-to-fact condition. Adolescents who have attained formal operations have no problem in reasoning that in a world in which coal is white, snow would probably be black.

Likewise, suppose we show a child four wooden disks colored green, red, black, and blue and ask them to arrange the disks in all possible combinations taking them one, two, three, and four at a time. The eight- or nine-year-old will try to arrive at the combinations by actually moving the disks around. With this strategy, however, they make mistakes of both omission and commission. They name some combinations more than once and fail to name others. One of their difficulties is understanding that lower order combinations, such as blue/green, can be part of a higher order combination of blue/green/red. Adolescents, on the other hand, usually come up with all sixteen of the possible combinations by looking at the disks and by writing down the various arrangements.

Syllogistic reasoning makes it possible for children to understand rules and to master the basics of reading, writing, and arithmetic. In a like manner, propositional logic enables adolescents to master the higher order rules required to learn advanced literacy and math skills. For example, we can ask an adolescent to interpret the simile, "My love is like a red, red rose" because she now understands that even though a rose is not a human being it can be likened to one with respect to its beauty, freshness, and delicacy. Likewise, in math young people can now understand that the algebraic equation $(x+y)^2 = x^2+2xy+y^2$ holds true for whatever values are substituted for x and for y.

This new ability to deal in possibilities extends to the young person's social interactions as well. Adolescents can engage in genuine debate because they can anticipate (conceive of) their opponent's possible arguments and prepare in advance to counter them. These new powers of argumentation are particularly evident if teenagers want something from their parents. When young people ask for permission to engage in an activity that they are sure we will veto, they prepare many arguments in advance to neutralize the arguments that they anticipate we will raise. It is also true, however, that adolescents sometimes argue for the sake of arguing. It is a way of practicing their newly attained abilities (not unlike the five-year-old who demands numbers to practice her computational abilities).

Formal operations also enable young people to think about and to conceptualize their own and other people's thinking—a higher level form of *metacognition*. We have already seen how this new ability, combined with the young adolescent's personal preoccupations, results in the imaginary audience and the personal fable. This ability to think about thinking appears in other ways as well. In my early studies of religious development, for example, I asked children and adolescents whether a dog or a cat could be a Protestant. Children were ambivalent. They said, "Well, he belongs to the family, so he could be, but if he went to church he would bark and the minister would kick him out, so I guess he couldn't be." In contrast, adolescents said that a dog can't think, so he doesn't believe in anything. Adolescents use terms such as *belief* and *understanding* that make it clear that they have conceptualized thought processes.

Another consequence of young people's ability to think about thinking is their new recognition that they can think one thing and say another. Children have difficulty in keeping secrets and in telling tales with a straight face. They have trouble saying one thing when they know that the opposite is true. Adolescents have no problems in this regard. As a consequence, adolescents become quite proficient at making up all sorts of stories to cover their tracks when, for example, they have engaged in forbidden actions. It is simply a fact that adolescents can dissemble with such great skill that one would almost swear that they were telling the truth, so convincing is their demeanor.

Closely related to her newfound abilities to think in terms of possibilities and to think about thinking is the adolescent's ability to deal with *multiple dimensions* at the same time. We see this clearly in the difference between children's and adolescents' approach to science. Although children can engage in simple science investigations, they cannot engage in experimentation. True experimentation involves keeping a number of variables constant while varying others. Adolescents can keep many variables in mind simultaneously, whereas children cannot.

Sometimes the adolescent's ability to deal with many different options at the same time can be frustrating. In school,

for example, a teacher asked her eighth grade class about
the climate they might find above latitude 30 degrees. A student replied, "Eskimos." The idea of latitude opened up so many possibilities that the student in effect forgot the question. Her response is an example of what might be called the *pseudostupidity* of the young adolescent. Because teenagers can think of so many different possibilities at the same time, it is sometimes hard for them to know how to choose the appropriate one. They give the wrong answer because they are too bright, rather than because they are too dense.

That is to say, learning how to use formal operations takes time and practice. Consider a young adolescent who is fortunate enough to have a number of different outfits to wear to school. One morning she is trying to decide what to wear. Unable to decide she asks her mother, who replies, "Wear the yellow sweater and brown skirt combination; that is a pretty outfit." The daughter then decides to wear jeans and a blouse! As we get older, we develop strategies for deciding what to wear, but young adolescents have not worked these out yet. As a consequence, they struggle with making decisions because they can entertain so many alternatives but lack a system for deciding among them.

A fourth characteristic of adolescent thinking generated by the emergence of formal operations is *relativism*. Children tend to think in terms of black and white, right and wrong. They have trouble, for example, in dealing with exceptions to rules that they regard as absolute. Adolescents, in contrast, because they can conceive of possibilities, begin to see the world in relative, rather rather than in absolute, terms. When a father says to his daughter, "Girls shouldn't date before they are sixteen," she might reply, "That may have been true in your day, Dad, but times change, and it just doesn't work that way anymore."

The adolescent's critical eye is also turned toward the school and the teacher. Whereas children may not like a teacher, they are seldom critical of him or her as an instructor. Children assume that the teacher is competent, and they may deny or ignore evidence to the contrary. Adolescents, however, are very critical of the teacher's knowledge and ability and are often quick to challenge an instructor who seems insecure and inept. Adolescents are much less concerned with how nice the teacher is and more interested in whether or not he or she knows the subject. This focus upon the teacher's knowledge and ability puts a new strain on teacher-student interactions. Adolescents often hit teachers where it hurts: their sense of adequacy and competence.

Toward middle adolescence, young people become concerned with general social issues and are a little less critical of their parents and teachers. During this age period, they turn their critical appraisals on government, the church, and other social institutions. Adolescents may now criticize other countries and societies as well as defend those countries and societies that appear to be victimized. This does not mean, necessarily, that the tension between adolescents and their parents and teachers diminishes. It does mean that adolescents disperse their attacks across a much broader front so that the force of any given attack is necessarily diluted.

Sometimes young people's eagerness to engage in relativistic thinking causes them to challenge everything and anything that they previously believed. In this regard, there is a parallel between the child's attainment of concrete operations and her skepticism regarding magicians, Santa Claus, and the tooth fairy and the adolescent's skepticism about adult social, moral, and political pronouncements. Some writers have suggested that a period of adolescent skepticism is a necessary prerequisite to attaining a more sophisticated understanding of our human condition.

Quantitative Facets of Adolescent Thinking

In addition to the changes in the quality of adolescent thought, there are changes in its quantititative aspects as well. Until a few decades age, psychologists thought that intelligence reached a peak in late adolescence and young adulthood and went into gradual decline thereafter. Today, however, researchers distinguish between *fluid* and *crystallized intelligence*. Certain fluid abilities—such as the ability to construct novel analogies or to memorize a list of unrelated words or to complete a complex series such as 32, 11, 33, 15, 34, 19—decline after age thirty. Other crystallized abilities, such as the ability to interpret written and verbal communication, actually increase markedly up until about the age of sixty, when these abilities too begin to decline. The extent of intellectual decline depends upon many different variables, such as intelligence and occupation.

Quantitative changes in intellectual functioning can also be described from the information-processing perspective. Looked at from this standpoint, adolescents are more capable of *selective attention* than are children. Adolescents, for example, may be able to do their homework while their parents are vacuuming the rug or mowing the lawn. They also have an improved capacity for *divided attention* and are able to carry on a conversation while playing a computer game. Divided attention makes it possible for adolescents to listen to a lecture and take notes at the same time.

In addition to improved attentional abilities, adolescents also give evidence of improved memory capacities. An interesting way of demonstrating this change in memory capacity is to have children and adolescents repeat a story that has been read to them. Children are much more likely than adolescents to engage in *leveling* and *sharpening*. For example, when children in one study heard, "On a sunny Saturday in May" they "leveled" the material and recalled only, "On a day in May." In contrast, the adolescents gave the exact rendering. This reflects an improvement in short-term memory from childhood to adolescence. When the story included the sentence "A green oily slime dripped from the monster's mouth," children "sharpened" the material and recalled, "A green gooey, oily slime was pouring out of the monster's mouth." Again adolescents give a more precise rendering.

Thanks to formal operations, perhaps, adolescents also demonstrate superior long-term memory compared to children. This is true because, as noted earlier, memory is not a simple storage of information, but rather an active reconstruction of the information that has been stored. With formal operations, adolescents are better able to reconstruct their past than they were when they were children. That is why many adolescents get angry at their parents for "crimes" committed against them when they were children. It is also true that young people's ability to reconstruct their past is facilitated by the dissipation of certain psychological defenses, such as repression and denial.

A third information-processing change in intellectual ability is to be found in the adolescent's ability to use *organizational strategies*. For example, adolescents can prioritize their assignments, responsibilities, and household chores so that they get them all done. An adolescent's schedule is often quite complex and requires a lot of planning as to when to do what. For example, an adolescent who has to do some shopping, go to the library, and drop some materials off at a friend's house might plan the route that would be most advantageous and efficient in terms of time. Children have difficulty making similarly complex and intricate organizational plans and strategies.

The Content of Adolescent Thinking: The Physical World

Changes in the quality and quantity of adolescent mental abilities clearly change the content of their thinking as well. Adolescents can now appreciate puns, for example. Puns may be the lowest form of humor, but they nonetheless require the highest level of intelligence. It is only with the attainment of formal operations that young people begin to read and enjoy *Mad* magazine, with its outrageous satires and cartoons. Puns, like algebra, require that the adolescent appreciate that one and the same symbol can have a variety of different meanings.

In adolescence, the young person's grasp of causality, space, and time expands once again. With respect to causality, she can begin to understand multiple causation. In studying economics, for example, she can comprehend the theory of value according to which the value of goods is determined by the cost of labor, materials, production, transportation, and so on. In the same way, she can now appreciate complex motivations in fictional characters and can recognize that individuals can be torn in many different directions at the same time.

With respect to time, formal operations enable adolescents to appreciate historical and celestial time. To really grasp historical time, the young person has to be able to understand the abstract concept of a century, which must be extrapolated from her knowledge of what a year entails. Likewise, the abstract conception of a light year has to be constructed from the concepts of speed and distance. Whereas children have to use concrete markers in order to understand historical or celestial time, adolescents can understand these forms of time in terms of abstract units of measure.

Young people's sense of space is also greatly expanded. They now have a much better grasp of geographical, topo-

graphical, and celestial space. Although, unfortunately, many
adolescents do not know a lot of geography—as national tests indicate—they are very capable of learning it and of using maps and globes. Children can identify the states and countries, but they often do so by their perceptual shapes, rather than through a conceptual understanding of where the places are located in real space. Adolescents can also appreciate microscopic space, a concept that is as abstract as celestial space.

The Content of Adolescent Thinking: The Social World

Formal operations also change the ways in which young people perceive other people. First of all, adolescents begin to perceive other people in more individualized ways than they did when they were children. When asked to describe other people, children tend to use fairly general terms, such as "He is old" or "She is kind of chubby," terms that apply to many different people. As they mature, however, adolescents are likely to describe individuals in much more specific terms: "She is a lot of fun to be with" or "He is really into country western music." This more individualized approach to others reflects the adolescent's ability to conceptualize abstract personality traits and categories of behavior.

Second, in comparison to those of children, adolescents' perceptions of others are more objective. Children tend to assume that everyone shares their perceptions (likes and dislikes, say) of others. In contrast, the adolescent comes to appreciate that the way she perceives and reacts to other people may not be shared by her friends. She eventually learns, and accepts, the fact that her friends may not like the same movie stars, sports teams, or music groups that she does. In many ways, this new objectivity mirrors the young person's emerging sense of her own individuality and separateness, a sense of uniqueness that she now extends to others as well as to herself.

These individualized and objective perceptions are necessarily more abstract perceptions as well. Children tend to perceive others primarily with respect to their physical attributes and observable actions. Adolescents, on the other hand, are more likely to perceive individuals as endowed with nonobservable traits and behaviors, such as thoughtfulness and generosity. Although these traits and behaviors are derived from the individual's actions, they are really abstractions from having observed many of the individual's past behaviors. They are not descriptions of particular concrete actions.

Fourth, the adolescent's perceptions of others tend to be inferential. Children can infer that their friends are unhappy when they see them cry or that they are happy when they see them laugh. The adolescent, however, uses more subtle clues. If a friend has done poorly on an examination, she will be supportive, even if the friend tries to not show her feelings. In such situations, the young person is able to reflect upon how she might feel in similar circumstances and infer that her friend would feel the same way. This form of supportive behavior also shows that the teenager is capable of a more differentiated and subtle understanding of social causality than is demonstrated by the child.

Finally, the adolescent is able to organize her individualized, objective, abstract, and inferential perceptions about others as well as about herself. That is to say, once the adolescent is able to construct a sense of her personal identity, she is also able to do something similar with respect to her friends. Just as she can now see herself as someone who, say, is good with animals but not with little kids, she can also see her friends as similarly differentiated and individuated. She constructs a sense of her own complex personality and comes to appreciate the complex personalities of other people.

The adolescent's new ability to see individuals in more personalized ways is correlated with an emergent ability to put herself in their position and to take their point of view. Harvard psychologist Robert Selman suggests that such perspective taking develops through a series of stages that are related to age. During the preadolescent years, young people are able to take the other person's position and to intuit his or her thoughts and feelings. They still lack a solid sense of social causality, however, and may have difficulty relating the other person's thoughts and feelings to circumstances or to the thoughts and feelings of others. Their ability to take the other person's point of view is still largely situational.

In early adolescence, the young person engages in *mutual* role taking. Now she has a beginning sense of social causality. She can understand how a cutting remark by one of her friends can be hurtful to another friend even when both girls seem to be smiling and acting friendly toward one another. Toward later adolescence, role taking reflects the adolescent's growing understanding of the *complexity* and *multilayeredness* of personality. She may appreciate that some of her friend's mannerisms are taken from her friend's parents, while others are uniquely her own. Toward the end of adolescence, the young person also begins to appreciate the limits of role taking, that is, how difficult it is to really appreciate another person's unique perspective.

We have already touched upon other facets of the adolescent's expanded social understanding in earlier sections of the book. In the domain of moral development, for example, adolescents come to appreciate the social origin of rules and the importance of such rules for social order. Young people also begin to appreciate religion as a set of beliefs to which one can choose to subscribe. In a like manner, their sense of social causality is much more differentiated, and they realize that much of our behavior is "overdetermined" and motivated by many factors and at many levels. This new broader social understanding also makes young people a little humble about their capacity to understand others and themselves. They begin to appreciate that understanding oneself and others is a lifelong undertaking.

During early to middle adolescence, then, young people begin to think in a new key. They have higher level mental powers than children, and their conceptions of themselves, their families, the larger society, and the world are correspondingly more multileveled and more abstract. The adolescent's thinking is now on a par with that of adults, but she is less practiced and competent in the use of these abilities and concepts than she will be later. By the end of this period, the major transition to adulthood has been accomplished, much of the trauma is over, and the period of adaptation and accommodation to the adult world begins in earnest.

Selected Readings

Elkind, D. (1984). *All Grown Up and No Place to Go: Teenagers in Crises.* Reading, MA: Addison-Wesley. Tries to show the relations between the adolescents' new levels of thinking and the quality of their social interactions.

Flavell, J. (1985). *Cognitive Development.* Englewood Cliffs, NJ: Prentice Hall. A thoughtful, well-written, and up-to-date review and interpretation of the literature on cognitive development.

Inhelder, B., & Piaget, J. (1958). *The Growth of Logical Thinking from Childhood to Adolescence.* Boston: Little, Brown. An overview of the development of logical thinking from infancy through adolescence with particular attention to the period of formal operations.

Kagan, J., & Coles, R. (eds.)(1972). *12 to 16: Early Adolescence.* New York: Norton. An excellent collection of essays on all facets of early adolescence by the leading figures in the fields of adolescent psychology, psychiatry, and sociology.

Montemayor, R., Adams, G.R., & Gullotta, T.P. (1990). *From Childhood to Adolescence: A Transitional Period?* Beverly Hills, CA: Sage. A critical examination of some of the established "truths" about adolescent behavior and development.

11

Age Profiles

All of the comments made earlier about age profiles pertain here. In a sense, these age profiles provide what might be called a microanalysis of development, a more fine-grained examination than a broader age span could provide. The analysis is limited, in part, because of the restricted socioeconomic sample upon which it is based. On the other hand, some principles of development hold across many social, cultural, and language boundaries. For example, the fact that the Piagetian stages hold for children in all parts of the world speaks to the hardiness of developmental phenomena. These profiles, then, are best seen as revealing patterns of development and not as standards against which to evaluate young people.

The Twelve-Year-Old

The average twelve-year-old tends to be outgoing, enthusiastic, and generous. She does not have her emotions in full rein, however, and often gets carried away. When she likes something, she really likes it, and when she doesn't like something, she really hates it. The twelve-year-old is still relatively uncomplicated emotionally. Parents and teachers generally find her open, friendly, and possessed of a sense of humor. She can laugh at herself, can engage in humorous, insulting banter, and may even sink to practical jokes.

At twelve, the young person makes efforts to demonstrate that she is no longer a child. One way she does this is to establish close peer friendships as evidence that she is capable of establishing nonfamilial attachments. She is also becoming a bit more objective about herself and her family. Although she may be critical of herself and her family, this criticism does not yet extend to society at large. She is relatively harsh in her judgments of her appearance. She may have difficulty accepting praise or admiration and often reacts with squirming and clowning. She is less self-centered than she was even a year earlier, but this new maturity has yet to stabilize. She is apt to alternate rather rapidly and dramatically from seemingly mature behavior to overtly childish modes of language and action.

Most twelve-year-olds relate comfortably to peers and nonparental adults. Preteens also get along reasonably well with their parents. This relationship is, however, less close than it was a year or two earlier. Daughters may develop a new flirtatious and worshiping attitude toward their fathers and may feel closer to them than ever before. Boys tend to move away from both parents but are often on better terms with their mothers than with their fathers. Twelve begins the trend toward ever-decreasing participation in family activities that will continue throughout adolescence. The twelve-year-old is also aware of her parents' new criticism of her and may respond by making joking criticisms of her parents. She may, for example, tease her father about his bald spot or criticize her mother for her dated hairstyle. Twelve-year-olds are also competitive with their parents in both sports and board games.

By the age of twelve, many girls are romantically interested in boys. This interest, however, is largely a matter of talk and more talk. A girl frequently expresses a liking for a boy whom she feels is her boyfriend, even though the boy may be quite unaware of the girl's interest in him. There are wide individual differences in heterosexual interest at this age. Most twelve-year-olds have not begun to date, although there are exceptions. Some girls of this age still maintain their childhood aversion to boys, whereas others seem not to be able to think or talk about anything else. Most girls of twelve are interested in making and keeping girl friends. Friendships at this age are still unbiased, and most girls can get along with most of their peers. Twelve-year-olds place a great deal of emphasis on best friends. They also complain a lot about their friends.

Boys at age twelve are beginning to be interested in girls and many claim to have a girlfriend. As is true for girls of this age, however, the "girlfriend" in question may be completely unaware that she has a secret admirer. The dominant mode of boy-girl interaction at this age is still often mixed-sex, adult-sponsored games and outings. Like twelve-year-old girls, twelve-year-old boys give a very high priority to making friends. They take pride in the number of best friends they have. Twelve-year-old boys also engage in a lot of fighting and arguing with their friends, and there are many shifting allegiances. Nonetheless, boys are usually friends with somebody most of the time.

The reading interests of twelve-year-olds tend toward sports, adventures, and the classics. At this age, young people don't like love stories and may regard animal stories as childish. These young adolescents watch television a little less than at an earlier age, perhaps because of their greater involvement with friends. When they do watch television, most twelve-year-olds prefer mystery or comedy programs, as they are tired of situation comedies and crime stories.

Young people show a similar pattern of preference in their choice of movies and videotape rentals. At this age, young people will watch the same movie or video over and over again if they really like it. Twelve-year-old boys are very sports-minded and may avidly follow professional sports. Girls, in contrast, often begin to lose interest in sports at this age. Although this is less true than in previous years, because of more opportunities for girls to participate in team sports, on the average girls are still less sports-minded than boys.

Twelve-year-olds are likely to take strong positions on schooling. They may claim to hate school or to love it, but there is no in-between. Young people of this age tend to be restless and fidgety, to engage in a lot of daydreaming, and to clown around with their peers. Note passing is also a very popular pastime. Although preteens will respond positively to a strong teacher, a teacher who lacks skill may easily lose control of the class. Successful teachers of this age level often use a lot of humor to keep young people involved. As a rule, it is not easy to get twelve-year-olds to work together as a group. In part this derives from the fact that at this age, every young person is an actor to herself, but an audience to everyone else. As a result, there are only actors, but no audience!

Part of the twelve-year-old's restlessness may be the result of transiting to a junior high and the novelty and freedom of going to a different room for each subject. That takes a lot of getting used to. Some young people may attend a middle school at grade six. True middle schools (not all middle schools incorporate the middle-school philosophy) are organized differently than junior highs and have greater continuity with the elementary school. That can make it easier on the eleven- and twelve-year-olds than the abrupt transition to the junior high school. Another factor may contribute to the twelve-year-old's restlessness at school. Many elementary school children tell me that what they dread most about going to junior high is the violence and aggression they expect to encounter there. Schools are not the safe havens they once were, and young people know it.

In many ways, the twelve-year-old is reminiscent of the six-year-old. Both are active, restless ages, outward looking and friendship seeking. The twelve-year-old's criticism of others, however, can have more sting because she has deeper insight into human personality. At this age, her friendships are based on interests rather than activities. She is also beginning to experience the effects of puberty, and these contribute to her restlessness and high activity level. In many ways, twelve is a highly anticipatory age; something is coming, but the young adolescent is not quite sure what it is and how it will turn out.

The Thirteen-Year-Old

Many thirteen-year-olds begin to turn inward and be preoccupied with themselves and with personal self-evaluation. As a consequence, the thirteen-year-old is often "touchy." At this age, the teenager is likely to sulk and go to her room when she is angry or upset. Alternatively, she may respond with sarcastic remarks. The thirteen-year-old often takes pleasure in other people's missteps and gaffes. In part, this may assuage some of the guilt she feels about her own mistakes. Thirteen-year-old boys and girls frequently have more vague "worries" than they do specific fears. This is a reversal of the situation at younger age levels. It reflects, in part at least, the thirteen-year-old's enhanced ability to anticipate the future.

In general, thirteen is introspective and is less happy than she will be in the succeeding teen years. This introspectiveness is evidenced by her search for self-understanding and acceptance. At this age, she agonizes over being too fat or too short or too tall or too hairy. She is worried about being liked and accepted by her peers and is constrained to dress and behave in the manner prescribed by the peer group. She also follows the peer group in her worries about having "brains" and "personality." At thirteen, as they discover the privacy of their own thoughts, boys and girls often keep to themselves while at home. They regard attempts by parents and siblings to engage them in conversation as a kind of prying. It is important to recognize and respect this secretiveness as constructive: It is necessary for the young person to consolidate her sense of self and identity.

The seclusiveness and secretiveness of the thirteen-year-old is often associated with a diminution in friendships. At this age, friendships are somewhat less close than they were a year earlier. Girls tend to form threesomes, and two of the girls will gossip about the third in her absence. Interest in friends may vary from day to day. Friends are now seen primarily as those in whom one can, with confidence, confide one's secrets. Boys, too, seem to have fewer friends at this age than they did at age twelve. They also seem more easily upset and angered by friends than they were just a year earlier. Although boys may engage in some group activities, even fairly close groups of boys may split up and go their separate ways.

Some girls may begin dating at thirteen (usually older boys), but this is the exception rather than the rule. At the other extreme are those girls who still regard boys as bad news. The majority of girls of this age, however, are romantically interested in boys without being "boy crazy." The fact that many thirteen-year-old girls are taller than many thirteen-year-old boys tends to exacerbate tensions in boy-girl interactions. Perhaps because of the size differential, some thirteen-year-old girls are often critical and dismissive of boys of the same age. Nonetheless, other girls may still act silly and giggle when their male classmates are around.

Thirteen-year-old boys show less interest in girls than do girls of the same age. Although they continue to be interested in girls, they move away from identifying a particular girl as a girlfriend. Few thirteen-year-old boys date, and many express themselves as confirmed girl-haters. Perhaps because of this ambivalence toward girls, thirteen-year-old boys may carry over childish ways of interacting with girls. At this age, boys may still pull a girl's hair, wrest away her books, or tease and plague her in other nefarious ways.

Perhaps because thirteen is more inner directed than she was at twelve, she reads more now than she did a year earlier. She reads and rereads her favorite books. These books often involve a lot of action, such as detective, adventure, and mystery stories. Many young people of this age still read comic books. As reading increases, television watching decreases, and adolescents are less devoted to particular programs. Television is now looked upon as a distraction, and thirteens are less selective in what they watch. Interest in video games, particularly among boys, takes the place of viewing television programs.

Thirteen-year-olds tend to go to the movies more than they did a year earlier. Telephoning is also becoming a very popular pastime, and parents who can afford it may put in a separate line in order to get their own messages. Thirteen-year-olds can stay on the phone for hours. At this age, boys tend to be more interested in outdoor activities and spend more time in sports than do thirteen-year-old girls. For many girls, walking and bike riding are still the major forms of outdoor activities.

At school, boys and girls are more settled at thirteen than they were at twelve. This is particularly true if the young people are in a junior high school and this is their second year. They have now become accustomed to moving from class to class every hour, and they find this freedom more liberating (time to socialize with peers) than disruptive. In general, young people of this age are better organized and use their time more efficiently than they did just a year before. Because of their concern with their own individuality, many thirteen-year-olds appreciate special projects and activities that reflect their unique personalities. At the same time, the thirteen-year-old may be shy and unwilling to read or perform in front of her classmates. Although adolescents can be critical of their teachers at this age, they still want and need direction. They are beginning to distinguish between a teacher's ability to teach and their own personal, subjective feeling of like or dislike of the teacher.

Like age seven, thirteen turns inward and works on herself rather than on her social relations. In some ways she is more mature than at age twelve, but she is not beyond showing more childish traits—often in the presence of the opposite sex. She needs time and respect for her privacy so she can do the inner work she needs to do before moving on to the next phase of her transition to adulthood.

The Fourteen-Year-Old

By the age of fourteen, many young people have become less introspective and reclusive than they were a year earlier. Now they are more outgoing and happy, less sensitive and touchy than they were at thirteen. They also get along better with their parents, siblings, and other adults. Overall, they seem more mature and self-confident than at their last birthday. Perhaps the inwardness and self-centeredness of the thirteen-year-old is a necessary phase in the preparation for the new maturity of age fourteen.

In many respects, the fourteen-year-old has worked through many of her anxieties about growing up and accepts her new "grown-up" status with zest and enthusiasm. She is happy much more often than she is sad. Occasionally, to be sure, she has her sudden and intense emotional flare-ups, but she now gets over these lapses with relative ease. At fourteen, she is much more likely to express her feelings and is not hesitant to show either anger or affection. She has fewer fears and worries, and those that she does have are more specific and targeted than they were at age thirteen. Fourteen is prone to have "pet" fears and "pet" worries. Perhaps most indicative of her ability to take herself less seriously is her humor. She now enjoys giving humorous birthday cards and engaging in light-hearted banter. Fourteen no longer takes herself, or growing up, with the die-hard seriousness that she did just a year earlier.

Along with her enhanced emotional maturity, fourteen also evidences a new level of self-evaluation and self-acceptance. Although she may still admire and want to be like a rock music star, she also finds much to like about herself, both in appearance and in personality. She now recognizes and accepts her positive attributes, such as her ability to get along with people and her sense of humor. At this stage, she takes pride in her athletic prowess and her academic skills. Fourteen does not brag about herself, however, and she dislikes those of her peers who do blow their own horn. So, although fourteen sees room for improvement in herself, she is also able to accept herself, warts and all.

At age fourteen friendship blossoms. Now, however, friendships are grounded differently than they were at earlier ages. Among fourteen-year-old girls, the clique, comprising anywhere from two to nine girls, becomes all-important. The basis for clique membership is not a matter of living near one another or of shared activities. Rather it is founded upon personal qualities, such as "She is fun to be with" or "She is thoughtful and kind." Fourteen-year-old girls do a lot of talking about themselves, and this talk often revolves about the personalities of their friends and about social issues. These discussions are far-ranging and include schoolwork and, inevitably, boys. Girls who are not a member of a clique often feel isolated and rejected. Many work hard to be accepted into the group.

Boys, too, show an increased friendliness at age fourteen. Yet they are more likely to be part of a loosely organized group than they are to be a member of a tightly bonded clique—just the reverse of what holds true for girls. Boys also begin to choose their friends on the grounds of personal qualities, rather than proximitiy or shared activities. Boys, however, may be less aware than girls of the reasons for their choice of friends. At fourteen, boys have a lot of good-natured fun with their friends. Each group seems to have boys who fit into more or less stereotyped roles. In each group, different boys assume the roles of comedian, activity leader, and Don Juan. These roles merely complement one another, so that by being in the group, the boy can vicariously live each of these roles. At this age, boys often display a degree of sympathy and compassion for those youngsters who are left out. A new student may be welcomed by some of the more outgoing members of the established group, for example.

Heterosexual interactions are also different than they were just a year earlier. At age fourteen, young men and women participate in socially acceptable and nonchildish activities, such as parties, dances, and dates. Boys and girls mix better now and are more able to carry on a meaningful conversation. It has become acceptable and commonplace for girls to ask boys for dates. Many girls also take the initiative in phoning boys just to talk or to plan activities. The boys whom fourteen-year-old girls date or inter-act with are likely to be several years older than they. In-asmuch as girls mature socially somewhat earlier than boys, they find older boys more attuned to their own level of social competency than boys of the same age. For example, fourteen-year-old boys are still prone to mess around at parties and dances, whereas older boys are more interested in talking and dancing with girls. Dating is more frequent among girls than among boys at this age. Fourteen-year-old boys have to be in the right mood, whereas girls are likely to go on dates as often as they are asked and as frequently as their parents permit.

Fourteen-year-olds tend to think about and plan their activities, not just for the moment, but for the whole year. They look forward to the different seasons and the activi-ties appropriate to each season. This reflects their new mental abilities and their new concepts of time and space. Boys are increasingly interested in sports and now anticipate the upcoming baseball or football season. Girls, who are interested in clothing, may begin to look forward to the different seasons in terms of the different outfits they will wear. They start to anticipate summer and the wearing of swimsuits, for ex-ample. This may occasion a period of dieting.

Fourteen-year-olds are also stronger and better co-ordinated than they were at thirteen. Boys are able to run faster and to hit and throw balls harder than they could even a year earlier. Boys are likely to set up a basketball hoop on the garage and play pickup games with their friends. Girls continue to be less interested in sports than are boys and do not spontaneously organize games as boys do. They are more likely to participate in sports that are sponsored by the school. Some young men and women of this age be-gin to actively compete in individual sports, such as ten-nis, swimming, ice skating, and gymnastics. Although they may have been training for many years, serious competi-tion begins in the early teen years.

By far the most important activity of fourteen-year-olds is socializing. Young people of this age spend the majority of their free time in social gatherings or on the phone. The structure of these social interactions is rather loose and free-floating, not unlike an adult cocktail party without the cocktails. A lot of this socializing goes on by means of the telephone. (Some high-tech teenagers even have their own pagers, which they take with them to school and elsewhere!) Girls tend to be more addicted to the phone than are boys. Boys use the phone, too, but their interest is now turning toward cars. They begin to experience a longing to drive and to own an automobile—a longing that will mount in intensity with each succeeding year.

Fourteen's interest in socializing is clearly evident at school. Note writing and passing have now become a polished skill. Sometimes, however, these notes are intercepted and read by the teacher to the class. It can be embarrassing, but fourteen-year-olds believe the risk is worth taking. At this age young people can work together cooperatively and may take pride in being a member of a particular class that has accomplished something special. As a result of their greater self-acceptance, these young people are more respectful of teachers. Their openness and outward orientation make them avid learners, eager for new information. Yet the fourteen-year-old's newfound enthusiasms may conflict with her interest in schooling per se. She may get so involved in producing the school paper, for example, that her grades may suffer.

The fourteen-year-old wants to learn on her own, to try out and to explore. She can tolerate failure if it is not coupled with criticism. At this age she is particularly interested in social studies, local and national politics, and current events. She is concerned with the study of humankind and likes biology, physiology, and even psychology. In contrast to the thirteen-year-old, the young person at fourteen likes to express herself publicly and to give oral reports, to engage in public speaking, and to perform in plays. At this age, the teacher's task is to exercise restraint and to rein in and channel the fourteen-year-old's exuberance and energy into educationally productive channels.

Fourteen, then, is beginning to manifest her new semiadult status. She is outgoing and self-confident and interacts positively and maturely with parents, peers, and teachers. She has become a truly social being and spends as much of her free time as possible with her friends. Heterosexual interests are well advanced, and she may begin to date older boys. The fourteen-year-old boy may be less ready for this form of heterosexual interaction. He is, however, ready and able to participate vigorously in individual and team sports. At fourteen, the young person is once again eager to learn and is respectful of teachers. In many ways, therefore, she is now much more an adolescent than she is a child.

The Fifteen-Year-Old

The exuberance and outgoingness of the fourteen-year-old give way, the following year, to a more somber, quiet demeanor. In many respects, the fourteen-year-old celebrates the establishment of a beginning sense of personal identity and of self-acceptance that is the groundwork for her adult personality. At fifteen, a new phase begins that has to do with separation from parents. The gloom and depression often displayed by the fifteen-year-old may reflect her heightened awareness that dependent childhood has gone and that she is now on the threshold of independent adulthood. Leaving home and being out on her own are no longer in the far distant future, but seem very near indeed.

Because of the contrast with the mood of the previous year, this age is often witness to what has sometimes been called the fifteen-year slump. The withdrawal of the fifteen-year-old is, however, more psychological than it is physical. The thirteen-year-old looks for a quiet corner in which to be alone. In contrast, the fifteen-year-old can be alone amidst a crowd. At such times she can retreat into her own thoughts and tune out the world around her. In addition to this mental absence, fifteen often appears apathetic and lethargic, as if she lacked the energy to do much of anything. Not surprisingly, adults often describe the fifteen-year-old as "lazy" and as "uncooperative." There are times, however, when fifteen can get out of her slump and show her subtle and mature humor. These subtle shifts reflect the fact that fifteen is, in general, more complex and difficult to fathom then she was the year before, when outgoing exuberance was the rule.

Fifteen-year-olds are more guarded about themselves than they were a year earlier. Although they are trying as hard as they can to understand themselves (they have discovered that self-control and self-knowledge are not as simple and as easily come by as they had imagined), they are relatively uncommunicative. When fifteen-year-olds do decide to converse, we can never really be sure whether their story is true or whether it has been concocted for our benefit. Fifteens are concerned that others will know too much about them, read their innermost thoughts, and judge these thoughts harshly. Although wanting to create a good impression, their secretiveness often has the opposite effect.

At this age, independence and freedom are uppermost in the young person's mind. She is resentful of anything that she construes as infringing upon her freedom. Questions as to her whereabouts and actions are often dismissed with phrases like "Out" or "Went for a ride." Her answers to questions as to her activities are equally unsatisfactory. Generally, she was just "hanging out" with her friends. It seems that fifteen's awareness of her impending adulthood makes her impatient with questions that suggest that she is a child who remains accountable to her parents.

Related to the fifteen-year-old's desire for independence and freedom is her desire for self-improvement. She may undertake rigid regimes of study, exercise, or diet or some combination of these. She may, at this age, decide to become a vegetarian. Fifteen is also thinking realistically about the future, however, of what she wants to do after she completes high school. Young people are marrying later today than in the past (about age twenty-five for young women and twenty-seven for young men), so that fifteen is thinking more about her occupation than she is about marriage. Adolescents still think about marriage, but they do not feel the pressure to marry early that adolescents of earlier generations did. They do think about relationships and begin to form an image of the kind of person they would like to be with.

Most fifteen-year-olds tend to absent themselves from the home a good deal. Insofar as it is possible, they also divorce themselves from family activities, such as picnics, shopping, and visits to relatives and friends. If they are forced to go on these excursions, they make their unhappiness very apparent. Fifteen-year-olds would like to be away from home as much as possible and would be out every evening if they were permitted to do so. The fifteen-year-old's need to get out of the house and to detach themselves from the family is often a source of friction with her parents. For parents, the adolescent's eagerness to dispense with the family is experienced as both a rejection and a example of flagrant ingratitude. Parents also feel (sometimes not without cause) that their fifteen-year-old is ashamed and embarrassed to be seen with them. It can be a very unpleasant period in family life.

Fifteen-year-old girls continue the trend, set at age fourteen, of moving away from intense one-to-one friendships and toward more dispersed, group friendships. Girls congregate where they can find some privacy, and the main activity is, as in the past, talk and more talk, often at a fairly high pitch. Boys continue to group at this age as well, but their gangs tend to be larger and to center around activities, primarily sports. Among boys of this age, there is a great deal of helping activity. One boy will help another at his job, with his chores, or with working on a bike or car.

Heterosexual interactions at this age level tend to be more involved. Dating is common, and double dating is more common (and more appropriate) than single dating. Fifteen-year-old girls tend to date older boys, but fifteen-year-old boys are not yet dating younger girls. Making out is a constant subject of discussion. Today, about 50 percent of fifteen-year-olds are sexually active. The age at which sexual activity is initiated, however, varies both with hormonal production and with the activity of friends. Accordingly, there is great deal of regional and community variation with respect to the age of becoming sexually active. In some communities and in some groups, sexual activity may begin at age thirteen or fourteen. In other groups, the norm may be seventeen or eighteen.

In addition to hormonal production and peer group mores, another factor that contributes to the age of sexual initiation is communication with parents. Those young men and women who talk with their mothers openly about sex tend to delay sexual activity longer than young people who do not engage in such discussions. Interestingly, young men who talk with their fathers about sexual matters are likely to initiate sexual activity earlier than young men who do not have such discussions with their fathers. For young women, but not for young men, the early initiation of sexual activity, before age fifteen, is associated with lower self-esteem and negative self-image.

With regard to other activities, fifteens are more narrow and restricted in their interests than they were at fourteen. They may engage in particular activities, such as listening to tapes or CDs or watching MTV or rented videos, until they are satiated or even disgusted with the activity. This tendency to media binges may explain why fifteens frequently take time to relax or to rest up. Although fifteens can get involved in recreational activities, they are generally not interested in taking lessons or in pursuing special hobbies. The exception is boys' enthusiasm for cars, which can become all-consuming. Spectator interest is also taking precedence over active participation for the majority of fifteen-year-olds. Girls tend to be less physically active than boys and to spend a lot of their leisure time talking in groups or on the phone or writing to friends and relatives.

Parties are frequent at this age, but a new issue has come up, namely drinking. Although the drinking age in most states is eighteen or older, many young people begin drinking at a much earlier age. Some young people are initiated into alcohol use with wine coolers and progress from there. Many fifteen-year-olds will not attend a party unless they are told that there will be something to drink. Sometimes adolescents "crash" parties and bring their own alcohol. It is very important for parents of adolescents to make sure that there is an adult present in the house when there is a party. The adult need not be in the same room but should be within earshot of what is going on. If teenagers insist that there is no party without beer, then perhaps there had better be no party.

Some of the negative attitudes that fifteen-year-olds direct toward home and family are also directed toward the school. It is an age when criticism of the school and of teachers is very frequent and harsh. Teaching this age group, accordingly, is not easy. The group spirit that animated fourteen-year-olds is much less evident at fifteen, when informal groupings and meetings are preferred to organized cooperative learning. Young people of fifteen like more fluidity in their social organization and are not enthused about such activities as participating in group projects.

At this age, young people need clarity; they want definitions, and they want details. Fifteen-year-olds want to know where they stand on social, moral, and political issues, and they want to know where adults stand as well. Some of their criticism of the school stems from their feeling that teachers do not know what they believe nor why. Alternatively, they may lack confidence that teachers are sufficiently committed to the positions they take, whether on politics, drugs, or sexual activity. Young people at this age want teachers who are enthusiastic about their subjects, who express opinions, and who are not threatened if a student challenges them. Some students may overattach to an admired teacher and unconsciously imitate the teacher's habits and speech patterns.

Fifteens are critical of school. Nonetheless, if teachers capitalize upon the fifteen-year-old's need for certainty and provide clear-cut values, goals, and standards, they can often enlist their students' energy and cooperation. However, if teachers do not stand firm, if they vacillate about their beliefs and their rationales for them, they will lose the respect of their students. This does not mean that teachers need to proselytize for their point of view. It does mean that they need to stand up for what they believe in and that they encourage young people to make their own choices after considering a number of alternatives.

Fifteen, then, is a period when the future seems to be rushing in upon the adolescent. She sees maturity, independence, and freedom looming, and this can be a little scary. Perhaps to help ease the transition, she finds fault with her family and tries to demonstrate her independence from it. Unfortunately, it is very easy for the adolescent of today to express this independence by engaging in risky activities once reserved for adults, namely, drinking and sexual activity. She will, however, usually not engage in this form of risk taking if she has been well parented and has internalized the values and standards her parents have set down from early childhood. Fifteen-year-olds are as critical of teachers and of the school as they are of their parents. At this age, young people want teachers to be leaders and to take firm stands.

Fifteen is a difficult age for parents and teachers. It is a period during which young people assert their independence by demanding that the adults in their world define themselves clearly and unambiguously.

The Sixteen-Year-Old

There is a clear parallel between the age of sixteen and the age of ten. At both of these ages, young people find a comfortable balance between the emotional and social growth forces with which they have been contending. At age sixteen, for example, the sulkiness and low mood of the fifteen-year-old give way to a remarkably even disposition. The sixteen-year-old doesn't get mad the way that she used to, and she is receptive to constructive criticism. She will take this criticism seriously and may make efforts to change if she thinks the evaluation is valid.

When sixteen is hurt by the remarks of others, she tends to cover up her feelings and wait for them to dissipate. With close friends, however, the sixteen-year-old will share her true feelings. In this respect, she has become quite adult in her handling of her emotional life. By and large, sixteen is less sensitive, happier, and more self-starting than she was at age fifteen. Balance and moderation, rather than extremes and exaggerations, characterize the emotional life of the sixteen-year-old.

This new equilibrium is also evident in the sixteen-year-old's self-concept. Her earlier concern with freedom and independence has given way to a sense of having "made it" and of a new autonomy from her parents and other adults. Fortunately, this new awareness of her individuality is coupled with a corresponding awareness of the relativity of independence. She shows an appreciation of the fact that personal happiness cannot be attained at the expense of others. A concern for self-realization is coupled with a commitment to social niceties and responsibility. As an outgrowth of these new attainments, the sixteen-year-old is more outgoing and sociable than she was a year earlier. She is now at ease when she performs the social graces, such as introducing her parents to friends. Social situations are, in general, more fun and less stressful than they were heretofore.

Just as the ten-year-old liked age ten the best, so does the sixteen-year-old like her present age. She recognizes and acknowledges her bad as well as her good qualities, and she is more accepting of both. Perhaps because of this new self-acceptance, the sixteen-year-old is not as concerned with choosing her line of work or her profession. She recognizes that she has many options and need not make an immediate choice. By age sixteen the young person has made up her mind as to whether or not to go to college. About 50 percent of graduating seniors do go on to college. The decision to continue schooling is dependent upon many different factors, including financial resources, aptitude, interest, and academic record. At sixteen, a schism begins to develop between those young people who are college bound and those who are not.

Adolescents at age sixteen exhibit more poise and convey a greater sense of equality in relationships with adults than was true at earlier ages. Both parents and their sixteen-year-olds are more relaxed about many issues that were the cause of violent conflicts just a year earlier. Parents now afford the sixteen-year-old more freedom and are less concerned about what hour she will return home. In part this stems from the fact that the sixteen-year-old tends to be more responsible and will call home if she is going to be later than expected. In addition, however, her new sense of autonomy and equality with parents means that the young person no longer has to defy or challenge her parents in order to demonstrate her independence.

Sixteen is more accepting of her mother than she was at earlier ages, and she now appreciates that her mother's concerns are genuine and are not just curiosity and prying. The situation is a little different with fathers. Although the sixteen-year-old is more willing to accept her father on his own terms, she is still a little cautious about being entirely open with him. A girl who is dating a boy of another religious faith, for example, may try to keep this fact from her father for fear of upsetting him. Fathers, on their side, seem to be accepting of the sixteen-year-old behaviors. They still lecture their sixteen-year-olds, but without the rancor they directed at her a year earlier. By and large, the sixteen-year-old's new sense of adulthood allows her to better understand and appreciate her parents. She is now able to share confidences and discuss issues on a more or less equal footing.

Sibling relations are also improved when the young person is sixteen. To be sure, the sixteen-year-old is so busy with her friends and is away from home so much that the decrease in friction may be simply attributable to diminished interactions. That is not the whole story, however, because the sixteen-year-old now enjoys the admiration of her younger siblings and begins to take a parental attitude toward them. Indeed, the sixteen-year-old may even intercede for her younger brother or sister and say such things as "Don't worry, Mom. He'll be okay. He knows what he is doing." With older siblings, sixteen feels more comfortable and on a more equal footing than ever before. The squabbling of the earlier years gives way to interesting discussions and to the discovery of one another as individuals. When they get to be this age, the adolescent's rivalry with older siblings is often replaced by sibling support.

Outside of the home, sixteen-year-olds have plenty of friends and spend more time with friends than with the family. Friendships are less superficial than at earlier ages, and now young people share confidences, discuss issues, and enjoy shared interests with their friends. Girls at this age are less preoccupied with boys than they were at earlier ages and are less concerned with a particular boy. They are also more discriminating. If a boy demands sexual relations and the girl does not want to engage in this activity, she will stop seeing him. At the same time, girls are beginning to develop platonic friendships with boys as people to talk to, as people who understand them, but in whom they have no romantic interest. Sixteen-year-old boys are less advanced in this regard. Most of their interactions with girls have romantic overtones. Boys at this age are usually interested in "playing the field" and are generally not interested in going steady.

Social interactions often occur at parties or dances, either put on by the school, religious organization, community, or by young people themselves. Sixteen-year-olds enjoy parties where everyone knows everyone else, where the music is loud, and where different activities—such as singing, dancing, and talking—are all going on at once. In some communities, this picture of teenage socializing is marred by the use of alcohol. When this happens, young people who drink too much can sometimes engage in embarrassing activities. One young woman of sixteen was given a number of beers and then encouraged to dance topless, which she did. The next day she found that none of her girlfriends would talk to her. It is essential that adults be around when adolescents have parties.

Although more than 50 percent of sixteen-year-olds are sexually active, most adolescents are not promiscuous. In the usual case, the young person will engage in sexual activity as part of an ongoing relationship. When that relationship breaks up the young person may enter into another where sexual activity may again play a part. The majority of adolescents thus engage in serial monogamy and do not have sex indiscriminately. Again, whether or not a particular young person becomes sexually active is very much dependent upon what is regarded as the norm by her peers. As one sixteen-year-old, who was being pressured by her friends to become sexually active, told me, "I just want to do it and get it over with." It should be said, however, that sixteen-year-olds are much more resistant to peer pressure than they were even a year earlier.

With respect to other interests and activities, the sixteen-year-old shows the same balance evident in other spheres of her life. Whether it be team sports, playing a musical instrument, or skiing, the adolescent has integrated these activities into her life-style. Many sixteen-year-olds obtain their driver's license and demonstrate both skill and responsibility in their driving. Parents respect this new demonstration of maturity and allow the young person considerable freedom with the family car. It must also be said that parents are somewhat relieved not to have to chauffeur their adolescent around anymore! Obtaining a driver's license is an important boost to the sixteen-year-old's healthy sense of self-confidence and mastery.

Many young people get jobs at the age of sixteen, the age when they can obtain working permits. By far the majority of adolescents work in fast-food restaurants. Although work had real benefits for youth at one time, this is no longer always the case. At fast-food restaurants, young people spend most of their time in cleaning up or in simple routine tasks, such as frying potatoes. Many may learn negative attitudes toward work. Moreover, young people who work more than fifteen hours a week may experience a drop in their school grades. Although the sixteen-year-old's work contributes to her sense of independence, it may not be as beneficial as it was when work was more meaningful and there was more mentoring by adults.

Not surprisingly, given all that sixteen-year-olds are doing, television viewing is relatively infrequent. Although many sixteen-year-olds express a great interest in reading, not much reading actually gets done. The exception is magazines, which young people read with great relish. Boys are likely to read magazines that have articles about sports, cars, boats, and computers—particularly when these articles are in magazines with nude centerfolds. Girls are more likely to read magazines that have to do with clothing, makeup, and diet and that include romantic stories as well. For the most part, sixteen-year-olds are so busy socializing or working that they have little time for activities such as television watching, going to the movies, or reading.

For many adolescents, sixteen is a turning point in their education. For those young people who are planning to go on to college, school becomes more interesting, and they feel they get more out of it. This may be due, in part at least, to the fact that they are often in smaller, advanced-placement courses that are taught by the best teachers. Other sixteen-year-olds find school dull and boring and drop out as soon as they are able to do so legally. The "forgotten half" of high school students, those who do not go on to college, are not well served by our high schools, which reinforce the schism between those who are college bound and those who are not.

In many ways, then, the sixteen-year-old is rather far along in her movement toward adulthood. She has attained all but an inch or two of her final stature, and she feels comfortable with her body size, configuration, and appearance. The first novelty and fear of sexual feelings and activity have passed, and many young people of this age are sexually active. Sixteen-year-olds feel in control of their desires and impulses and can resist peer pressure to engage in sexual activity or to use alcohol if this is not in keeping with their sense of themselves.

Sixteen feels more or less equal with parents, older siblings, and other adults. She can discuss issues and share activities on an equal footing. To be sure, the sixteen-year-old will meet new problems, as well as old ones, as she continues to grow and to mature, but she will meet them in an adult fashion. Childhood is past without regrets, and the future beckons her with promise and excitement.

Afterword

This last decade of the twentieth century is a difficult time in which to be a child or a parent. There has been a major shift in emphasis on the part of families and society away from meeting the needs of children and youth and toward meeting the needs of adults. Although this trend may have corrected an overconcern with the welfare of the young that was evident during the first half of this century, the correction has gone much too far. Many children in our society today are being deprived of many of the stages of development I have described in this book. These stages are developmental, rooted in our biological heritage, and cannot be hurried.

To be sure, we cannot and should not try to return to what family and society were in the past. What we can do, however, is recognize that children do need time to grow, to experience the ebbs and flows of inwardness and outwardness, of self-confidence and self-doubt, of liking self and others and of not liking anyone, including the self. Although we may not be able to protect children and youth in the ways that we once did, we can do something. If we take the time and make the effort we can give children and youths some opportunity to experience the rhythms of development that are so important to a fully realized adulthood.

One thing we can do as parents is to share ourselves with our children. Because we often have little time for our children, we sometimes believe we need to spend the time we do have with them in some fun, enriching experience, such as taking them for lessons. Yet if we have little time for our children, the most important thing we can do is to share ourselves with our them. We can do with them the things we have to do or that we love to do. This may mean doing the laundry, mowing the lawn, going to a ball game, or cooking. Whatever it is, we give our children the best experience when we share ourselves, our chores, and our loves with them.

The second thing we need to do is to look at each child as a unique individual, on his or her own terms. Although it is hard to separate our own hopes and ambitions for the child from what he or she is and can be, we have to make the effort to do so. We can do this if we take the time to observe and to know our children. For example, if we watch what they do in their leisure time, what they choose to do on their own, it will give us clues to their interests. We can then follow their lead and encourage and support these spontaneous interests. In this way we contribute to our children's self-realization along the path that is most comfortable for them.

The last thing we can do is as much for ourselves as for our children. Childhood and adolescence, in prospect, are long and tedious. In retrospect, when our children are older, it seems like an instant, like a dream. So one thing we can do for our children and for ourselves is to enjoy them and their growing up. Perhaps the most important trait for successfully rearing children and adolescents is a sense of humor. One of the reasons I have included the growth profiles in this book is so you can watch and enjoy the changes in your child as he or she moves toward maturity. Most important, if we enjoy our children while they are growing up, we ensure that they will enjoy their childhood—and their adulthood—as well.

Index